TOURISM INFORMATION TECHNOLOGY

WI T Library

DEDICATION

To my parents
Stanley and Helen Sheldon
for their loving support.

Tourism Information Technology

Pauline J. Sheldon, PhD
Professor of Tourism
School of Travel Industry Management
University of Hawaii
USA

CAB INTERNATIONAL

CAB INTERNATIONAL
Wallingford
Oxon OX10 8DE
UK

CAB INTERNATIONAL
198 Madison Avenue
New York, NY 10016–4314
USA

Tel: +44 (0)1491 832111
Fax: +44 (0)1491 833508
E-mail: cabi@cabi.org

Tel: +1 212 726 6490
Fax: +1 212 686 7993
E-mail: cabi-nao@cabi.org

A catalogue record for this book is available from the British Library, London, UK

Library of Congress Cataloging-in-Publication Data
Sheldon, Pauline J.
 Tourism information technology / Pauline J. Sheldon.
  p.   cm.
 Includes bibliographical references and index.
 ISBN 0–85199–181–5 (alk. paper)
 1. Tourist trade—Information services. I. Title
G155.A1S485   1997
025.06'3384791—dc21

97–15284
CIP

ISBN 0 85199 181 5

Typeset in 10/12pt Melior by Columns Design Ltd, Reading
Printed and bound in the UK by Biddles, Ltd, Guildford and King's Lynn

Contents

Preface

Tourism and information technology are two of the largest and most dynamic industries in the world today. Separately and together they are changing the way society operates. The intersection of these two industries has held my fascination for the last eight years, and is where I have spent most of my teaching and research during this time. This book represents the fruition of those activities and addresses the synergy between the two industries. More specifically it examines the applications and impacts of information technology to the very information intensive field of tourism. The book covers both the operational and managerial uses of information technology in tourism enterprises.

The book has three potential audiences. The first audience is tourism industry professionals who want to better understand the use of information technology in their institutions and in the industry in general. The second audience is information systems professionals who may be interested in applying their expertise to tourism enterprises. The third audience, of course, is students. Students in tourism programmes of all types and particularly those with courses on information technology will benefit from the book. Students of business management, in particular the management of services, will gain some insight into the technological applications and impacts on the service sector.

It has been suggested that 'no player in the tourism industry will be untouched by information technology' (Poon, 1993). This book examines how information technology is being applied to and is touching each sector's operational and managerial functions. Eight case examples are used throughout the book to integrate the discussion of the text with real world applications. These cases will be helpful to academic readers as a basis for classroom discussion, and to non-academic readers in better understanding specific applications in tourism firms.

The book begins with an overview of tourism and information technology and discusses the synergy between the two industries. The unique characteristics of tourism that make it so information intensive are explained, and different typologies of tourism information are discussed. The airline industry, being the first tourism sector to intensively use information technology, is covered first in Chapter 2. The passenger reservation systems it created in the 1960s which have had significant ramifications on the rest of the tourism industry are a significant part of this chapter. Decision support systems and operations management systems are also discussed in this chapter. The application of information technology in airports to handle passengers and aircraft more effectively is also covered. The chapter ends with a case example of Singapore Airlines. Chapter 3 examines how travel intermediaries, such as travel agents, tour operators and speciality channellers are using information technology, and how the structure of this sector is changing as a result of information technology. The resultant changes in the travel distribution channel are addressed at the end of the chapter, followed by a case example of Rosenbluth Travel which has creatively used information technology to become one of the largest corporate travel agencies in the world. Chapter 4 examines the use of information technology in surface transportation modes such as road, rail and water transportation companies. Intelligent Transportation Systems (ITSs) are discussed as a framework of how information technology is making road travel safer and more efficient. The chapter ends with two cases – one on National Car Rental and one on Royal Caribbean Cruise Lines. Chapter 5 covers consumer access to travel databases, which are being used to bypass the traditional travel distribution channel. Public access networks, the Internet and the World Wide Web, interactive TV, videotext, CD-ROM and voice recognition systems will be discussed. A modified travel distribution system is presented at the end of the chapter. The case for this chapter examines the Internet Travel Network, a company who has made significant contributions to consumer access to travel databases.

Chapter 6 investigates how the hospitality sector (accommodation and food service) is utilizing information technology, both in its operations, marketing and reservations handling. The many specialized systems used in this sector and their interfacing are explained. Telecommunications and teleconferencing are addressed with discussions of the impact of teleconferencing on tourism and travel in general. The case example at the end of this chapter is on Swissôtel. Chapter 7 examines how information technology is being used in the attractions and entertainment sector of the industry. Systems used to control ticketing and access to entertainment facilities are discussed as well as information to create or enhance the visitors' experience.

Applications used by theme parks, ski resorts and gambling casinos will be given particular attention, and the chapter ends with a case from the Polynesian Cultural Centre, a cultural theme park in the Hawaiian Islands.

Chapter 8 examines how government tourist offices use IT to better manage and market their destinations. Destination Information Systems are a core component of this chapter but other electronic applications are discussed. Various systems to collect and analyse tourism statistics are presented. The chapter ends with a case study of how the Finnish Tourist Board is using information technology to improve its operations. Chapter 9 gives the reader a more detailed picture of how data communication networks (in particular ARINC and SITA) link the travel industry together and span the globe. It discusses the different standards and protocols used by systems and sectors and important issues in their connectivity. A description of electronic document interchange for tourism ends the chapter. Chapter 10 examines some future trends underlying information technology applications in tourism. These include the increased intelligence in the form of expert systems and robotics, the increased use of multimedia and virtual reality, and more global connectivity. It also comments on industry changes as a result of technological implementation.

This is the first book attempting to cover how all sectors of tourism are using information technology. I have tried to keep the coverage as international as possible, making the book appropriate for readers all over the world. The cases have been carefully chosen from different parts of the world, with Asia, North America and Europe being represented. A slight bias towards North America may exist in the text, but this is mostly due to the fact that many of the new developments in information technology are occurring there. I hope that the reader, having read this book, will be better prepared for the technological changes ahead as the tourism industry enters the new millennium.

Acknowledgements

Like most worthwhile projects, this book was not accomplished alone.
Many people helped on different levels. Discussions with colleagues
were critical in the formation of some of the ideas in the book and
many of them reviewed drafts. I am deeply grateful for the insights
they provided. The need to be updated on the latest systems required
input from many firms and organizations in the tourism industry.
Some of this information resulted in case examples that are presented
at the end of the chapters. I would like to thank all who contributed
their ideas and opinions on travel industry perspectives, and materials
and information on their company's products. Their cooperation and
time were given graciously and made significant contributions to the
book. My sincere gratitude goes to all of these people. They include
but are not limited to the following:

Discussions and reviews of drafts:
Michael Baker, University of Surrey
Hong Mei Chen, University of Hawaii
Richard Eastman, The Eastman Group
Doug Finlay and others for discussions on the Infotech.Travel
    electronic bulletin board
Thomas Loane, Alamo Car Rental
Bill Remus, University of Hawaii
Randy Smith, Lanyon
Thomas Tunstall, Sabre Technologies

Materials for cases
Kandy Akina, Singapore Airlines
Oliver Bernet, Swissôtel
Dante Cayaban, Sheraton Hotels in Hawaii
Terry Gordon, Avis Rent-a-Car

Diane Koh, Singapore Airlines
Inkeri Starry, Finnish Tourist Board
Rich Steck, Royal Caribbean Cruises
Various staff, Rosenbluth International
Christian Wilson and Les Moore, Polynesian Cultural Centre

Others
Jacques Bernier, Virtual World
Carol Boden, Steamboat Ski Resort
Lucy Chew, Abacus
Karlen Dong, American Airlines
Marcus Endicott for InfoTech.Travel which provided valuable
    information and discussions
Begonia Gosh, Amadeus
Bill Hakason, International Travel Technology Association
Roger Hansen, ARINC
Yousaf Hafeez, SITA
Hansheiri Hubert, Laax Ski Resort
Karen Lennon, Worldspan
William Lew, Abacus
Owen Miyamoto, Honolulu International Airport
Don Murray, Ecosign: Mountain Resort Planners
Kris Nelson, Gaming Systems International
Rachelle Noroyan, Apple Computer
Barbara Okomoto, Hawaii Visitors and Convention Bureau
Peter Ramadge, Travel Industries Automated Systems Pty, Australia
Sheri Schwebach, Sabre
Pat Scanlon, BRC Imagination Arts
Donna Teboe, Angus Reid
Jennifer Wong, American Airlines
Vivien Wright, Galileo International
Dick Zunkel, Recognition Systems Inc

I would also like to acknowledge the School of Travel Industry
Management at the University of Hawaii for supporting this project,
and the students who caught errors and made suggestions on earlier
drafts. Especially I would like to thank Carol Chu and Sandy Man Woo
who did an outstanding job of helping with layout and other typo-
graphical assistance at the end of the project.

My husband Bill Remus has offered loving and continuing support
throughout the two and a half year writing process, and throughout
my academic career over the years. He has provided excellent feedback when asked for it, and kept wisely quiet when not asked. I am
deeply grateful for his support.

Any book has the potential for errors and omissions; and any book on technology runs the danger of being immediately out of date. Any errors, omissions or outdatedness I take on as solely my responsibility.

Abbreviations

AAA: American Automobile Association
ACARS: Aircraft Communication and Reporting System
ADNS: ARINC Data Network Services
AGV: Automated Guided Vehicle
AI: Artificial Intelligence
ALC: Airline Line Control
APN: ARINC Packet-Switched Network
ARC: Airline Reporting Corporation
ARINC: Aeronautical Radio Incorporated
ATB-2:   Automated Ticket and Boarding Pass
ATM: Automated Ticket Machine
ATMS: Automated Traffic Management System
ATPCO: Airline Tariff Publishing Company
AVL: Automated Vehicle Location

BT: British Telecom

CAD: Computer Assisted Design
CAM: Computer Assisted Manufacturing
CAS: Call Accounting System
CPE: Communication Processor Equipment
CPU: Central Processing Unit
CRS: Computer Reservation System
CTI: Computer–Telephone Integration
CUTE: Common Usage Terminal Equipment

DCIES: Dishonoured Cheque Information Exchange Service
DCS: Departure Control System
DIS: Destination Information System
DSS: Decision Support System

EBB:	Electronic Bulletin Board
EDI:	Electronic Document Interchange
EDS:	Electronic Data System
EFT:	Electronic Funds Transfer
EIS:	Expert Information System
ETDN:	Electronic Ticket Delivery Network
FAA:	Federal Aviation Administration
FECP:	Front End Communication Processor
FIDS:	Flight Information Display System
FIT:	Free and Independent Traveller
FTB:	Finnish Tourist Board
GCU:	Group Controller Unit
GDN:	Global Distribution Network
GDP:	Gross Domestic Product
GDS:	Global Distribution System
GIS:	Geographic Information System
GMDSS:	Global Maritime Distress and Safety System
GPS:	Global Positioning System
GTO:	Government Tourist Office
HCC:	Hotel Clearing Centre
HEDNA:	Hotel Electronic Distribution Association
IATA:	International Air Transport Association
IMP:	Interface Message Processor
IPS:	Integrated Property System
ISDN:	Integrated Services Digital Network
IT:	Information Technology
ITN:	Internet Travel Network
ITS:	Intelligent Transportation System
LAN:	Local Area Network
LCR:	Least Cost Routing
MCP:	Meeting and Convention Planner
MDNS:	Managed Data Network Services
MIS:	Management Information System
MPINet:	Meeting Planners International Network
NMC:	National Marketing Company
NTO:	National Tourist Office
OAG:	Official Airline Guide

OR: Operations Research

PARS: Programmed Airline Reservation System
PBX: Private Branch Exchange
PC: Personal Computer
PCC: Polynesian Cultural Centre
PMS: Property Management System
PNR: Passenger Name Record
POS: Point-Of-Sale
PROMIS: Professional Marketing Information System

RCC: Remote Communications Concentrator
RISC: Reduced Instruction Set Computer
RNG: Random Number Generator
RT: Rosenbluth Travel

SABRE: Semi-Automated Business Research Environment
SAS: Statistical Analysis System
SDLC: Synchronous Data Link Control
SI: System Integrator
SIA: Singapore Airlines
SITA: Société Internationale Télécommunications Aéronautique
SLC: Synchronous Link Control
SMDR: Station Message Detail Recording
SNA: Systems Networking Architecture
SPSS: Statistical Package for the Social Sciences
SQL: Standard Query Language

TA: Terminal Address
TCP/IP: Transmission Control Protocol/Internet Protocol
THISCO: The Hotel Industry Switching Company
TIS: Tyrol Information System
TPF: Transaction Processing Facility

UATP: Universal Air Travel Plan
UPS: Uninterrupted Power Supply
URL: Uniform Resource Locator

VICS: Vehicle Information and Communication System
VIO: Visitor Information Office
VR: Virtual Reality

WAN: Wide Area Network
WWW: World Wide Web

X.25:   Packet-switched network protocol

Tourism, Information Technology and their Synergy

1

1.1 INTRODUCTION

Planet Earth is experiencing some of the most dramatic social changes in its history. Borders are dissolving and countries, societies, people and firms are connecting more and in different ways than they ever have in the past. Increases in international trade agreements, global business activity, telecommunication networks and personal and educational travel are linking the planet together like never before. These linkages are being forged and supported essentially by two of the largest and fastest growing industries in the world today – tourism and information technology (IT).

Tourism is well documented as the world's largest industry (Waters, 1995), contributing significantly to many national and regional economies. In 1995, it was responsible for over 200 million jobs worldwide, and by 2005 that is expected to increase to 300 million. Tourism is also responsible for 11.4% of the global GDP for 1995 with a total output of US$3.4 trillion (World Travel and Tourism Council, 1995). Tourism is also a powerful force in arenas other than economics. Much travel is motivated by educational, cultural, business as well as leisure and adventure needs, thereby having an enormous impact on the social fabric of the world. All travel, however, causes people to interact and communicate in new and different ways, thereby giving rise to more connectivity.

The information industry is equally significant and powerful. It is responsible for 50% of the jobs in the industrialized world and in 1992, the information technology industry generated 10% of the US GDP. The information industry moves, stores, processes and displays information with the help of information technology (IT). IT includes computers, peripherals, data and voice communication lines and equipment, and software of all kinds. The rapid pace of development in IT is creating millions of electronic connections around the globe, connecting people, the business community, industries, regional and international communities. The travel and tourism industry is a heavy user of these connections and some of the largest telecommunication networks spanning the globe carry travel information. IT, therefore, provides the information backbone that facilitates tourism.

This book is about these two industries and their synergy. It describes how the different sectors of the tourism industry are applying IT to their operations, and using it to improve connectivity across the industry. The book also examines the impact IT is creating on travellers, firms and the entire industry. This first chapter sets a foundation by examining the nature of the tourism industry and presents various typologies of tourism information. Its synergy with information technology is explained and ways in which the two industries interlock and support each other are discussed. Issues relating to the strategic management of information and IT within a firm are also discussed.

1.2 TOURISM: AN INFORMATION INTENSIVE INDUSTRY

The size of the tourism industry alone suggests that it generates large volumes of information to be processed and communicated. For each person embarking on a trip, scores of messages and pieces of information must be exchanged: itineraries, schedules, payment information, destination and product information, and passenger information. The airlines alone process on average 25 transactions per net booking (Amadeus International, 1994). But the tourism industry exhibits many other unique characteristics which give rise to an intense need on the part of travellers, companies and tourism agencies for information and IT to process it. This section will first present a model of tourism information flows and then discuss the characteristics which make tourism so information intensive.

1.2.1 A Model of Tourism Information Flows

Information flows exist between various sections of the tourism industry and various agents in tourism. Figure 1.1 models these flows by identifying the agents which receive and produce information and the connections between them. Three main agents receive and produce travel information – they are suppliers, travel intermediaries and travellers as shown in the centre of Fig.1.1. Travellers (whether they be pleasure, business, group, free and independent travellers (FITs) or

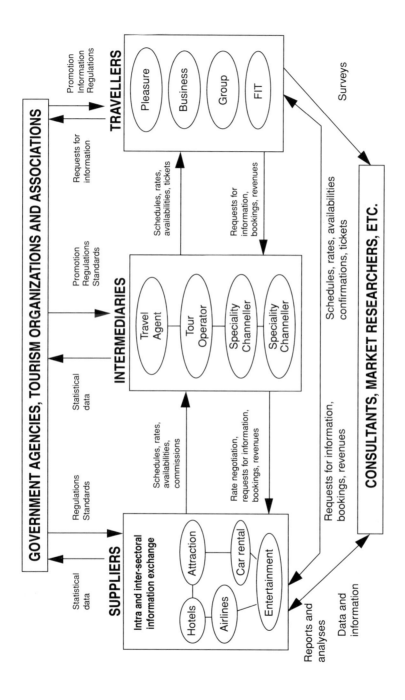

Fig. 1.1. Information flows in the tourism industry.

any other type) require information in the form of product information, schedules, fares, rates, availabilities and bookings. They can
acquire this from either travel intermediaries (travel agents, tour operators, corporate travel agencies or other speciality channellers), or
directly from the suppliers. In return, the intermediary or the supplier
needs information on the traveller to create the reservation. These
information flows are represented by the horizontal arrows in Fig. 1.1.

There are also vertical lines in the intermediary box which represent information flows when more than one intermediary is used to
organize a trip. For example, a travel agent may book a client's trip
using a tour operator causing information to flow between those two
intermediaries. Information flows are also critical between and within
the suppliers' firms as shown in the supplier box. For example, car
rental companies need to communicate with airlines to coordinate
travel itineraries, and hotels and attractions must sometimes communicate with each other. In addition, there are many needs for information flows within a firm and between its offices in different locations.
Accounting information, customer information, and marketing information are examples of these information flows. Therefore, various
intra- and inter-organizational information channels are needed
within and between international, national, regional and local travel
suppliers.

Suppliers, intermediaries and travellers operate in a larger environment of governmental (national and international) agencies,
tourism organizations and associations which themselves provide and
receive information. Their information flows are shown at the top of
the figure. Many governmental bodies provide information on regulations and standards for travel such as customs regulations, health regulations and currency controls. Also, suppliers are often regulated by
government agencies requiring business licences, health and safety
standards, and certification of employees. Information on these topics
must flow easily between the interested parties. Tourism organizations
also generate and communicate large volumes of information about
the destination and its facilities to travellers and travel intermediaries.
They typically collect statistical data on travellers to their destination
and produce reports for the industry to use for analysis and planning
purposes. The travel industry also has numerous associations at the
global, national and regional levels. The role of many of these
organizations such as the World Tourism Organization and the Pacific
Asia Travel Association is to coordinate the collection and transmission of tourism information and statistical data and to publish promotional information. There are many other associations in tourism
which deal with information on various levels.

Consultants and market researchers (shown at the bottom of Fig.

1.1) are also important links in tourism information flows. They assist suppliers in organizing corporate and client data into meaningful reports and analyses. They examine the impact of environmental factors on the firm or industry, and survey travellers in various ways to obtain market information. They may also provide governmental agencies with information.

The above model demonstrates the many and varied sources and forms of information that lubricate the travel industry. They also emphasize the industry's information intensity. The next section will discuss the characteristics of the industry that contribute to this information intensity.

1.2.2 Characteristics of Tourism

The tourism product (or trip) is a unique type of product. Some of the characteristics that differentiate it from other products and make it so information intensive are its heterogeneity, its intangibility, and its perishability. The international scope of the industry, and the fact that tourism is a service industry also contribute to its information intensity. Each of these characteristics will be discussed below.

Heterogeneity
The tourism industry, and hence the tourism product, is complex and consists of many component parts. The US Standard Industrial Classification System has identified at least 35 industrial components that serve the traveller (Gee *et al.*, 1994). To research and plan a trip, travellers must interact with many private sector firms and public sector agencies. Coordination and cooperation between each of these firms, agencies and the consumer is necessary to create the heterogeneous product called a trip. This requires efficient, accurate and timely information flows to piece together the multifaceted trip. Information and information technology provide crucial links between the different industry sectors to make the traveller's planning and experience seamless. If the links break down or are too slow, information is not transmitted in a timely manner and the industry does not function maximally. The more complex and international the trip, the more information is required.

Intangibility
The second characteristic of tourism which makes it so information intensive is its intangibility. Potential consumers are unable to see, touch or feel a vacation or a business trip and its components before they purchase it. Instead, they need detailed information about the

destination or product to substitute for the lack of tangibility. This information can be presented via many different media. Travel product and destination information often come in the form of brochures, leaflets, and videotapes. Increasingly, however, electronic media are being used. Global Distribution Systems (GDSs) are currently the primary electronic media for travel agents. CD-ROM discs provide travel agents and consumers with multimedia presentations on destinations and travel products, giving a more vibrant 'sample' of the trip. The Internet and the World Wide Web (WWW) are other voluminous sources of electronic travel product information. Virtual reality can even be used to provide the consumer with a more tangible experience of the product before making a purchase. The intangible nature of the tourism product has brought the IT and tourism industries together to creatively market the product and make it more tangible. Information also serves to reduce the risk associated with some travel and therefore is valued by most consumers. Some travellers, however, prefer and feel challenged by trips which they know little about before departing.

Perishability

The third factor which makes the tourism product information intensive is its perishability. If an airline seat is not sold on a given flight, that particular seat can never be sold again. It, or rather the revenue from it, has perished. This is true for almost all products in the tourism industry (accommodations, attractions, transportation), and is due to the time-sensitive nature of tourism products. This characteristic has implications for the application of information technology. IT can assist with monitoring product inventories more carefully, and dynamically adjust prices to maximize load factors, occupancy and attendance rates. Many computer reservation systems (CRSs) in tourism use yield management systems to assist with the challenges created by product perishability. Also the use of high speed data communication networks can assist firms in the distribution of last minute information about available products to sell them before they 'perish'.

International

By its very nature the tourism industry is one of the most international industries in the world. This characteristic contributes further to its information intensity. International travel generates large volumes of information not found in domestic industries. International travellers must have access to information on border controls such as visa and passport regulations, customs regulations, arrival or departure taxes, currency controls and health regulations such as immunization requirements. In addition, they require information on such diverse topics as cultural practices, driving regulations and language translations. For example, travellers from France visiting Peru have higher information needs than travellers from New York to San Francisco. Both leisure and business travellers are expanding their horizons and travelling more globally requiring access to this kind of information. This geographic dispersion requires data communication networks around the globe to link countries, tourism firms and travellers together. Without IT, the tourism industry would not function as efficiently at the international level.

Service industry

The tourism industry is essentially a service rather than a manufacturing industry. One of the greatest challenges facing managers in the West today is to increase the productivity of service and knowledge workers (Drucker, 1990). In the past there has often been resistance to automation in service industries due to a misconception that the quality of the customer's experience would decline. But in the 1990s with the change in lifestyle and priorities, time has become an important commodity. This has led to service expectations of a different nature, where speed is increasingly important. In fact, information has been identified as one of the most important quality parameters for efficient service (Schertler, 1994). IT applications are necessary to more rapidly serve tourists, whether it be to check a guest out of a hotel or to change their flight reservation. Because of these consumer expectations, time has become an important focus for competitive activities in tourism demanding the application of IT.

In summary, the tourism industry is highly information intensive and information is its lifeblood. The application of information technology to its operations therefore is critical to its growth and success. A deeper investigation of tourism information reveals different typologies of information. The next section discusses three of those typologies.

1.3 TYPOLOGIES OF TOURISM INFORMATION

Tourism information, in addition to being very voluminous, is very diverse in nature. A sampling of information that the industry produces and needs is shown in Box 1.1. Some information is static and some dynamic, some is used by travellers prior to their trip and some during their trip. Some is produced by private sector firms and some by public sector agencies. These different types of travel information require different information technologies to process and distribute them, and are discussed below.

Box 1.1. Examples of tourism information needs.

by Consumer:	about destinations, facilities, availabilities, prices, border controls, geography/climate
by Travel Agents:	about consumer trends in the market; about destinations, facilities, availabilities, prices, border controls, tour packages; about other branches
by Suppliers:	company information; about consumers and travel agents; about competitors
by Tourism Offices:	about trends in the industry; about the size and nature of tourism flows; policies and plans for development

1.3.1 Static Versus Dynamic

Some tourism information does not change very frequently and therefore is relatively static. Other information changes frequently and is intensely dynamic. Examples of static tourism information which may change in the long run but not in the short run are: product descriptions, transportation routes, maps and location information. Static information lends itself to distribution and access on hard copy, video, CD-ROM, or other off-line media. On-line electronic media to distribute this information is not essential. A large volume of tourism information, however, is dynamic, and needs electronic media for frequent updates and rapid distribution from supplier to consumer. Examples are product availability, schedules, fares and rates, and environmental conditions such as weather, snowfalls on ski-slopes or surfing conditions. Some dynamic information changes daily, some weekly, some monthly and some seasonally. Information systems to process this type of information must be on-line, real-time systems with the ability to easily capture the changes. These systems are more difficult to implement and more costly to operate. Adequate resources and personnel to ensure that information is continuously and accurately updated must be part of any dynamic information system.

1.3.2 Pre-Trip Versus In-Trip Information

Information is needed by travellers in different times and different places. Pre-trip information in the planning phase of a trip is required in the traveller's home or the prior destination. It tends to be more static and is required in the earlier stages of the trip decision-making process. The later stages of the trip decision-making process and once the traveller embarks on the trip tend to require more dynamic information. The type of information (pre-trip versus in-trip) required at different times depends on the type of tourist. For example, adventurous travellers or impulsive travellers will need little or no pre-trip information, whereas risk-averse travellers and those with long planning times will need pre-trip information to be both static and dynamic. In general, travellers are leaving more of their decisions until they are at the destination. This need for more in-trip information is spawning new applications of IT. Destinations are developing creative information systems to make visitor information easily accessible in the destination. Information kiosks, and TV-based systems in various forms are common. Along with this trend, however, needs for pre-trip information are not necessarily diminishing. Static, pre-trip information is usually distributed with brochures, guide books, and CD-ROM, whereas static, in-trip information is typically distributed using kiosks, guidebooks and brochures. Dynamic pre-trip and in-trip information requires the on-line connectivity of fax, e-mail, computer reservation systems, interactive TV, the Internet, and Destination Information Systems (DISs). Figure 1.2 shows these various dynamic and static information media for pre-trip and in-trip needs.

	STATIC	**DYNAMIC**
PRE-TRIP	Brochures Guidebooks CD-ROM	Phone, fax, e-mail Travel agent access to GDS Internet
IN-TRIP	Kiosks Guidebooks TV channels in hotels	Phone, fax, e-mail Destination Information Systems Internet

Fig. 1.2. Types of tourism information media.

1.3.3 Private Sector Versus Public Sector

Some tourism information is provided by the public sector and is more general to the destination, and some by the private sector which is more specific to a given product or brand. The public sector, however, may provide specific product information, as when a public tourism office distributes information on specific attractions or accommodation in response to general requests. Also some private sector firms may provide more general information on the destination. They may do this in their advertising to entice consumers to purchase their product. Other examples are tour operators and hotel concierge desks who can enhance their customers' experience by providing general destination information. Sources of public sector information are government tourist offices at the regional, national or state level. They tend to provide more objective, unbiased information on both public and private tourist facilities. Information contained in guidebooks can also be objective and unbiased if the author has no affiliations with the product. Information provided by private companies tends to be more promotional, and more specific to their individual products.

All of the above typologies of tourism information help to shed light on the types of information technology appropriate for the various applications.

1.4 STRATEGIC MANAGEMENT OF INFORMATION

This section focuses on the role of information within the operation of a given firm or organization, rather than in the industry at large. The management of information in tourism firms is especially critical to their success, given the information intensity of the travel product. IT was initially introduced into firms to reduce the costs of processing transactions and to facilitate record keeping, but has more recently become an important strategic weapon for competitive advantage (Ribbers, 1994). Firms that have benefited the most from the use of IT are ones who recognize that information truly is an important resource that must be carefully managed. Firms have traditionally operated with the economic resources of land, labour and capital. With the recognition of information as a fourth resource, firms must carefully combine information with the other three to maximize output and profitability, in addition to providing the best levels of service to travellers.

Information, however, differs in numerous ways from the other three resources (Cleveland, 1985). First, information is neither scarce nor depletable. Instead, it expands as it is used. As one traveller gives information to another about a favourite hotel, museum or beach, that information is duplicated and not lost by the giver. This information expansion can create opportunities or threats depending on the nature of the information and the receiver. The expansion of factual information serves to enhance a firm's or a destination's position as its level of awareness is increased. The spreading of subjective information can create positive or negative impacts depending on the perception of the information giver. Negative perceptions can of course damage, and positive ones can further enhance a firm's position.

Second, information and information technology can actually be used by management to substitute for the other three resources of land, labour and capital. When these three are in short supply or are expensive, the creative application of IT can be used instead. Telecommuting is an example of using IT to substitute for land since firms whose employees telecommute need no longer rent or purchase so much high priced land in expensive districts. IT can also be used to substitute for labour in many ways. In repetitive, lower level tasks in travel firms IT can reduce the number of employees needed to perform the task. At higher levels of operations, IT can augment human resources with decision support systems, expert systems, and other applications of artificial intelligence.

A third characteristic differentiating information from the other three resources is its tendency to 'leak'. This can cause security problems and requires management to create particular policies to prevent untoward situations. Information is a highly prized resource and so care must be taken to ensure its security. The careful use of passwords and policies must be used to ensure that traveller information is protected. For example, hotels will not give guest room numbers to casual requests, nor will airlines release information of passengers on a specific flight. The travel industry generates much personal information that must be carefully secured to avoid misuse.

These are just three of the ways in which information differs from the other resources. There are numerous others discussed in Cleveland, 1985, but all point to the fact that companies must carefully examine information and treat it as an important resource. Maximizing its use for their competitive advantage is an important challenge to managers operating in this information intensive industry. Appropriate applications of IT at the strategic level have served to increase the success of many travel firms, as will be demonstrated in this book.

The strategic use for IT can take many forms and have many effects. Some IT applications affect the production of goods and services and others have more impact on the marketing process. A model has been developed to show how different industries can use IT to

improve both their production and marketing (Cash *et al.*, 1992). The
model uses a two-by-two matrix in which the horizontal axis represents IT's impact on marketing activities and the vertical axis represents its impact on the production of goods and services. The model
suggests that industries further along on the horizontal scale will tend
to be ones where product choice is complex, quick customer decisions
with confirmations are essential, and where customer tastes and pricing are volatile. Industries will tend to be high on the vertical scale if
high technology is embedded in the product, if production requires a
long design process, and if time and cost savings are possible through
automation. The authors of the model place certain industries on the
matrix as shown in Fig. 1.3. The defence industry is placed high on
production impact and low on marketing impact since the product
tends to be highly technical and needs no marketing. High fashion,
however, is placed high on the marketing impact scale, with moderate
impacts on production.

An analysis of various travel industry sectors and their use of IT in
marketing and production can position them on the matrix relative to
other industries. The travel industry sectors placed on the matrix are
airlines, travel agents, tour operators, hotels, and attractions (in bold).
Most sectors are placed on the right side of the matrix since IT has a
strong impact on marketing all tourism products. Travel sectors are
positioned from high to low on the production axis since its impact
here is not so clear. Insights into the positionings are discussed below
and create a foundation for the rest of the book.

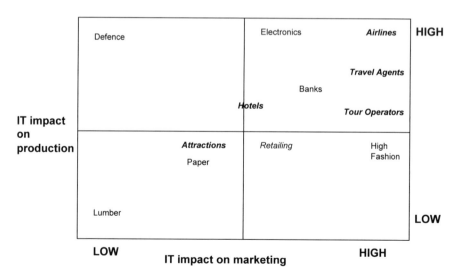

Fig. 1.3. Impact of IT on different industries. Adapted from Cash *et al.* (1992).

The airline sector is the highest on both dimensions and was placed there in the original matrix of Cash *et al.* Global Distribution Systems, frequent flyer databases, yield management programs have been heavily used by the airlines to distribute and market their product. IT has also effectively been used in production activities, for example in the design, operation and maintenance of aircraft, and in luggage handling. Other transportation sectors such as trains and car rentals are not quite so high on the marketing axis, but are equally high on the production axis since new technologies are always being implemented to provide better transportation.

Travel agents, tour operators and other travel intermediaries are perhaps the most information intensive of all travel sectors. They deal almost exclusively with information and have no tangible product of their own. Product choice is complex, quick decisions and confirmations are often necessary and customer tastes and prices are volatile, placing them high on the marketing axis. There is also a high impact on production activities since their product or service is the provision of information.

The accommodation sector is high on both scales, but not as high as the airlines. Computer reservation systems including guest history systems assist in the marketing of hotels. IT's impact on production, however, is less. Hotels traditionally have not embraced technology as readily as the airlines, but this is changing. More and more accommodation units are installing property management systems, electronic locking systems, energy management systems and guest room technology to make their operations more efficient. The hotel industry therefore has, over time, moved higher and further to the right of the matrix.

The attractions sector is difficult to position since some attractions use technology intensely in their production (e.g. theme parks) whereas others use it hardly at all in production (e.g. natural attractions). Therefore it is placed in the middle of the production axis. It is also positioned in the middle of the marketing axis.

The strategic management of IT is necessary whether it is used for marketing or production in any sector of the industry. It will not bring the firm maximum benefits if simply applied to operational problems. It has been suggested that IT can be applied in a systematic way to tourism firms (Poon, 1993). Applications would include distribution and sales, management, service production and service delivery. A strategic direction would be necessary for this level of implementation, and there are numerous ways that the strategic implementation of IT can be ensured (Haywood, 1990). First and foremost, there must be a commitment from top management to support the implementation of IT, by giving it adequate resources, and creating a corporate structure to maximize its implementation. Vice President for Information Systems is an increasingly common position in firms that prioritize the information function rather than placing a Data Processing Manager on the organizational chart at a lower level. When information technology is given this level of visibility and resources, its power can truly be realized. Adequate training of employees to operate the systems is critical to IT's implementation. The constant evaluation of new technologies to determine their appropriateness to the firm's strategic direction is also necessary. This should involve input from all employees in the firm, who should be invited to provide feedback on current systems. Funding IT purchases and keeping systems updated even when cash flow is tight is recommended to prevent a firm from falling behind.

The case studies in this book show how successful firms continuously strive to use IT to provide customers with a better experience, or to meet their needs in some way. It becomes harder and harder to be ahead of the competition with IT applications, but if firms keep their strategic direction in mind, their purchases and applications will be easier to make.

1.5 SUMMARY

This chapter has stressed the importance of information and information technology to tourism. It has shown the reasons why tourism is so information intensive and presented a model of tourism information flows, and different typologies of tourism information. Issues to be considered by management in the strategic application of IT to the firm were also discussed. The ideas presented in this chapter pave the way for the rest of the book which examines IT applications in the specific travel industry sectors. The air transportation sector is covered in the next chapter. It is covered first since its IT applications have impacted upon not only the airlines but also the entire travel industry. The other sectors of the travel industry are covered sequentially in the book.

Information Technology in the Airline Industry

2

2.1 INTRODUCTION

Air transportation systems worldwide are being dramatically affected by technological developments. Some of these technological developments focus on the design of the vehicles themselves (e.g. aircraft design, and rail track design). Others focus on the use of information technology to improve the efficiency of operations. This chapter will discuss the various applications of IT to the management and operation of airlines and airports but will not cover vehicle technology. Chapter 4 will discuss the use of IT by surface transportation modes, such as intelligent transportation systems, car rental systems and IT applications to rail and cruise operations.

Since the early 1950s when air travel became a mass phenomenon, airlines have dealt with large amounts of diverse information. This complexity led them to examine how IT could assist their operations earlier than other travel industry sectors. It is a daunting task to keep track of thousands of flights, fares, seat inventories, crew, passengers, cargo and baggage without automation. The larger the airline operation and the more complex the route structure, the more critical the use of IT became.

The first application of computer technology to airline operations was in the 1950s when computerized reservation systems (CRSs) were designed. In subsequent decades, there has been an increasing use of IT by airlines in other areas, such that today, most aspects of an airline's operations are computerized. Airlines now have some of the largest computer installations in the world and are responsible for some of the largest and busiest data communication networks. In 1987, the airline industry spent more than any other industry on data communication networking (2% of its revenue versus 0.6% for other industries) (Desmond, 1988). The airlines are often cited as companies

15

who have strategically used IT to survive in a very competitive environment. This chapter discusses many of the applications that have led to that recognition. Applications range from automated operations such as reservations, check-in systems and baggage handling, to the computer modelling of operations (scheduling and control problems), to decision support systems, yield management systems and expert systems to assist management in strategic decision-making.

2.2 PASSENGER RESERVATION SYSTEMS

A passenger reservation system is the most common and necessary application of IT to an airline. At the core of a reservation system is a database of flight schedules, seat inventories and passenger information. Prior to the development of computer reservation systems, airlines used various manual methods to keep track of seat inventories. American Airlines, in the 1930s, used a 'request and reply' system whereby reservation agents phoned a central location for availability information. They received responses by teletype (Tunstall, 1996, unpublished). Other airlines' reservation offices used wall-sized availability boards to monitor and process seat reservations. When passengers or travel agents called to make bookings, the reservation agent referred to this availability board which was kept updated by manual workers. When a flight was sold out, a telex was sent to all reservation offices and the flight's originating city to terminate the selling of that flight.

Another manual method used was the 'Lazy Susan' which stored coloured cards with pencil markings on them to record the bookings. Agents referred to these cards to respond positively or negatively to an availability request. By 1952, American Airlines used an electrical/mechanical system called a Reservisor with random access memory drums to perform arithmetic calculations. Figures 2.1 and 2.2 show photographs of agents using both of these systems.

Despite these attempts at controlling seat inventories, the reservation process was still intensely manual and cumbersome and posed disadvantages for the airlines in the form of significant under-booking and over-booking of flights. The inefficiencies of these methods provided a strong impetus for airlines to investigate computer technology as a way to improve their efficiency and profitability. (For a more detailed description of the historical development leading up to computer reservation systems see Copeland and McKenney, 1988.)

Fig. 2.1. Photograph of 'Lazy Susan' technology. The Lazy Susan reservation system used coloured cards placed on a large revolving table. Cards were marked with pencil when seats were received. Photograph permission of American Airlines.

2.2.1 Design Issues

In 1953, American Airlines and IBM began a partnership to develop the first computer system to handle airline reservations, ticketing, schedules, seat inventories, and passenger name records (PNRs). This development effort, which involved years of research and development, and over $40 million investment, was called SABRE (Semi-Automated Business Research Environment) and represented a significant breakthrough in computer system design at the time. The various design challenges that had to be overcome created solutions that have subsequently been adopted by other industries such as the pharmaceutical industry and the banking industry (Kay, 1989).

At least four major design challenges had to be overcome to create a computer system which would process air reservations efficiently. First, the reservation system had to be a real-time, inquiry-response system so that agents could receive immediate responses to their questions on seat availability and fares. The guideline used for the maximum response time to queries was less than three seconds. To meet this requirement a new operating system was developed called Transaction Processing Facility (TPF). TPF's ability to process large volumes of transactions quickly was revolutionary at the time, and is still at the core of airline reservation systems today even though they have evolved to become more comprehensive and diverse. In today's computer environment, TPF has certain limitations. It is a 6-bit processing language, has one-tenth the efficiency of fourth generation computer

Fig. 2.2. Photograph of American Airlines' Magnetronic Reservisor. The Magnetronic Reservisor offered random access memory drum and arithmetic. Photograph permission of American Airlines.

languages, and requires large investments in human resources to keep updated. One airline employs 1200 programmers each paid approximately $100,000 to keep the system going (Feldman, 1994).

A second major challenge was to create a large, geographically dispersed data communications network to connect all users of the reservation system to the central site. In the 1950s there were few networks of this size, and so a pioneering effort was required to create such an extensive data communications network. It involved working with telecommunications companies to lease or build data pathways and nodes across the US and eventually the world. Originally the leased lines were slow at 2400 bits per second. As the technology advanced, high speed data lines was used with data transfer speeds at 96,000 bits per second or more. Hardware to manage these networks was placed in the central site and in cities where airports and airline offices were located. A specialized communication protocol was developed for airline data communications called ALC (Airline Line Control). It is a full-duplex, synchronous communications protocol specific to the airline industry and different from many other communication protocols. The ARINC network (Aeronautical Radio Incorporated) and the SITA network (Société Internationale Télécommunications Aéronautique) were also used by the airlines to transmit their messages from city to city. ARINC and SITA are, respectively, a domestic and an international data network linking travel industry computers together and will be discussed in more detail in Chapter 9.

A third challenge at the time was to keep the systems continuously operational. Because of the geographic distribution of terminals, the computers had to be operational for close to 24 hours to accommodate different time zones. Short periods of downtime were, however, necessary to update flight and fare data. This was scheduled at a time when the fewest people were affected. Limiting downtime and delays due to hardware problems or software errors was another consideration. Hardware redundancy in the form of numerous backup CPUs was built into the system design. Modern installations use fault tolerant systems which have redundancy in the hardware and software, so that recovery from errors is easier and quicker. This feature is particularly important in real-time inquiry-response systems such as airline reservation systems. Backup generators and uninterrupted power supplies (UPSs) also contribute to the performance of the central site hardware by catering for power outages and emergencies. Systems today report an uptime in the 99% range.

Data processing capabilities provided by 1950s hardware platforms were adequate since most airline requests are simple, short database searches with no complex calculations. The messages from terminal to mainframe are typically short and discussions between the passenger and the agent occur between data inputs. The data storage requirements of an airline reservation system, however, were unusually large and posed a fourth challenge to the designers. Data on thousands (now millions) of flights, schedules, fares and passengers were needed on-line to respond to incoming inquiries. The media chosen for storing large volumes of on-line data were magnetic disc packs or drums.

American Airlines and IBM met all of the above design challenges and more, and Sabre was fully operational by 1964 as the first computerized passenger reservation system. The original Sabre installation consisted of two IBM 7080 mainframes – one for real-time processing and one for batch processing of low priority jobs. On-line storage consisted of six magnetic drums, and terminal connections into the mainframes were through voice grade lines at 2400 baud (Copeland and McKenney, 1988). After Sabre's completion, IBM created Programmed Airline Reservation Systems (PARS) which incorporated application software into the TPF operating system. Many airlines used this for their computerized reservations. Eventually by the 1970s, Delta, Continental, Northwest, Western, PanAm, Eastern and United Airlines also had created their own systems similar in function to Sabre.

2.2.2 Central Site Hardware

The typical configuration of an airline computer reservation system is shown in Fig. 2.3. Each system consists of a central site which houses the computer systems, network hardware and the personnel to oversee its operation. The central site is usually heavily secured because of its immense value to the airline, and is designed to withstand natural disasters such as fire, flood or earthquake in addition to bomb attacks.

The site houses several large mainframe systems linked together to handle the high volume of message traffic. A typical installation has at

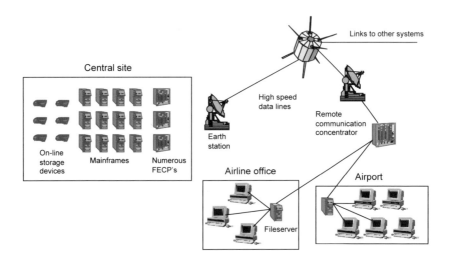

Fig. 2.3. Hardware components of an airline reservation system.

least ten systems; typical systems are IBM 3090s, Unisys 110 and 2200 and Amdahl mainframes. There are also numerous on-line storage devices with faster access than the drums in the original design. Solid state discs which are 30–35 times faster than magnetic discs are used in more recent applications and meet the speed requirements to adequately handle the thousands of requests per second (Henderson, 1991a). Robotic technology is now being used to rapidly access storage devices (tapes, cartridges, discs) (Musselwhite, 1996a). Robotic arms can be programmed to reach for storage devices. Many airlines also store duplicates of their data in remote locations for added security.

Sabre, Apollo/Galileo, Worldspan, SystemOne/Amadeus are some of the largest airline reservation systems. The central site of Sabre, which is located in Tulsa, Oklahoma, US, for example, claims to be the biggest computer installation in the non-military world. It has 12 on-line mainframe CPUs and one backup with a total of 1380 disk storage units able to store 1875 gigabits of data. The central site of Amadeus, which is located near Munich, Germany on a site of 30,000 square metres houses seven mainframes (4 IBMs, 1 Amdahl and 2 Unisys computers) with 3.3 terabits of disc storage (148 tape cassette drives and 30,000 tapes). Worldspan's site in Atlanta, Georgia, houses 6 large mainframes and over 30 FECPs (front end communication processors) and hundreds of disc storage units to store 4220 gigabits of information. Apollo and Galileo (previously housed in Swindon, UK) have now combined their hardware in a central site in Denver, Colorado, US. Figure 2.4 shows a typical central site.

FECPs, communication concentrators and network nodes control the data communication networks at each central site. The number required depends on the volume of message traffic. FECPs monitor messages coming into the central site from thousands of terminals located around the world in airports and airline ticket offices. Sabre, for example, handles approximately 3000 messages per second from over 110,000 terminals worldwide. Over 1 million kilometres of circuitry are used to connect terminals to the central site mainframes. Amadeus processes 480 transactions per second, Galileo 2000 and Worldspan 1500 transactions per second

The front end communication processors have numerous other roles. One is to poll the network. Polling is a method of controlling data traffic on the network by sequentially requesting on-line terminals to send messages to the central site. In the event of messages arriving with errors (either due to incorrect data entry or network problems) the FECP performs error detection and correction procedures. Messages may come in to the central site at different speeds, requiring the FECPs to handle message speed differences. The FECPs also serve as storing and forwarding devices if the message volume is

Fig. 2.4. Photograph of the SystemOne central site. The central site facility of SystemOne GDS. Photograph permission of SystemOne.

too high for the CPUs to handle. This is likely to happen at peak travel times and when fare wars are announced. The FECP also forwards messages to other travel computer systems for processing when necessary.

The network hardware in the central site is connected to thousands of terminals in airports and airline offices through data communication. From the central site the messages start the journey to the terminals on high speed satellite or fibre optic data lines. In the case of satellite transmission, earth stations close to the central site send the messages to a satellite. Remote communication concentrators (RCCs) located in key cities receive the high speed data stream from earth stations and distribute the message over lower speed local lines to the originating terminals. RCCs receive and consolidate requests from reservation terminals in a given geographic region. They then boost the speed of the incoming messages and send the consolidated signal on high speed data lines back to the central site.

2.2.3 CRS Versus GDS

Until the mid 1970s, airline computer reservation systems (CRSs) were used only for proprietary airline information. The airline's major selling agents, however, were travel agents, who also needed access to the computer reservation systems of many airlines to more efficiently research and sell seats. But having a reservation terminal for each airline on a travel agent's desk made no sense. Therefore, in 1975, in the US, an attempt was made to create a single industry reservation system that would give travel agents access to all major airline information. This effort called Joint Industry Computer Reservation System brought together the major carriers to plan such a system for travel agent use (Copeland and McKenney, 1988). After considerable discussions, no agreement was reached and the effort failed. Shortly after, Apollo and Sabre augmented their systems to provide information on other airlines and leased their systems to travel agents in the US. Sabre and Apollo chose different strategies at this point. From the beginning Sabre treated its CRS as an independent business and targeted the largest travel agencies, whereas Apollo viewed its CRS more as a utility for travel agents booking United flights (Tunstall, 1996, unpublished).

Other airlines such as Delta, Eastern Airlines and TWA followed with reservation systems called DATAS, SystemOne and PARS respectively. By the 1980s travel agents wishing to automate had a choice of these five systems. A merger between DATAS and PARS created a new system called Worldspan and reduced the number to four by the early 1990s.

In Europe and Asia, more airlines were computerizing their operations but until the 1990's no computer reservation systems were available for travel agent use (Farris *et al.*, 1991). Videotext technology was used in a number of countries (Britain and Germany, for example) to process travel agent bookings. Eventually two consortia of European airlines and one of Asian carriers each developed multi-carrier CRS for travel agent use. The two European systems are called Amadeus and Galileo and the Asian system is called Abacus. Subsequent mergers occurred between Galileo and Apollo and between SystemOne and Amadeus expanding the global reach of the systems. The four systems now available to travel agents may well reduce to three or even two in the future. Chapter 3 discusses in more detail the subsequent developments in the automation of travel agents. Table 2.1 summarizes some of the significant developments in the history of airline GDS.

As a result of the above events, two categories of airlines emerged. Airlines affiliated with a computer reservation system used by travel agents for multi-carrier (and later multi-product) information and booking, and those without such affiliations. The first category is referred to as 'vendor' airlines and the second as 'non-vendor' airlines. Computer reservation systems affiliated with vendor airlines have

Table 2.1. Significant developments in GDS history.

Year	Development
1976	Apollo (United), Sabre (American), and PARS (TWA) offer terminals to their systems to US travel agents.
1981	SystemOne Direct Access (SODA) formed by Eastern Airlines.
1982	DATAS II formed by Delta Airlines.
1987	Galileo and Amadeus formed in Europe and offered to travel agents there. Abacus formed in Asia and offered to travel agents.
1988	Axess formed by Japan Airlines.
1990	SystemOne purchased by EDS (a non-airline company). Worldspan formed from merger of PARS & DATAS II. Infini formed by All Nippon Airways and Abacus in Japan.
1993	Galileo and Apollo merge to form Galileo International.
1995	SystemOne merges with Amadeus.

Source: adapted from Tunstall, 1996, unpublished.

become known as Global Distribution Systems (GDSs) and those affiliated with non-vendor airlines are called Computer Reservation Systems (CRSs). All GDSs (except Sabre) now have multiple carrier affiliations and all provide important electronic distribution channels for a variety of travel products. The affiliations are shown in Table 2.2

Much controversy has occurred in the US about the impact on airlines' competitiveness and profitability as a result of being affiliated with a GDS. The success of many airlines can be attributed to their substantial investment in information technology, particularly to their computer reservation systems. Table 2.3 shows the huge market value of these systems. Non-vendor airlines often feel they are at an unfair disadvantage without their own electronic channels to the travel agents. After much legislation in the US, rules are now in place to fairly and equally represent all airlines on the GDS screens. Benefits (called 'halo effects') still accrue to the vendor airlines, however, in a number of ways. More recent legislation to address this issue is now in place. The US Department of Transportation has required that airlines with a GDS must separate their own airline's seat inventory from the GDS as a further move to reduce any perceived unfairness (Eastman, 1996). In Europe in the late 1980s when it became clear that travel agents needed access to some kind of GDS, great concern was expressed and care was taken to prevent domination by one or two airlines due to their CRS. Both European-developed systems are multiple-carrier owned.

The events to date have removed much of the perceived unfair advantages of vendor airlines. However, non-vendor airlines are still

Table 2.2. Airline affiliations with GDS.

SABRE	American Airlines	100%
GALILEO	United Airlines	38%
	British Airways	15%
	Swiss Air	13%
	KLM Royal Dutch Airlines	12%
	US Air	11%
	Alitalia	8.7%
	Olympic	1%
	Air Canada	1%
	TAP Air Portugal	1%
	Austrian Airlines	0.1%
	Aer Lingus	0.1%
AMADEUS	Lufthansa	29.2%
	Air France	29.2%
	Iberia	29.2%
	Continental Airlines	12.4%
WORLDSPAN	Delta Airlines	38%
	Northwest Airlines	32%
	TransWorld Airlines	25%
	Abacus	5%

Table 2.3. Estimated market value of major GDS.

GDS	million US$
Abacus	650
Amadeus	600
Apollo	1100+
Galileo	400
Sabre	1500–2000
SystemOne	500
Worldspan	500

Source: Green, D. 'Airline Ticket Shops Bridge the Atlantic', *Financial Times*, March 9 1996

left with the decision of how to best make their seat inventory electronically available to travel intermediaries. Non-vendor airlines can reach the travel agent electronically in two ways. First, they can become co-hosts with a vendor airline by listing their flight information and seat inventories on a section of the GDS hardware, for which they pay a fee. The airline, then, does not need its own hardware and software and yet has direct access to travel agents. Approximately

50% of the 1100 airlines in the world that are computerized are hosted on a GDS mainframe system (de Pommes *et al.*, 1995).

Second, an airline can develop its own computer reservation system in-house and then link that CRS with one more GDS. Or it can purchase a system from a computer vendor or another airline and again link with the GDS. Cost will often be a deciding factor in choosing one of these options. Arkia Israeli Airlines, for example, chose to create its own system in-house, because the cost of co-hosting with a GDS was too high (Borovits and Neumann, 1988). Airlines who decide to purchase their own system have the advantages that come with more contemporary architecture than that used by GDS. In any case, all non-vendor CRS need to create data communication links from their systems to the GDS. This is a complex process that is modelled in Fig. 2.5.

The airline must first be certified and receive a two-letter code from International Air Transport Association (IATA). After receiving this code, an airline in the US must file its fares with the Airline Tariff Publishing Company (ATPCO) and its schedules with the Official Airline Guide (OAG). (The rest of the world has equivalent organizations where the airlines must file this information.) Its fares and schedules are loaded into the GDS by OAG and ATPCO once a day along with 40 million other fares and schedules (Feldman, 1994). To receive bookings from the GDS, the airline's own CRS must be equipped with message switching hardware and software and connected through data communication links to GDS. These links can be provided by ARINC

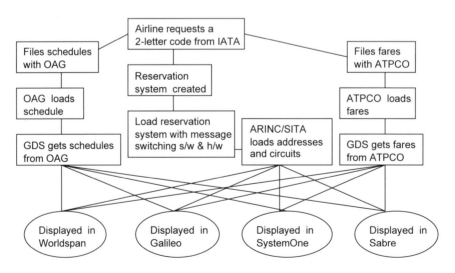

Fig. 2.5. GDS linkup for airlines. Source: Frontier Airlines.

or SITA or the non-vendor airline can create its own direct access links to provide faster confirmations and last seat availability to the travel agents. Once connected, any booking that comes through the GDS into the airline's own system requires a payment ($2–$3) to the GDS processing the booking. These substantial charges are causing airlines to investigate alternative methods of selling seats.

All airlines and GDSs are now creating a presence on the Internet and using that as an important distribution channel especially to consumers. This move is requiring changes in hardware and communication protocols – away from ALC toward TCP/IP (the Internet protocol). Airline home pages on the WWW vary in design and composition, but most allow consumers to view schedules, fares, fare rules and to book flights on-line. The displays are simpler than the ones on GDS screens, and are easier to follow. Frequent flyer club information such as award levels is also commonly found on airline home pages. Seat preferences can be requested, however, seat assignments are not yet given on-line. Payments with credit cards are possible for customers willing to give their numbers over the Web. Business travellers are especially eager to book their own flights. This direction, along with ticketless travel is irrevocably changing airline distribution channels. Chapter 5 will discuss these developments in detail.

The next section will discuss the core functionality provided by most airline reservation systems, which has remained relatively consistent despite changes in hardware platforms and operating systems.

2.2.4 Functionality of Airline Reservation Systems

The technological environments discussed above serve to provide important functionality for the users of the systems. The users are airline agents for the CRS, and both airline and travel agents for the GDS. Even though each airline's reservation system may have unique features the majority of the functions performed are similar and are discussed below.

Flight schedules and availability
Perhaps the most important function of airline CRS is to display flight schedules and availability in response to passenger and agent requests. A CRS will show one airline's schedules, whereas a GDS shows many carriers' schedules. A typical GDS availability screen (one of many generated for each request) is displayed in Fig. 2.6. Each screen contains information on the airline two-letter code, flight numbers, classes of service and number of seats available in each class, arrival and departure times of the flights, the type of aircraft and the meal service

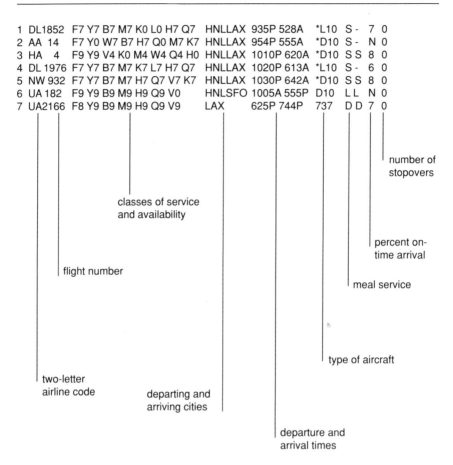

1 DL1852 F7 Y7 B7 M7 K0 L0 H7 Q7 HNLLAX 935P 528A *L10 S - 7 0
2 AA 14   F7 Y0 W7 B7 H7 Q0 M7 K7 HNLLAX 954P 555A *D10 S - N 0
3 HA   4   F9 Y9 V4 K0 M4 W4 Q4 H0 HNLLAX 1010P 620A *D10 S S 8 0
4 DL 1976 F7 Y7 B7 M7 K7 L7 H7 Q7 HNLLAX 1020P 613A *L10 S - 6 0
5 NW 932 F7 Y7 B7 M7 H7 Q7 V7 K7 HNLLAX 1030P 642A *D10 S S 8 0
6 UA 182   F9 Y9 B9 M9 H9 Q9 V0   HNLSFO 1005A 555P D10 L L N 0
7 UA2166 F8 Y9 B9 M9 H9 Q9 V9   LAX   625P 744P 737 D D 7 0

number of stopovers

classes of service and availability

percent on-time arrival

flight number

meal service

two-letter airline code

departing and arriving cities

type of aircraft

departure and arrival times

Fig. 2.6. Sample availability screen from a GDS. (Data taken from an Apollo screen.)

provided. On-time performance of the flight is displayed in the next to last column (e.g. 8 signifies an 80% on-time record). The number of stopovers is displayed in the last column.

The order in which the flights are displayed in a GDS is regulated to prevent bias. Flights higher in the screen displays are more likely to be booked by travel agents, and so the ordering of the display must instead reflect passenger convenience. It has been suggested that travel agents book 50% of flights on the first line of the first screen and 90% of flights from the first screen (Boberg and Collison, 1985) To avoid this carrier bias, algorithms are written to sort flights based on three criteria. The first criterion is whether the flight is non-stop, direct, or connecting. Non-stop flights are listed first, followed by direct and connecting flights. The second criterion is to list flights with the shortest displacement time first (displacement time is the difference between the requested and actual departure times). The third criterion is to list the flights with the shortest travel time with higher priority.

From this multiple-screen listing, the agent chooses a flight and makes a reservation request. The request is transmitted to the central site and is either processed directly by the GDS mainframes and confirmed (if the seat inventory is stored there), or it is forwarded by the FECP to the mainframe computer of the appropriate carrier's CRS to receive a confirmation. Reservations can be changed or cancelled in the same way. Seat maps of the various aircraft can be displayed on screen to assist with seat selection. Recently, in an attempt to board planes more quickly, some airlines chose not to assign seats for short haul flights. Instead passengers are given a number representing their arrival sequence at the airport which is used for boarding. Printouts of itineraries are generated from the systems.

Passenger information

Each reservation stored in a CRS or GDS must have passenger information attached to it. A passenger name record (PNR) contains information including the passenger's name, address, phone number, payment details, ticketing deadlines, frequent flyer number (if appropriate) and seat preferences (e.g. aisle or window). Other special requests such as special meals (e.g. vegetarian, kosher, diabetic), wheelchair requests, and assistance for unaccompanied minors are stored with the PNR and then transmitted to the appropriate departments. The systems also track the history of communications and requests to that PNR to monitor the reservation, including any special remarks that an agent might add. The PNR usually interfaces with the airline's frequent flyer database and reports the miles flown into the customer's account. This interface also facilitates the creation of a PNR since passenger information is already stored in the frequent flyer database. Detailed customer preferences can also be stored in the frequent flyer database to provide better customer service. Airlines use these databases for direct marketing campaigns, and to improve service.

Fare quotes and rules

Airline reservation systems contain large databases of fares and fare rules for each class of service for each itinerary. These have exploded in size and change frequency since airline deregulation in the US in 1978. An individual airline's CRS need only list its own fare information but a GDS must provide fare information on all carriers. Fare rules regarding reservation and ticketing deadlines, stopovers, maximum or minimum length of stay, and blackout dates are stored for each fare.

Fare basis codes are used to identify each fare and its appropriate set of rules. Fare displays can be sorted into ascending order, to accommodate travellers looking for the cheapest fare. For international itineraries, fares may need to be constructed considering multiple segments, multiple currencies, taxes and sets of regulations. This complex operation is performed either by specially trained staff at international faring desks or more recently, by expert systems (to be discussed more fully in Chapter 10). Fare quote software is one of the most challenging for airline programmers to design. Fares are often determined by yield management systems which run on separate computers outside the TPF environment. These sophisticated programs monitor the demand and supply of seats and use algorithms to generate the least fares to maximize revenues. Once determined, these fares are fed into the CRS or GDS for display.

Ticketing

Until recently, airlines have required passengers to travel with tickets to validate their reservation and payment. Airline CRS/GDS generate tickets and boarding passes on special printers in airline offices, travel agent offices or satellite ticket printers located in corporate offices or public areas (see Chapter 3). Ticket technology has changed from the multi-paged carbon ticket to a ticket and boarding pass with a magnetic strip on the back called the ATB-2 ticket (automatic ticket and boarding pass). These tickets, when fully utilized, significantly streamline check-in and information processing for reporting and analysis purposes. The magnetic strip encodes pertinent information such as passenger name, flight numbers and bare base code. Passengers insert the ticket into a machine as they board the plane. The machine reads the flight and passenger information encoded on the magnetic strip and feeds it into a computer database. After take-off, ground personnel no longer need to manually tally ticket coupons. Instead, the information is already in the database ready to produce the necessary reports.

The era of airline tickets, however, may be dying. Ticketless flights are now common, particularly for domestic and single carrier itineraries (Flint, 1995). In order to maintain security, the passenger is given a confirmation number at the time of booking and receives an itinerary in the mail. On arrival at the airport, the passenger gives the agent the confirmation number and a picture ID, and receives a boarding card. As with ATB-2 tickets, no ticket coupons need to be manually processed; thereby increasing the efficiency of both check-in and postflight data analysis. For itineraries on multiple carriers, ticketless flights are much more difficult to implement because of the necessary communications between the carriers.

2.3   OTHER AIRLINE APPLICATIONS OF IT

Reservation systems are the most predominant computer applications, but many airlines have invested millions of dollars in information systems to automate other areas of airline operations and management. These applications fall into two basic categories. One is the use of the computer to streamline operations, the other is the use of decision support systems to aid in decision-making. This section will discuss these two areas of application.

2.3.1 Computerization of Operations

Some airline operations are tedious and yet need to be performed as rapidly and accurately as possible. Such traits create a natural environment for computer technology to assist and are discussed in this section. The applications of IT to the three areas of baggage and cargo handling, cabin automation, and safety systems, all exhibit these traits.

Baggage and cargo handling systems

Airlines and airports operate together to efficiently move baggage and cargo from the check-in areas to the planes. They also attempt to prevent lost baggage and to track it if lost. These tasks can be accomplished with a combination of database systems of bag information databases and computerized equipment to handle the bags. Baggage tags with optical bar codes which record the tag number, flight segments and destination of each bag are the core of the bag tracking systems. At check-in, the tag information is read into a database of bags in transit. This may be a centralized database for use by multiple carriers as the one created by SITA called Bagtrac, or an airline may have its own. A lost bag can be readily tracked with the tag retained by the passenger. The optical bar code on the tag is used to access the record in the database and to determine the bag's location. Success of the system requires that when unretrieved bags are discovered, their information be consistently entered into the baggage tracking database.

Computerized baggage handling systems, which are the responsibility of the airport, again use the tags to transport baggage efficiently through a network of tunnels under the airport. Optical scanning technology in electronic eyes reads bag tags as they move along conveyor belts connecting check-in counters, baggage check-in points and aircraft at gates. These systems minimize the amount of lost baggage and transport the bags more rapidly from place to place.

Many airlines carry cargo and therefore need IT to handle both reservations and tracking systems separate from the passenger systems. As with passenger baggage, optical bar codes are used to track the cargo's journey. Moving the cargo, which is often larger and more cumbersome than passenger baggage, is an arduous task suited to automation. Automated cargo movement systems use automated guided vehicles (AGVs) to move the cargo. The AGVs are programmed to pick up cargo from a predetermined location, take it to a storage area, loading dock or departure area and place it down within 6 mm of the required location (Nelms, 1992).

Cabin automation

Activities in the aircraft cabin can be automated to enhance passenger experience and to improve the efficiency and quality of service. Small point-of-sale systems in the form of hand-held computers can be used to facilitate the sale of beverages, movie headsets, and duty-free products on board. Labour costs may also be reduced as fewer flight attendants are needed. The variety and quality of cabin meal service can also benefit from computer applications. Passengers often experience little variety in cabin meal service. This can be traced to slow communications between airlines and their caterers. On-line connectivity between the computers of caterers, airline catering staff, suppliers and purchasers, has been shown to improve the timely revision of menus. (Henderson, 1991b).

The passenger seat is becoming a hub of computer technology. Many seat backs now include video screens, phones with datajacks and fax transmission capabilities, and in some first class seats, laptop computers are provided. Passengers can use the seat-back telephone not only to place calls, but also for data input and to receive audio input through headsets. Video screens in the seat back can be used to watch videos on demand, to view the aircraft position display or airport layout, to shop for duty-free or mail order items, to send and receive e-mail, to play video games and even to gamble. One airline has found that the revenue from the gaming activities on board can offset the installation cost of the equipment ($3.5 million per aircraft). Gambling losses and winnings are limited to moderate amounts to avoid overreaction by passengers. Interactive video screens in seat backs may entertain passengers so that the need for attendants to service passengers is reduced. It is predicted that video screens will be in all seats in all wide-bodied planes by the year 2000 (Reamy, 1995).

An additional cabin service provided by some carriers is the visual geographic information system (GIS) display which shows the location of the aircraft and its progress on a video screen. Information on aircraft speed, time to arrival and outside temperature are shown on the display either in the seat-back screen or the main cabin screen.

Safety systems

Safety is a major concern in all aspects of airline operation and computer technology can improve it. Regular maintenance of aircraft is one of the most important applications where computers can help. Computerized systems ensure that all aircraft receive maintenance on schedule (Gray, 1993). Databases which contain information on each aircraft and its component parts, and the time schedule for maintenance for each part can be used to generate reports so that no mistakes are made. These systems also reduce repair costs, particularly for airlines with older fleets needing more maintenance. The case at the end of this chapter shows how one airline has computerized its maintenance operations. Safety is also increased by computer systems which check the weight of each aircraft and its content prior to take-off.

Databases which record incidents where safety was at risk can also enhance an airline's safety record. Examples of such incidents range from pilot error, to accidents in the cabin galley, to oil leaks. As events occur which endanger safety, employees enter data into the computer system. This provides an important data bank for pilots and other employees assigned to work with a certain aircraft. They can search the database for potential safety problems and reduce the likelihood of a problem occurring (Nelms, 1992). The computer serves as a memory of safety violations and allows the company to better understand where their operations need attention. Such a system does depend, however, on the diligent entry of safety violations as they occur. Another aspect of computerized safety occurs in the airports. It is essential that certain areas of an airport are accessible only to bona-fide staff on duty. Computerized locking and entry devices are used to maintain the security of these areas.

2.3.2 Decision Support Systems

Airline managers are faced with many complex decisions about the airline's flight activity. A particular type of computer system can be used to analyse such situations and recommend solutions to problems, particularly scheduling and control problems. These systems are based on sophisticated models called Operations Research (OR) models. These models use 'What-if?' and sensitivity analyses to investigate the impact of various factors on operational and logistical problems. They also maximize or minimize variables given certain constraints. Skilled staff with OR training are needed to build and use these models. Successful applications of OR models can provide airlines with substantial savings. For example, an OR model of booking control was implemented by Scandinavian Air with an estimated net potential revenue increase of about $2 million per year (Alstrup *et al.*, 1989).

Decision Support Systems (DSSs) based on OR models constitute a significant amount of airline computer applications. They run on different hardware platforms and software environments from the reservation systems. Hardware platforms are often parallel computers running specialized optimization and simulation software. Large volumes of data are needed for the model development and testing, and graphical user interfaces are used to facilitate data input (Gray and Kabbani, 1994).

The following section will discuss the OR applications of flight scheduling, crew management and gate management.

Flight scheduling and planning

Flight scheduling requires a careful determination by airline management of their route structure. This includes an examination of the most profitable routes, the frequency with which to serve those routes, and the aircraft to fly on each route. The route structure (hub and spoke or point-to-point) must also be determined. OR models are used to support these decisions, which for a large airline are very complex.

Flight demand is an important input to the models, and sophisticated forecasting models using econometric techniques are used to project demand for each route. Other important inputs are competitive factors such as other airlines flying a particular route and the fares they charge, economic factors such as household income, and business trends and cycles, and available resources such as crew, planes and gate accessibility. Exogenous and more erratic factors such as weather, air traffic control delays and technical failures must also be considered by the programmers in the creation of these models. The model's outputs are flight schedules which maximize load factors and revenues under the given constraints. Flight scheduling is an ongoing task since schedules fluctuate with market and competitive forces and seasons. For more detailed information on flight scheduling systems see Abara (1989), Henderson (1991c) and Gray and Kabbani (1994).

Crew scheduling and management

Once the flight schedules have been determined, the pilots and flight attendants for each flight must be scheduled. Computerized OR-based DSS models are used to assemble flight packages (called bidlines) for each crew member for a given period of time. To determine the best assignment of crew to a flight, OR models work with various inputs to create the best schedules. Examples of inputs are crew requests for their preferred routes, crew member seniority, and their base city. Other constraints in the model are work rules (such as maximum number of hours of work stipulated by the FAA (Federal Aviation Association) and other bodies) and cost parameters such as salaries and budgets. Optimization models generate the best schedules and pairings for pilots and flight attendants for all flights for a given time period. For a fuller discussion of crew scheduling systems see Jones (1989) and Gershkoff (1989).

Gate management and departure control

Once flights have been scheduled and the crew assigned, flight arrivals in airports must be coordinated with airport facilities. Each flight needs a gate assignment upon arrival and must utilize the gate efficiently to depart on time and not cause delays in other flights. An arriving aircraft has numerous needs: a skyway to disembark the passengers into the terminal and access for vehicles to service the aircraft in preparation for another flight. Examples of such services are food service, cleaning, fuelling and maintenance.

In determining the best utilization of gates, OR-based computer models consider arrival times, aircraft types, turnaround time, gates of connecting flights (particularly for hub and spoke route structures) and cost. The best gate pattern for arrivals is determined such that all resources are used most efficiently. In larger airports, some airlines have their own terminals making gate assignment simpler than when multiple carriers share the same terminal. Many airports, however, do not have enough gates to accommodate the number of incoming flights. Often airlines must deplane on the runways, bus the passengers into the terminal, and service the plane on the tarmac. Computer technology can mitigate the inconveniences caused by gate shortages by ensuring maximum use of available gates.

When different airlines share gates, they also must share the use of the computer terminals located at the gates for check-in. This creates a special problem. The terminals cannot be connected to an individual airline's computer system as when the gate is dedicated to a particular airline. SITA has therefore developed a technology called Common Usage Terminal Equipment (CUTE) which allows any airline to use a terminal to access its own computer reservation systems. CUTE terminals are connected on a local area network in the airport allowing airlines to access their own departure control systems regardless of their location in the airport (Saunders, 1994).

In summary, the application of IT to airline operations is ubiquitous, comprehensive and dynamic. Because airlines depend heavily on the airports they fly into, the next section of this chapter will discuss airports' use of information technology.

2.4 AIRPORT USE OF IT

Airports are complex webs of IT applications. They house the hubs of data communication networks for air traffic control, airline and airport use, in addition to the many and varied applications inside the terminal for passenger use. This section will focus on those technologies which are enhancing passengers' experiences in increasingly busy and complex airports.

2.4.1 Flight Information Display Systems

When travellers find themselves in unfamiliar airports, they have a critical need for information on airport activities and facilities, preferably in their own language. Information on arriving and departing flights, gates and baggage collection are the most critical. Electronic signage plays a role in providing this information and making airports easier to navigate. Flight Information Display Systems (FIDS) display flight departure and arrival times, gate assignment and baggage carousel locations on large wall-sized displays or individual monitors. The information is taken from airlines' individual computer systems, and entered into a central database by airport staff, which is then sorted and transmitted to numerous display boards in various locations around the airport. Denver International Airport, the newest airport in the US, for example, has 1200 flight or baggage information display monitors throughout the airport (Denver International Airport, 1996).

Many FIDS now incorporate multimedia and graphic displays (Musselwhite, 1996b). Smaller display monitors in kiosks are also being introduced to provide the traveller with more diverse information and the ability to control their information search, rather than viewing a generic display. In addition to flight information, these kiosks can also include information on airport facilities and on the city destination's tourist industry.

2.4.2 Electronic Immigration Control

One of the most arduous and time consuming tasks in international gateway airports is the processing of passengers' visas and immigration documents. At busy airports when numerous flights disembark at the same time, delays can be long, and tired passengers become frustrated. Numerous agencies (including the World Travel and Tourism Council) are looking to information technology to improve this situation.

A computerized system called INSPASS, using hand geometry, is now in use in some US airports to speed immigration procedures.

A frequent traveller wishing to minimize their waiting time at international airports can apply for an INSPASS card prior to travel. Enrolment requires the traveller to place a hand in a geometry reader which generates a three dimensional template of the enrolee's hand. This image is stored in a database accessible to immigration officers across the country, and is encoded onto a card which is given to the traveller. Upon arrival at a US border the traveller inserts the card into a kiosk, and then places the hand onto the reader. If the hand image matches the one in the database, the traveller can pass through with no further examination. If not, the passenger is asked to proceed to an agent. Even though such systems will not be used by all travellers since prior enrolment is not always possible or practical, waiting time for remaining passengers is shortened because some travellers will use the automated system (Zunkel, 1996). Figure 2.7 shows a photograph of the reader.

Some governments have also computerized immigration control to a lesser degree. They have databases which contain information on individuals they do not wish to enter the country. These databases are accessed when travellers show their documentation upon entry into a country. The digitization of passports and visas is another trend to facilitate the processing of passengers through immigration control.

2.4.3 Passenger Service Applications

As travellers spend more time in airports due to flight delays, congestion and hub route structures, they need access to more facilities. These facilities are needed for refreshment and entertainment and some to allow travellers to do business. Entertainment and refreshment are provided by shops and restaurants, all of which use IT in the form of point-of-sale systems to record and process transactions. Duty-free shopping in particular requires information processing to ensure merchandise is sold only to bona-fide travellers. Boarding passes with magnetic strips can be used to allow access to the stores. Computer connections to flight information are needed to deliver the merchandise to the passenger's flight.

Business travellers have special needs in airports. Many travel with their own laptop computers and need access to data communication facilities. Airport lounges often provide facilities such as fax machines, phones with data jacks and personal computers. Airports are a natural meeting place, some also have meeting rooms set up with teleconferencing facilities which can be rented for use. In the terminals

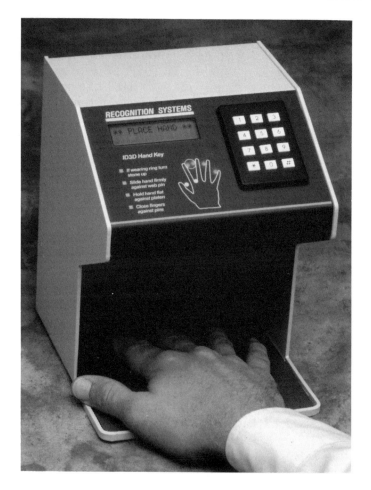

Fig. 2.7. Photo of hand imaging kiosk. The traveller places their hand into the machine at immigration control. Photograph permission of Recognition Systems Inc.

themselves, telephone/data terminals are being installed for passenger use. These 'pay-as-you-go' electronic mail terminals are connected to the Internet. Travellers can use them with a credit card and a touch screen terminal to send messages worldwide to transmit and receive data, and to surf the Internet.

2.5 SUMMARY

The airline industry has used IT intensely and creatively to thrive in a very competitive and volatile market. Its need for massive information processing and data communications has created the many systems discussed above. In the process, the airline industry has become a classic example of the successful application of information systems to operations, marketing and management. There are many types of airline reservation systems and the technology is constantly changing. Those which operate in the TPF environment and use ALC communication protocols are vulnerable to the newer technologies and connectivity. The TPF environment continues to exist today partly due to the extensive investment in hardware and human resources needed to maintain the systems. This investment is likely to slow down the transition to the next generation of airline reservation technology. But other players are entering the travel distribution market. IBM, Microsoft and EDS are investing in alternative systems to the GDS, and it is questionable how long the GDSs will enjoy the dominant position and substantial profits they have in the past. As demands on airlines and airports increase, airlines need to continue to investigate and invest in new technologies to improve the efficiency, comfort and safety of air travel. Significant areas of development now for airlines are artificial intelligence and expert systems (to be discussed in Chapter 10) and the use of the Internet and ticketless travel to market directly to the end consumer (to be discussed further in Chapter 5).

2.6 CASE – SINGAPORE AIRLINES

Singapore International Airlines (SIA), one of the world's most profitable airlines and a frequent recipient of consumer and industry awards, is an example of an airline committed to the use of information technology in its operations. It is the national airline of Singapore established in 1972 with routes to over 70 cities in 41 countries. It has a fleet of 77 aircraft (for both passenger and freight transportation) with an average age of approximately 5 years, making it the world's most modern fleet. This fleet carries ten million passengers annually. SIA is committed to investing in cutting-edge technology as it strives for excellence in product innovation and in providing quality in-flight and ground services.

SIA uses many of the computer applications discussed in the text including flight operations and cabin crew management (flight planning, airport analysis, crew assignments, fuel management) and corporate and financial applications (budgeting, crisis management, complaint tracking, document handling). Like most airlines, SIA's passenger and cargo reservations are extensively automated. Its own CRS called Kriscom performs all of the functions discussed in the chapter such as availability displays, service requests, check-in, gate boarding, weight and balance, seat requests, in-flight sales, the ability to perform post departure investigations, and frequent flier information. Kriscom also has direct access data communications with other CRSs and GDSs.

A yield management system, called Krismax, is currently being developed to improve revenue and inventory control. It controls, on a flight segment basis, the amount of space available for different classes of seats from the various booking sources. It also determines time periods when these different classes and fares are available. Fares generated from this system will be fed into the CRS. The system will also incorporate a module which handles group requests. SIA's reservations from travel agents are taken care of with its major investment and involvement with Abacus, the Asian GDS, which has over 12,500 terminals in 5000 travel agencies.

New computer systems are being introduced to smooth SIA's airport operations. A system to improve pilot and cabin crew rostering is one such system. Another is the cargo tracking at Changi Airport in Singapore which is also connected to cargo systems globally. A mainframe TPF-based Departure Control System (DCS) is used to handle passenger check-in, seat allocation, issuance of boarding passes, printing of baggage tags, and the tracking of boarded passengers. This system also ensures that departing aircraft are properly trimmed prior to take-off. A PC-based interface to DCS (called Krischeck) is now in place with a graphical user interface freeing users from the cryptic entries necessary to use the host system directly.

SIA provides maintenance for its own aircraft and on a contractual basis for other airlines and has developed computer applications for aircraft maintenance with a system called 'Integrated Technical Documentation and Production Control System'. The system was progressively implemented beginning in 1996 after extensive design and development efforts to improve all of its maintenance activities. Technically, the system is superior to its predecessor since it is an open system compliant with the many data standards used in the industry. A Project Management Committee was set up to oversee the project including senior management, engineers, users, and a System Integrator (SI). The SI was brought in to simplify SIA's communications with the multiple software and hardware vendors involved with the project. Also the SI assisted with training of SIA's IT personnel. The SI worked closely with the project management team in resolving operational problems, and assisted with training of SIA's personnel.

The system consists of three components. The first two, called Technical Documentation and Maintenance Planning, are designed to automate technical documentation for aircraft maintenance for SIA's own varied fleet required by manufacturers and local authorities. Technical documentation such as the Aircraft Maintenance Manual and Service Bulletins from aircraft manufacturers are accepted and input in digital format. Maintenance schedule information formerly on tape can also be accepted by the system. This system significantly reduces the man-hours required by maintenance engineers, who no longer must manually refer to technical manuals during aircraft maintenance activities. Instead, each employee is given up-to-date job cards generated from the system containing detailed work descriptions and graphic illustrations of the aircraft components.

The third subsystem is a Production Control System called AIRMAN which focuses on third party aircraft maintenance provided by SIA for other airlines. It includes four modules:

Job Control: this provides real-time comparisons between planned and actual time spent on tasks highlighting delays and bottlenecks.

Labour Resources Management: this module continuously updates records of total labour resources by skill and qualification and identifies where these resources are currently employed or needed in the future.

Inventory Management: this module deals with customer part handling and the management of spare parts

Commercial and Administration: this module produces quotations, maintains contracts and individual sales orders, monitoring of these orders in production and the transformation of costs and charges to produce an invoice.

SIA is also using technology in the cabin for passenger use. It recently introduced a global in-flight telephone and fax service and a global in-flight television news service. On some of its bigger aircraft, SIA has implemented an interactive in-flight entertainment system called KrisWorld, providing passengers with a library of audio-visual material, including computer games, in-flight shopping and real-time financial and news updates.

Information Technology Applications to Travel Intermediaries 3

3.1 INTRODUCTION

This chapter examines the application of information technology (IT) to travel intermediaries. Travel intermediaries are firms who distribute the travel product to the end consumer. There are different types of travel intermediaries: travel agents, tour operators and speciality channellers. Travel agents arrange and distribute travel mostly to individual travellers, although some specialize in certain market segments or products, and some design and sell their own group package tours. Tour operators and tour wholesalers design package tours and sell them either directly to the traveller or through an agent. Speciality channellers distribute travel products to special interest groups – examples of such firms are meeting and convention planners and corporate travel planners.

Travel intermediaries of all types use information intensely and therefore need IT to process that information. Indeed, information on travel products, destinations, schedules, fares, rates and availabilities is their most important product and defines their existence. The more information the travel intermediary can access electronically, the more timely, accurate and efficient service can be provided to the client. It has been estimated, for example, that sales per travel agent increase by approximately 25% by automating the reservation function. The application of IT, therefore, is critical to increase the efficiency, productivity and market reach of travel intermediaries. Travel agencies, tour operators and speciality channellers also use computers to process internal information. Examples are to create tour packages and to organize meetings and conventions. This chapter will discuss all of these IT applications, the hardware and software configurations, and their benefits and impacts.

IT poses a potential threat to the existence of travel intermediaries since electronic connectivity can bring products directly into the hands of the consumer. IT applications can be used to mitigate that threat by creating value-added products and by integrating IT into their strategic planning. The last section of the chapter examines how IT is impacting upon the travel distribution channel. The chapter ends with a case example of a travel agent that has been particularly successful in its strategic implementation of information technology.

3.2 TRAVEL AGENCY USE OF IT

Travel agents are the most ubiquitous travel intermediaries varying in size from multinational, multi-branch mega-agencies to small, independently owned offices. This section describes their use of computers for information retrieval and reservations, the various hardware configurations that different sized travel agencies use, the application of CD-ROM technology to travel information distribution, electronic ticketing and computerized back office systems. The chapter will cover applications and impacts internationally, but because North America is where many of the new technologies are being applied and developed, a little more attention will be given there.

3.2.1 Global Distribution Systems

The first and most prevalent application of IT to travel agents is the GDS terminal (as discussed in Chapter 2). These terminals were first placed in travel agents' offices by major airlines to facilitate airline bookings in the mid 1970s. Prior to that, travel agents had to rely on the phone and telex for reservations or the printed Official Airline Guide (OAG) for schedule and fare information. Some travel agents were given blocks of seats to sell in 'desk sets' but the system was not efficient. Since then, more and more travel agencies have acquired computer terminals for information retrieval and reservations and the terminal's functionality and product availability has dramatically increased over time. Today, in the US and increasingly around the world, GDS terminals are the major information and booking tools used by travel agents for all types of travel products. The speed of the GDS data networks linking the terminals to the mainframe can return confirmations to travel agents in seconds. Owners and managers of travel agencies usually find it easy to justify the costs of installing such systems as the benefits are numerous.

Available systems

The major systems available to travel agents worldwide (as discussed in Chapter 2) are Sabre, Apollo/Galileo, Worldspan, SystemOne/ Amadeus, and Abacus. The recent interconnectivity of the US, European and Asian systems, both technically and organizationally, gives the travel agent global access to travel suppliers from any one of these terminals. Further background on the development of these systems and their role in travel distribution can be found in Sloane (1990) and Truitt *et al.* (1991). Of all US travel agents 98% have automated their reservations with GDS terminals. Sabre and Apollo/Galileo are the most commonly used systems with Worldspan and SystemOne having a smaller share of the market. The number of terminals per agency varies but on average there are five per travel agency location (Harris, 1994). Many large corporate travel agencies may have terminals to more than one system.

In Europe, the use of GDS terminals has been more recent and is not yet so prevalent as in the US. Travel agents have instead relied either on phone bookings, telex or videotext systems to make bookings. Airline reservations could be made through a terminal of the national airline's computer system, and tour packages could be booked through tour operators' videotext terminals. In the UK, however, a system called TRAVICOM has been used. This is a multi-access reservation system owned by British Airways. Travicom Skytrack is another booking tool for UK travel agents providing direct videotext links with over 40 airlines. The national videotext system called Prestel has also been used in the UK for travel agent booking (Bennett, 1988). In Germany, a system called START was designed and implemented jointly by travel agencies, German Rail, Lufthansa and a tour operator to give access to more than just airline seats. It has subsequently joined with Amadeus, but provided good accessibility to booking travel products in Germany until the more widespread use of GDS systems occurred.

More recently, agents are installing GDS terminals of SystemOne/ Amadeus and Apollo/Galileo, with some installations of Sabre and Worldspan. A goal in the development of the two European GDS (Amadeus and Galileo) was to create systems which fairly represented multiple carriers. They had seen how the travel industry in the US had wrestled with systems originally affiliated with only one airline. A comprehensive discussion of automated reservation systems in UK agencies can be found in Bennett (1988) and a similar discussion of automation of French travel agencies can be found in Guyomard (1994). In Europe, the average number of terminals per agency is just over three, and the most commonly used system is Amadeus/ SystemOne. Some agencies still use the videotext systems.

Even though the US and Europe represent the largest number of GDS terminals, they are now used all over the world. In total, GDS terminals are installed in 125 countries with 98,000 locations representing nearly 250,000 terminals (Schaeffer, 1994). In most cases, GDS vendors are setting up national marketing companies (NMCs) to distribute their product in each country. The NMC knows the needs and cultural differences of the specific country's travel industry better than the GDS vendors and so can more effectively market the GDS. In Asian countries (the next most automated area after US and Europe), on average 40% of agents use GDS terminals. Abacus is the most commonly used GDS in Asia since it is owned and developed by Asian carriers. It is marketed through NMCs in Australia, Brunei (where it is the only available GDS), Hong Kong, India, Indonesia, South Korea, Malaysia, Philippines, Singapore and Taiwan. Abacus is now in a joint venture with Vietnam Airlines to set up a NMC in Hanoi. In Japan, Abacus and All Nippon Airways have set up a joint venture GDS called Infini of which Abacus has a 40% equity stake.

In Australia, travel agents have the choice of three systems. Sabre is distributed in Australia by Fantasia which has 43% of the market. A company called Southern Cross has the marketing rights to the Galileo system which has 52% of the Australian market. The distribution of the GDS in Australia is done under the auspices of TIAS (Travel Industries Automated Systems, Pty). In New Zealand, all four major GDSs are represented but Galileo and Sabre have 80% of the agencies and 95% of the bookings.

In some lesser developed countries, the GDS vendors are aggressively trying to capture the market. In India, for example, the Sabre system is being marketed under the name SITAR, and is being distributed through NMCs. In Latin America, SystemOne is well represented, with two of the national airlines (Varig and Aerolineas Argentina) being part of the Amadeus consortium. Numerous countries (e.g. Myanmar, Sri Lanka, Bangladesh, Pakistan) as yet do not have travel agent access to GDS due to the lack of telecommunication infrastructures, and cost and demand factors.

Now that GDS vendors are offering their products competitively in most countries, each travel agent must make a choice of which system(s) to use. The next section addresses important factors to be considered in that choice. Table 3.1 shows the GDS reach throughout the world.

System choice

A travel agency's choice of GDS involves the consideration of many factors. Even though all GDSs have much in common, there are variations in the product and in the contract that must be considered. The

Table 3.1. Worldwide usage of GDS.

	ABACUS	AMADEUS/ SYSTEMONE	GALILEO	SABRE	WORLDSPAN
NORTH	0	6,796	10,842	15,218	8,475
AMERICA		27,240	50,668	74,087	34,000
EUROPE	0	17,590	7,827	4,694	2,900
		47,300	29,344	13,481	7,700
ASIA/PACIFIC	3,000	470	4,029	1,476	0
	7,000	1,151	12,222	5,325	
AFRICA &	0	265	1,345	526	380
MIDDLE EAST		470	5,677	1,299	680
LATIN AMERICA	0	4,275	872	980	625
& CARIBBEAN		6,803	1,547	2,289	750

First figure is number of locations and second is number of terminals.
Source: Vendors' statistics, 1995.
Data for Galileo includes Apollo.

goal of most agencies acquiring GDS access is to have easy access to the most relevant updated information, the most flexible contract at the lowest cost, and good support for service and training.

Travel agents need access to complete, unbiased information so that they can advise their clients well. Information presented on the screens of GDS terminals in the US used to be heavily biased towards the airline sponsoring the system, thereby heavily influencing the travel agent access to information and subsequent bookings. The vendor airline would place its own flights on the first few screens, putting other carriers out of easy reach of the travel agent. Since travel agents tend to book flights off the first screen (90% of the time) or even off the first line of the first screen (50% of the time), non-vendor airlines received substantially fewer bookings, and vendor airlines received more, creating a 'halo effect' for that airline (Boberg and Collison, 1985). In 1984, the Department of Transportation ruled that flight availability screens must be unbiased and cannot be sorted based on carrier identity. Other variables such as displacement time (difference between requested and actual departure time), whether the flight is a non-stop, a direct or a connecting flight, and elapsed time of the journey are all variables that can be used. The systems' sorting algorithms are checked by the Department of Transportation regularly to ensure compliance with the non-bias ruling.

Although bias in the flight availability screens is no longer legal, other information sections of the GDS often reflect some bias in the

form of more detailed and up-to-date information on the vendor airline. Therefore, the more bookings a travel agent does with an airline,
the more likely they are to use its GDS. In Hawaii, for example, where
United Airlines has been the major carrier, more agents use the
Apollo/Galileo system than any other GDS since they book more
United flights. The European and Asian systems designed their systems to be unbiased from the beginning. This choice was made by both
the European Commission which oversees the European systems and
by the management of Abacus after seeing the controversy created by
biased systems in the US. No regulation exists about bias in display
screens for other travel products such as hotels, car rentals, or tour
packages. In most instances the display order is random amongst those
suppliers that pay to be listed, and each subsequent information
request generates different screen responses.

Another factor influencing the access to information and therefore
system choice is the number of direct access links the GDS has with
other travel computer systems. As discussed in Chapter 2, direct
access links between reservation systems tend to create quicker communication, faster confirmations and access to last seat/room availability with non-vendor airlines and hotels. Direct access allows the
travel agent terminal to look and book directly into the computer of
the other supplier, empowering the travel agent to provide better service to clients by working with more complete and updated information on that particular vendor's products. Travel agents therefore
prefer a GDS to have direct access links with as many of its major suppliers as possible. For example, if the agent has a large volume of
bookings with a particular hotel chain, a direct access link facilitates
communication and bookings with that chain's reservation system.
Most GDSs have more than a hundred direct access links with other
travel industry reservation systems and more are being added over
time.

The next important consideration in choosing a system is the content of contract the agent must sign with the GDS vendor to obtain terminals. This contract, originally very restrictive on the travel agent
(and often referred to as the 'golden handcuff'), has, over time, become
more flexible. The term 'golden handcuff' refers to the fact that the
very tight clauses in the contract left the travel agents feeling 'hand-
cuffed' to the vendor. The term 'golden' refers to the fact that travel
agencies gained significant benefits by signing these contracts in terms
of productivity. Prior to 1984, the contracts included the following
clauses:

1. The contracts were of infinite length giving the agent no option to
discontinue or switch systems without paying high liquidated damage

costs. A typical formula for calculating the liquidated damage (LD) costs is: LD = # terminals × 200 × (average revenue per booking approx. $2.50) × # months remaining. These costs can be substantial for a large agency wishing to switch systems.

2. The contract required exclusivity on the part of the travel agent (i.e. the agent could not use more than one vendor's GDS).

3. GDS vendors required a certain minimum usage level of the terminals (at least 200 bookings per month) otherwise they were pulled from the agent's office and leased to more productive agencies.

4. Productivity pricing was part of the contract, meaning that if the agent used the terminal to book very large volumes of transactions, they were charged less by the GDS vendor.

In 1984, after much input and debate from the travel agents and the non-vendor airlines, the Department of Transportation investigated GDS practices. They ruled that contracts with agents could be for no more than 5 years and that exclusivity was illegal. In 1992 further legislation reduced the maximum length of contract to 3 years, and removed the minimum use clause. An attempt to remove productivity pricing was unsuccessful and large productive travel agencies can still be automated at no or low cost if they generate a certain number of bookings. There have been instances where extremely high booking levels can entice the GDS vendor to pay them per booking instead (Poling, 1992).

Travel agents can now have more than one vendor's GDS in their office if they choose since the exclusivity clause has been lifted. Many large agencies do so to ensure totally updated and comprehensive information on multiple carriers, thereby allowing them to serve different large corporate clients who prefer different airlines. It is clear from the above discussion that travel agency contracts for GDS terminals are complex. The need for travel agency managers to carefully analyse the clauses when signing a contract with a GDS vendor cannot be overemphasized.

Other important decision factors are the level of service and training provided by the GDS vendor. Service for both software and hardware problems are often provided with tollfree numbers into the GDS central site to troubleshoot problems. Some GDSs also offer on-line troubleshooting. If hardware must be repaired or replaced, GDS vendors typically contract with local companies to provide on-site service. With systems such as Galileo which are installed in many countries, a national service company is designated by the GDS vendor to service the travel agent clients, removing the need to have GDS employees worldwide. Training may be done centrally or locally, and the amount of training included in the contract needs to be considered by the travel agency. Issues such as the number of agents that will be trained and the availability and cost of the training must be known. Most systems have computer-aided instruction modules in the GDS so that agents can train themselves. With the introduction of more user-friendly interfaces in the future the training issue may be less critical.

Another issue for multinational travel agencies to consider is whether the GDS vendor will permit their branches in different parts of the world to access and/or change passenger name records (PNRs) and itineraries created by a branch in another country. As many travel agency mergers are taking place across international borders, this is an important consideration. Fortunately the global merging of the GDS vendors is happening concurrently. For example, Apollo and Galileo are now making this possible. If Apollo sets are used by a company in the US to create a PNR, branch agencies in Europe using Galileo sets can access and change that PNR if that is what the travel agency wants.

The specific functionality of the systems, although somewhat similar, also plays a role in the choice of system. The next section will discuss the various functions performed by GDS terminals, and will list the functions offered by the vendors.

Functionality

The functionality of a GDS is immense, and many of the features were discussed in Chapter 2. Travel agent terminals connected to the host mainframes are programmed so that information displayed on their screens is different from screens and functions used by airline agents. The following section discusses some of the GDS functions most used by travel agents to facilitate their booking and information retrieval:

Air features

- Flight Information: Access to information on availability, schedules, fares, fare rules, and bookings for thousands of flights on hundreds of carriers.
- Passenger Information: Ability to create, modify and store PNRs, itineraries, frequent flier information and special requests.
- Document Printing: Facilities to print tickets, boarding passes and itineraries.

Non-air features

- Booking car rentals, hotels, cruises, rail and tour packages.
- Ordering foreign currency or theatre/event tickets.
- Checking the weather worldwide by connecting with weather computer systems.
- Accessing Department of State Travel Advisories.

- Accessing information on international border controls through TIMATIC. This subsection of the GDS provides information on visas and passports, health, customs, currency controls, and departure taxes.
- Accessing destination information through TravelFile and other databases.
- Electronic mail and fax facilities.

The GDSs have traditionally been command-driven requiring the use of formats and codes to request information and to perform the transactions mentioned above. Command-driven systems are often faster for expert users than menu-driven systems and so are still used. Recently, however, Windows applications with 'point and click' user interfaces are being developed by the vendors to facilitate use and increase productivity further by reducing the number of key strokes required and therefore time for transactions. The Windows environment also allows agents to move between applications, PNRs or functions more easily, and generally increases the user-friendliness.

The GDSs provide additional tools to increase efficiency. One of these is the queuing function which queues messages to a particular agent's terminal from the GDS host computer. These queues are like a filing system that contains information about actions needed to be taken by the agent, such as when to ticket reservations in the computer. Another software feature of the GDS is scripting. This allows a sequence of commands to be stored (often in the function keys) so that often-used research and booking functions can be performed more quickly. A simple example of script use is the sign-on required to log on to the GDS that can be programmed into one function key. A more complex example is the sending of a flight request to a special fax processor that will send a fax of flight information to the client's fax, removing the need for the agent to read flight options over the phone. Table 3.2 shows the various features of each of the major systems.

The GDSs are used extensively for booking all travel products (as shown in Table 3.3), but airline seats still represent the products most likely to be booked through a GDS. Other products such as cruises and tour packages tend to be booked less through a GDS because of their complexity, the need for more detailed information, and because agents' confidence in electronically booking those products is still being established. Booking of these various suppliers has, however, been facilitated by the direct access communication links created between the GDS and the host computers of each supplier.

Costs are involved for each supplier to be listed on the GDS. Therefore, even though most travel sectors can be booked through the

Table 3.2. Functions offered by the major GDS systems.

	ABACUS	AMADEUS/ SYSTEMONE	APOLLO/ GALILEO	SABRE	WORLD-SPAN
CD-ROM				SabreVision	
Fax	Abacus Easi Manager	SystemOne Easylink	Apollofax	SabreExpress	Fasttrack
Windows	N/A	Amadeus Pro	Focalpoint	Sabre for Windows	Worldspan for Windows
Corporate	Abacus View Abacus Easi-Access	SystemOne Access	Corporate Apollo	Corporate Sabre	Commercial World
Consumer	Abacus View	HomePro	United Connection	Eaasy Sabre	Travel Shopper
Car	Care System	Amadeus Cars	Car Master		Car Select
Hotel	Hotel Source	Amadeus Hotels	Hotel Master		Hotel Select
Cruises	Cruisematch	Cruisematch	Cruisematch	Cruisematch	Cruise Source
Tour Packages	N/A	Tour Source	Leisure Shopper	Tourlink	Tour Source
Destination Information	Timatic	Weissman Travel Reports	TravelFile	TravelFile	Worldspan Travel Suppliers
Direct Access Links	Abacus Easy-Access	Amadeus Access	Easylink		Worlddial Link

Source: Vendor's information as of 1996.

Table 3.3. Travel product bookings made through GDS terminals.

Travel product	Percentage of bookings through GDS
Domestic Air	95%
International Air	86%
Car rentals	77%
Rail	61%
Hotels	57%
Tour Packages	14%
Cruises	10%

Source: Harris, 1996.

GDS the smaller, lower-priced travel products tend to be under-repre-sented, whereas the larger suppliers are well represented. More com-prehensive destination information systems are being developed by tourism offices to fill that gap by representing all the destination's facilities. These will be discussed in Chapter 8.

Hardware configurations

The configuration of computer hardware appropriate for a particular travel agency depends on agency size and the applications desired. All hardware configurations begin with at least one GDS terminal. Each terminal has a terminal address (TA) so that the host computer knows how to communicate with each terminal. Originally the terminals were dumb terminals leased from the GDS vendor, acting as send and receive devices only. After the 1992 legislation by the Department of Transportation (referred to earlier), travel agents can use third party hardware for the terminal as opposed to hardware that had to be leased from the GDS. The European Commission also permits European travel agents this flexibility so they can use whatever hard-ware they choose.

A terminal processing unit or gateway is needed if there is more than one terminal in the office. This piece of hardware consolidates the messages from each terminal so that they can all be transmitted out of the office on one dedicated phone line. A modem and a printer are also needed in all configurations. In most agencies numerous work-stations are connected together by a local area network (LAN) using network software. The file server is then connected through a gateway, modem and a dedicated phone line to the host central mainframe. The size and type of machine used for the file server varies with agency size and the number of software applications being used. Figure 3.1 shows a typical configuration.

Of agents' reservation terminals, 57% are now intelligent work-stations used for word processing, spreadsheet, database, desktop pub-lishing, e-mail and any other software applications (Harris, 1996). The additional functions provided by intelligent workstations, and the per-centage of agencies in the US using each function are described in Table 3.4. Business applications such as word processing and spread-sheets are used by the majority of travel agents. Data communication functions such as accessing distant databases, for fax transmission, or e-mail are used by a small minority of agencies. This is likely to change as agents realize the power that interconnectivity provides.

Hardware configurations have become more flexible since the GDS vendors no longer control terminals. Products are available which pro-vide multiple access from one travel agent LAN to numerous different travel industry CRSs. They can also provide software that will show

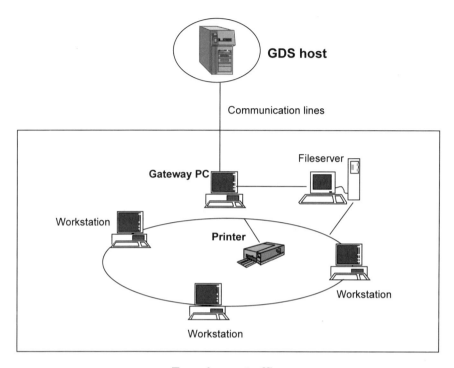

Travel agent office

Fig. 3.1. Typical travel agent LAN hardware configuration.

Table 3.4. PC use in travel agencies.

Word processing	78%
Database management	72%
Accounting tasks	69%
Accessing CRS for booking	60%
Fax to clients	56%
Spreadsheets	52%
Booking travel by fax	40%
Training programmes	33%
Accessing database outside agency	31%
Faxing to other agencies	28%
Electronic fare auditing	25%
Viewing data from CD-ROM	23%

Source: Harris, 1996.

information from up to eight different GDSs or CRSs in eight different windows on one terminal simultaneously. This is done by installing special terminal emulators and protocol conversion software on the gateway PC, and a special communications board to ensure smooth communications. In addition, it is possible for agents to have floating terminal addresses that can be used by, for example, management staff working on their own workstation, who need temporary access into a GDS. When the need is no longer there the TA can be released and picked up by another user on an independent LAN. This is accomplished by splitting the GDS line into two as shown in Fig. 3.2, and installing special boards and software on the gateway PC. This configuration allows a workstation on the independent LAN to become a GDS terminal if the agency has purchased enough TAs from the GDS vendor.

Of all US agencies 16% are using some kind of third party access software and more are expected to in the future. The usage of third party access software by agency location and agency size is shown in Table 3.5. The larger travel agencies located in city centres are most likely to use third party access software, possibly because in order to service a large volume of demanding clients, access to more than one GDS is necessary. A higher level of computer expertise is required by agencies wishing to follow this route. Management should ensure that

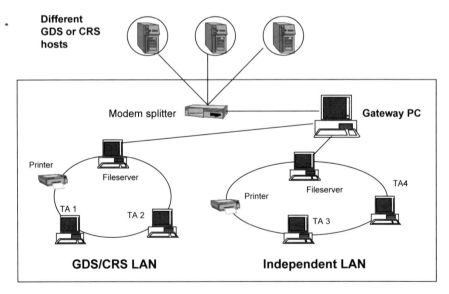

Travel agent office

Fig. 3.2. Multiple access hardware configuration.

Table 3.5. Third party access software usage by US travel agents.

AGENCY LOCATION		
	Central City	19%
	Suburban	15%
	Rural	8%
AGENCY SIZE	Under $1 mn	8%
	$1–2 mn	16%
	$2–5 mn	18%
	Over $5 mn	34%
TOTAL AGENCIES		16%

Source: Harris, 1994.

some computer literacy exists in the employees, and have at least one employee who is technically competent to manage the day-to-day operations of the network. This is not necessary when leasing GDS hardware.

3.2.2 CD-ROM Applications

Textual information on the GDS terminal is rarely sufficient to adequately represent and effectively sell many travel products. Multimedia presentations including colour photographs, sound and video clips are far more effective. This requires that the agency install a machine with multimedia capability. A CD-ROM drive, a high resolution colour monitor, speakers and a sound board are necessary to display multimedia information. A recent survey found that 35% of all travel agents in the US now have multimedia capabilities whereas only 21% did in 1993. The GDS vendor supplied 66% of those units – the remainder were purchased by the agents themselves (Harris, 1996).

The installation of CD-ROM capability is important for agents as an increasing amount of travel information is distributed in CD-ROM form, a medium which can store much higher volumes of information (700 megabytes or the equivalent of 500 floppy discs). Many are created by destinations to describe and market the destination's facilities. Others are produced by travel associations, individual travel suppliers, or independent publishing companies to market products. They are mostly interactive, consisting of sound, text, maps, colour pictures, graphics and video clips on the product or destination. Some are offered free to travel agents, some are sold. Standardization of the information presentation on the CDs and the user interfaces needs to be addressed, otherwise travel agents will be required to learn numerous different formats to access the information on each CD. Attempts are being made to produce CDs on the major destinations of the world in standard formats.

Videos on destinations are also utilized by travel agents but, since they are neither interactive nor digitally stored, they tend to be inferior to CD-ROMs. CD-ROM technology, however, is itself limited because it is a static medium and much travel information is dynamic. The use of Integrated Services Digital Network (ISDN) and other broadband networks which can deliver on-line multimedia product information into the travel agent office will be an important development in the future (Tuenissen, 1995).

3.2.3 Electronic Ticketing

Computer technology is enhancing ticket printing and distribution. Many airlines and GDS vendors now use magnetic strip tickets requiring travel agents to have International Air Transport Association (IATA) approved ATB-2 (automated ticket and boarding pass) printers to print them. ATB-2 ticket printers are designed to print information on the front of the ticket and encode the magnetic strip on the reverse side with the information using a magnetic head. These tickets contain passenger, fare and itinerary information on the magnetic strip and facilitate the check-in process and information collection and control. Machines at the boarding gate are ready to accept the tickets and extract from the magnetic strip the information required. Staff then no longer need to tally the information from the ticket stubs after the plane departs. ATB-2 tickets are also more convenient for travellers as the boarding pass is attached, and will soon be mandatory.

The delivery of tickets to travellers is also being affected by computer technology. Travel agents can electronically send tickets to designated satellite ticket printers in the offices of their corporate clients. These printers allow corporations to receive tickets immediately without waiting for mail deliveries yet they must be affiliated with a registered travel agency. Since 1992, an electronic ticket delivery network (ETDN) in the US provides that remote printing to the individual traveller. The ETDN is a non-proprietary shared ticket printing network to serve travel agents and their clients. Travel agents can, for a small fee, send tickets electronically to a printer in a distant location convenient to the traveller (see Fig. 3.3). The booking is still made through the travel agent's GDS terminal and is sent to the host in the normal way. The ticket image is then sent from the host computer to the chosen printer where it is printed out. Simultaneously, audit coupons are

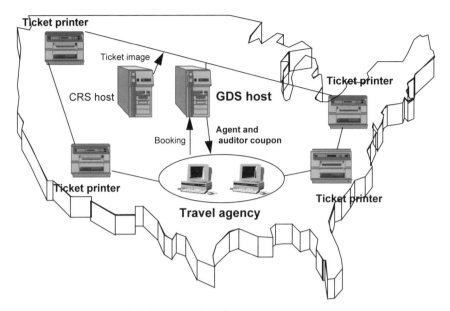

Fig. 3.3. Electronic ticket delivery network.

printed in the travel agent location where control of the sale is maintained. The travel agent receives the commission and must record the sale in their ARC (Airline Reporting Corporation) reports as usual. ETDN connects travel agents to hundreds of printers throughout the US in locations such as airports, shopping malls, hotel lobbies, grocery stores and office buildings.

Each ETDN machine has its own code number which is cross-referenced with the host agency code, and must meet certain standards to ensure the safety of the ticket stock inside. Customers activate the machine with either a credit card or an identification card or number provided by the agency. Some more recently developed ticket printers have on-line videoconferencing connection to a travel agent for last minute advice. They are then guided through steps to print the ticket. ARC permits four different types of ticket printers on the ETDN as shown in Table 3.6, ranging from moderately secure to extremely secure, and varying with the accessibility to the machine.

ETDNs have numerous benefits. First, for the traveller the ability to receive tickets quickly and conveniently is valued. Second, the travel agent experiences increased geographic market coverage, by allowing agents to service clients anywhere ETDN printers exist. Also with Types II and IV the hours of operation are extended. But technology changes rapidly and often leapfrogs itself. Even as the ETDN is

Table 3.6. Types of ETDN ticket machines.

	Location	Users	Times	Security
TYPE I	Private office	Authorized parties	Business hours	Door contact alarm, tickets removed and stored overnight.
TYPE II	Common area of business	Employees and guests	24 hours	Security personnel on site, door contact alarm, resistance to movement of 750 lb.
TYPE III	Public setting	General use	Business hours	Under observation by 'responsible' person or door contact alarm, resistance to movement of 1500 lb.
TYPE IV	Public setting	General use	24 hours	Door alarm, resistance to movement of 5000 lb., tickets automatically retrieved in 30 seconds.

Source: 'Highlights of ticket delivery machines', Anonymous, *Travel Weekly*, 1992.

being established in the US, ticketless flights are common, perhaps reducing future need for the ETDN. Ticketless travel requires the airline to give the passenger a confirmation number at the time of booking. When the passenger checks in they must show a picture identification and give the confirmation number. Ticketless travel began on domestic flights for some carriers but has now also been extended to international travel.

3.2.4 Internet Usage by Travel Agents

Travel agencies have an unusual relationship with the Internet. It is both a threat since it could remove much of their business, but it also provides additional business opportunities. Some travel agencies offer services on the WWW, giving them a much broader geographic consumer base than if they operated traditionally. They can receive bookings from clients through the Internet and can either send tickets electronically through the ETDN or book the passenger on ticketless flights. Communication with suppliers can also be done via e-mail.

Travel agents can also use it as an important research tool in addition to their GDS. This may be particularly important in the future as some travel products become available only via the Internet. Of US travel agents 60% use the Internet to research products and destinations, 55% use it to receive e-mail from clients, and 23% use it to make bookings for clients. In addition, 24% have set up a home page on the Web, and 42% access news groups through the Internet (Harris, 1996).

New types of travel agencies or reservation services which exist only on the Internet are also emerging. Some examples are PC Travel, Internet Travel Network, TRaX Air Res System and TPI On-Line Booking Request. PC Travel, for example, has written an interface which allows their on-line clients to access the Apollo GDS mainframe. Bookings are sent through Apollo, but PC Travel tickets the travellers and gains a commission through them. Internet Travel Network (ITN) has done a similar thing, but sends the booking through the travel agency of the client's choice. ITN also sets up Internet presence for traditional travel agents if they choose. The case at the end of Chapter 5 examines ITN more closely. All travel agencies must consider the Internet carefully in their strategic planning. If it is not embraced as an opportunity, it will become a threat.

3.2.5 Travel Agent Back Office Systems

Travel agencies also need computers to automate their back office functions, thus relieving employees from performing many of the tedious accounting and reporting functions, and releasing staff time to service clients. Back office software is available from numerous vendors – both GDS and third party vendors. The functions that are part of most back office computer systems include:

1. Commission tracking: to track and analyse commissions on bookings; to report bookings by agent and commissions due by a given time period.
2. ARC reporting: to calculate and print Airline Reporting Corporation (ARC) reports (such as the ticket summary and the weekly report) and refund notices.
3. Cheque writing: to print cheques for trade refunds and expenses.
4. Accounts payable: to track payments due to suppliers (non-ARC).
5. Accounts receivable: to track corporate and leisure accounts.
6. General Ledger: to generate financial reports per location, or consolidated reports for multi-branch agencies.
7. Report Writer: to generate operation, management and marketing reports. This can allow the design of the agency's own customized reports.
8. Rebate analysis: to analyse sales and potential rebates leading to improved sales strategies and increased profit.
9. Database marketing: using a relational database to capture information on clients for better customized marketing. A relational database can also be used to manage frequent traveller programs.

10. Mailing: to connect to word-processing applications to assist in marketing to clients and potential customers with promotional mailings.

Much of the information required for back office reports and functions is located in the PNRs in the host GDS, and must be downloaded for analysis purposes. It is imperative, therefore, that the travel agent has an interface between the back office computer and reservation system. To accomplish this, the GDS vendor must ensure that PNRs are in a format that can be transferred to the back office system of third party vendors as well as their own. GDS vendors install most back office systems, and it is likely, but not necessary, that a travel agency will install the back office system from their GDS vendor (Godwin, 1987). There are also a number of independent vendors of back office systems. The major back office systems offered by GDS vendors are:

Sabre: Agency Data Systems and Travel Base
Apollo: TS2000XL and Travel Manager
SystemOne: Max and PCMax
Worldspan: WorldLedger

Back office systems usually run on separate hardware from the reservation terminal, but can also run on an intelligent GDS terminal. If separate hardware is used it can be one of numerous platforms depending on agency size and preference. Systems vary from single user DOS machines to larger AS/400 and UNIX systems. There is a trend towards using more open architecture, and most larger agencies use a client-server configuration.

3.3 TOUR OPERATOR USE OF IT

This section will examine how tour operators and tour wholesalers use IT. Tour operators' function is to design and package tours which they then sell through the travel distribution system, making them both suppliers and intermediaries in the travel industry. They still need access to GDS terminals to book tour components, but in addition their computer systems must perform numerous other functions. Software vendors provide custom designed comprehensive tour operator packages for purchase, but creative operators can use spreadsheets, relational databases and financial packages to perform some of these added functions. The functions provided by tour operator software vendors typically include package creation software, systems to help in the distribution of packages, and systems to handle reservations and customer management. Each will be discussed below.

3.3.1 Package Creation

The creation of a tour package involves the identification of travel products and their combination into a tour. Computer technology can assist with this process by facilitating negotiations. Negotiations with suppliers in the various destinations lead to reduced rates due to their volume bookings. Electronic communications, such as electronic mail, file transfers or meetings assisted by technology such as videoconferencing make the negotiation process smoother and less costly. Software is also used in the costing of tours. This may be spreadsheet software, accounting software, or in the case of larger companies, software written specifically for the purpose. Such software must be able to cost the tour components and the entire tour, and to do sensitivity analysis. It must also handle the tour inventory, each tour itinerary, and group tour quotes for special groups.

3.3.2 Distribution of Tour Packages

Tour packages are traditionally distributed using brochures. Computers can assist in in-house brochure creation with the use of desktop publishing software. Brochures, however, represent a significant expense for agents and so many are looking to distribute brochures to agents electronically using high bandwidth data communication lines, thus allowing full colour pictures and text to be transmitted to an agent's terminal. Integrated Services Digital Network (ISDN) is an example of a technology that could facilitate electronic brochure distribution. A pilot project called Eurotop funded by the European Commission and backed by tour operators, computer service companies, and telecommunication operators throughout Europe focused on the distribution of electronic brochures. The goal of the project was to digitize tour operators' brochures and distribute them to travel agents across international borders, using ISDNs. Text, images and data describing operators' tour packages were electronically distributed to travel agent screens. Reservations were then transmitted back to the tour operator reservation system directly from the travel agent's terminal. Figure 3.4 shows this system.

Electronic distribution of tour packages can also be done with CD-ROMs, videotext, GDS, or the World Wide Web. In Europe, videotext systems have been a common method of information retrieval and booking for tour operators such as Thompsons and Thomas Cook. Both the travel agent and the consumer at home can use videotext to book tour packages. Many tour operators also place their inventory on the GDS as a way of facilitating travel agent bookings. Tour operators

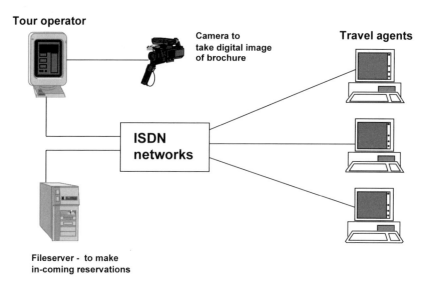

Fig. 3.4. Electronic distribution of tour brochures.

with their own reservation system can connect to systems such as TourLink, TourSource or Leisure Shopper which are features accessible to GDS users, or they can connect directly with the GDS vendor's mainframe. To accomplish this connection, a gateway and protocol converter must be used so that the two reservation systems can exchange information. The World Wide Web is a natural medium for tour operators to distribute information on their products. Mountain Travel Sobek was one of the first to develop their WWW presence. On-line bookings for tour packages are likely to be small because of the significant financial outlay that many tour packages represent compared to other travel products.

3.3.3 Reservations and Customer Management

Tour operators need computers to handle reservations and payments at two levels. First, to handle the outgoing reservations for tour components from suppliers, such as the hotels that are part of a tour. Second, to handle incoming reservations from travellers for their own inventory of tour packages. To make block reservations and payments with the component suppliers, a GDS terminal may be used, particularly for air reservations. Some GDS (Amadeus and Worldspan) provide tour operators with a feature of the GDS called Reverse Access.

This gives the tour operator the ability to retrieve flight information and availability and create PNRs and advance seat reservations for their groups themselves (Weber, 1995).

Reservations for their own inventory of tour packages require an internal computer reservation system which can either be designed in-house or purchased from a third party vendor. This database contains information on tour availability, description of tour itineraries and components, payment and booking deadlines, costs, travel agent commissions, credit card processing and customer profiles. The system should also ideally contain a yield management function and a multi-lingual and multi-currency support module if it is to be used in an international context. Some tour operator software permits the tour operator reservationists to switch between the GDS and their own reservation system, or in a Windows environment, to view both.

Many tour operators offer independent tours with modular components allowing customers to construct their own tour from an array of accommodation, event and flight options. This requires more flexibility on the part of the reservation system; instead of having an inventory of tours for customers to choose from, an inventory of tour components is there for selection and combination into packages. The reservation software must allow the easy building of a tour and the ability to modify independent selections when necessary (Weber, 1995). Tour operator reservation systems should also ideally interface with the GDS so that travel agents can transmit bookings to their in-house reservation systems.

3.4 SPECIALITY CHANNELLER USE OF IT

Speciality channellers are travel intermediaries that serve a particular 'special' section of the travel market. Two of the most common are meeting and convention planners and corporate travel offices. The following section will discuss the applications of IT to their operations.

3.4.1 Meeting and Convention Planners

Meetings and conventions represent a significant and growing sector of the travel market generating $75.6 billion in the US in 1992. Usually the organizers of meetings and conventions do not use travel agents as their intermediary but use speciality channellers called meeting and convention planners (MCPs). The MCP organizes all aspects of the meeting, including transportation, accommodation, food, special events, meeting rooms and equipment, and convention registration for delegates. The information needs of such companies are huge, and require the handling of many lists, schedules, orders and plans. Project management software which analyses the component activities, the sequencing and the time taken to accomplish each task can be very useful in this context.

Special software exists to handle the needs of meeting and convention planners. Computer programs are designed to assist with the following functions:

Site selection: One of the first decisions that must be made is to choose a site for the meeting. Databases of hotels with the room capacities, dimensions and contact information of each hotel help meeting planners choose and book hotels with the best facilities in a particular destination.

Housing tracking: Once the site is chosen, conferencing attendees must be assigned to hotel rooms. Software is available to automate the room assignment process from the list of conference registrants in the computer.

Function room scheduling: Software to schedule conference sessions and activities for function rooms while also tracking presenters, their audio-visual needs, and food and beverage requirements is also needed.

Floor plan design: Each meeting or convention has room set-up requirements. Software to generate function room floor plan designs is available. There are numerous floor plan options such as theatre style, classroom, banquet, hollow-square and U-shape configurations which can be pulled up on the computer screen and requested.

Meeting registration: From the time the attendee makes a reservation until arriving at the site, much information must be processed. Software to handle confirmation letters, rosters, sign-in sheets, registration and payments are examples of the myriad tasks. Such software also can generate name badges, labels and other printed materials for the meeting or convention.

Time/cost management: Software to project and track the full cost of conducting a meeting can be very helpful. Computer simulations which allow planners to see the impact of hypothetical time frames and expenses can help MCPs make decisions in the early stages of the planning process.

Special event management: Many meetings include special events and software is available to assist in their management.

In addition, some property management systems in hotels also offer features to assist in meeting management. Figure 3.5 shows the essential activities needed to organize such a meeting and the companies responsible for each activity (Laetz, 1994). As the diagram

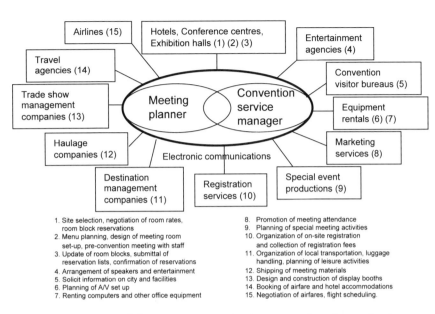

1. Site selection, negotiation of room rates, room block reservations
2. Menu planning, design of meeting room set-up, pre-convention meeting with staff
3. Update of room blocks, submittal of reservation lists, confirmation of reservations
4. Arrangement of speakers and entertainment
5. Solicit information on city and facilities
6. Planning of A/V set up
7. Renting computers and other office equipment
8. Promotion of meeting attendance
9. Planning of special meeting activities
10. Organization of on-site registration and collection of registration fees
11. Organization of local transportation, luggage handling, planning of leisure activities
12. Shipping of meeting materials
13. Design and construction of display booths
14. Booking of airfare and hotel accommodations
15. Negotiation of airfares, flight scheduling.

Fig. 3.5. Application of electronic communication to meeting planners' tasks. Source: Laetz, 1994.

shows, this involves many important functions requiring the use of communications technology. Electronic mail, electronic file transfer and Electronic Document Interchange (EDI) all facilitate the jobs of the MCP and the Convention Service Manager in the hotel. The meetings and conventions industry also has an electronic bulletin board called MPINet offered through CompuServe which provides a communication link for all members of the industry. In the future it plans to provide desktop videoconferencing, downloading of suppliers' electronic brochures, or viewing files of three-dimensional graphics of meeting facilities.

3.4.2 Corporate Travel Planners

Travel agencies that service corporate clients or corporate travel offices are another type of speciality channeller which has special automation needs. The most important of these is software to monitor reservations and ensure that they comply with standards required by the corporation. One example is travel policy software. Travel policy systems allow the agent to input and store corporate travel policies in their computer systems to ensure adherence to the policies laid down by the corporation when bookings are made. Examples of travel policies are the use of a preferred vendor, the use of a predetermined contract rate, the class of service booked, and upgrade policies. The software then filters the reservation as it is made to ensure that the policies of the corporation are applied. It can also be used to store individual traveller preferences. Some travel policy software can also track frequent traveller miles for corporations requiring employees to return miles to the corporation rather than keep them for personal use. This software is provided by the GDS vendors at additional cost.

Fare auditing software is another IT product used mostly, but not exclusively, by corporate agencies. The software assists with the accurate calculation of fares for a given itinerary. It ensures that the fare that is booked is both correct and is the best fare for a particular itinerary. Other quality control software is available to ensure best seat assignments, to clear waiting lists, and to upgrade passengers in compliance with the airline rules. Approximately 36% of travel agents in the US use such software. These agents tend to be the larger ones since the smaller agents cannot justify the high software cost. Fare auditing software is available from either third party vendors or from reservation system vendors. GDS vendors may also provide the capability for corporate travel offices to store their own negotiated fares. Rosenbluth Travel, one of the largest and most successful corporate travel agencies, credits the strategic use of IT for their success, and will be discussed at the end of this chapter.

3.5 IMPACT OF IT ON THE TRAVEL DISTRIBUTION CHANNEL

Much debate has ensued in the last few years about the continued viability of travel intermediaries, particularly in the light of new technological developments. Consumer access to travel databases creates an immediate threat to the existence of travel intermediaries as consumers book and research their own trips (to be discussed more in Chapter 5). The rapid growth of the Internet, the World Wide Web and other public access networks is having a profound impact on travel product distribution and therefore on travel intermediaries.

But a simple economic analysis would suggest that the consumer benefits by still using a travel agent. To access these databases the potential traveller expends both time and money (subscription and connection charges), whereas travel agent services have until recently been free of both. Despite this rationale, consumers are starting to book their own travel, obviously finding additional benefits such as control over their search and the knowledge that they have found the best product to match their needs. In addition, since travel agents are now starting to charge for some services, consumers have further incentives to be independent in their travel planning.

Travel intermediaries can respond to this threat in numerous creative ways. For example, many travel agents and tour operators now offer their services to consumers on the Internet, significantly increasing their geographic reach. Some travel agencies exist solely on the Internet, realizing that physical location is irrelevant in today's electronic marketplace. A recognition that the Internet connects them directly with upper income, highly educated consumers, an ideal target group for travel, is causing some to take this medium seriously, and market their value-added products this way. Some agents, recognizing the need to keep abreast of the information their potential clients are accessing themselves, are training their staff to use the Internet as an additional research tool. Another strategy used by some travel agents (less favoured) is to participate in the various travellers' forums and bulletin boards on the Internet where individuals discuss their trip plans. Some travel agents are responding to queries about travel products by contacting the individual through the electronic mail address attached to the message. This generates unsolicited contacts and may not be appreciated by the consumer.

There remains, however, one important fact pointing to the continued existence of travel intermediaries. Initial studies suggest that most consumers who use the Internet to research trips still tend to use a travel agent to verify the information and to book. The need to have a third party take responsibility for the booking, and the hesitancy to put credit card information on the Internet are possible reasons for this. The agent benefits since the time necessary to research clients' trips is shortened considerably and the booking still generates a commission. The extra time can be used by the agent to create value-added products to increase their profitability. This is an important consideration in a time where agents are being threatened by lower commissions. In the future, as consumer booking over the networks becomes easier, travel intermediaries will have to continuously redefine themselves.

3.6 SUMMARY

To exist and thrive in an information intensive industry, travel intermediaries must learn about and embrace all aspects of information technology. Most travel intermediaries have come to rely on computerized reservation terminals. They must now learn to fully utilize other hardware and software applications. This requires careful analysis of when and how IT can provide the opportunity for travel intermediaries to offer value-added services to their clients. The development and marketing of those services will redefine the role of the travel intermediary in the future. In particular, the major challenge for most intermediaries is to use the growing data communication networks to their advantage. Specialization, increased professionalism, and improved travel counselling skills are strategies for travel agents to survive in the increasingly competitive environment. In each case, information technology, when used appropriately, will assist in accomplishing those strategies. It can also be used creatively to turn threats into opportunities.

3.7 CASE – ROSENBLUTH TRAVEL

Travel intermediaries who recognize they are in the information business tend to embrace new information technologies readily. One company that has led the industry in this regard in Rosenbluth Travel (RT). RT is a privately held, worldwide travel management company offering comprehensive corporate, vacation and meeting travel services. It began as a family business, established in 1892, and has subsequently become a multinational, multimillion dollar corporation with 825 locations in the US and representatives in 41 countries worldwide.

RT's main intent in IT investment is to better service clients' needs. It has used IT extensively to design products and services that save clients' time, money and effort, thereby giving themselves a competitive advantage (Clemons and Row, 1991 and Clemons *et al.*, 1992). All of their IT products serve to provide the customer with needed information as rapidly as possible. In order to be successful in their endeavour, certain prerequisites and characteristics of the company were helpful. First, commitment by top management to support IT developments was critical. This allowed the creation of an information systems department which was well funded and staffed. This department designed and implemented IT applications which have positioned their company as one of the largest and most successful corporate travel agents. Some of the strategic applications they designed are discussed below.

READOUT: RT's first major IT product was READOUT. This system constantly downloads information from the GDS and reorganizes it so that the agents' screens show flights ordered by fare rather than departure time for hundreds of city-pairs. This service is appreciated by corporate clients who are able to receive the information they need much more quickly than from agents who use the traditional GDS displays.

VISION: This is a back office system which downloads passenger information from the GDS and reorganizes it so that corporations can use it to analyse their employees' travel activities. VISION-DIRECT was recently designed so that corporate clients could use it on their own PC to access and analyse the same data. Without this system, corporate clients had to typically wait over a month to get it from the GDS vendor.

ULTRAVISION: A more detailed travel management software that allows RT to give better service to clients was their next product. It checks the fares of all booked itineraries up until the flight departs and rebooks the passenger in the lower fare class. It also tracks waiting lists against flight availability and automatically clears waiting lists when possible. Travel policy features are another important part of this software, ensuring that a corporate client's travel policies are adhered to.

Trip Monitor: This is fare auditing software which prices itineraries at the lowest rate independently of the GDS, thereby ensuring the best fares.

E-Res Connection: For clients finding it more convenient to book business travel through e-mail rather than through phone, E-Res Connection provides this capability. The reservation is sent to the RT office directly where it is processed by the RT agents and replied to by e-mail.

PRECISION: Allows RT to work with suppliers to get negotiated fares from their suppliers based on volume. PRECISION circumvents the airline's yield management system, and stores and displays negotiated fares.

Global Distribution Network (GDN): This is a network connecting all RT offices electronically. It allows sharing of negotiated rates with all offices around the world, and the sharing of PNRs worldwide so that clients can be serviced by any RT office. Information relevant to world events that might affect travel is also disseminated to agents through GDN.

RT continues to investigate ways in which IT can provide them with a competitive advantage. They have a strong presence on the World Wide Web and are currently investigating teleconferencing and virtual reality, both of which are potential threats to tourism. By embracing them and incorporating them into their product offerings they hope to turn these threats into opportunities.

Information Technology in Surface Transportation 4

4.1 INTRODUCTION

This chapter covers the use of computer technology by surface transportation operators. Road (car rental, bus and taxi), rail (regular and subway) and water transportation (cruise ships and ferries) will each be discussed separately. These transportation modes are an important part of the tourism infrastructure since they not only provide the utility of moving from place to place, but also a direct touristic experience (e.g. cruises and special train journeys). Surface transportation companies vary in size and scope. Some may be small and some large, some local and some international, and some operated by private companies (tour bus, cruise lines, taxis) and some by public agencies (bus, rail, subway).

Whatever the mode or type of company, surface transportation operators use IT in various ways to support their operations, but in general with less investment than the airlines. Road transportation in many locations, however, is now requiring substantial investments by public agencies to better handle traffic flows with Intelligent Transportation Systems (ITSs). This chapter will first discuss ITSs since they provide a framework for the application of information technology to increase the efficiency of land transportation systems. The chapter will then go on to discuss the specific applications of IT to private and public transportation operators such as car rental companies, railroads and cruise lines.

4.2 INTELLIGENT TRANSPORTATION SYSTEMS

The movement of tourists via ground transportation systems is becoming more challenging as traffic volume increases. This is particularly

70

true in large cities, on heavily traversed highways, and in popular touristic areas where congestion and delays are commonplace. As highways become more crowded, they also become more difficult for drivers to navigate, particularly for tourist drivers in unfamiliar surroundings. Crowded conditions compromise safety and generate more accidents. Individual transportation operators can do little to solve such problems, and so public transportation agencies need to become involved at the strategic planning level to create Intelligent Transportation Systems. The cooperation and commitment of private transportation operators in the implementation of such systems are also needed to maximize their benefits. As an example of an ITS, the National Automated Highway System Consortium in the US is working on deploying a national automated highway system by early next century (Intelligent Transportation Society of America, 1995).

ITS is a term used to describe a combination of information technologies applied to the management of ground transportation and the provision of route information to travellers. They are relevant to this book on tourism information systems since they help tourists have safer, faster and more enjoyable journeys, whether in rental cars, buses or taxis. An ITS can include many different technologies but the ones of most relevance to the tourist industry are: route guidance systems, traveller information systems, automated vehicle location systems, fleet management systems, and automated traffic management systems. The following sections will discuss each of these technologies and their relevance to the tourism industry.

4.2.1 Route Guidance Systems

Route guidance systems (also called in-vehicle navigational systems) assist drivers in determining the best route to a given location while they are in the vehicle. This requires that the vehicle be equipped with an on-board computer which retrieves data from a central database located elsewhere. The database is a Geographic Information System (GIS) which stores graphical information and maps of a given region. GISs have multiple uses of which a route guidance system is just one. The information from the database is communicated to the car's computer via a satellite. A colour monitor on the dashboard displays the information and a touch panel allows the driver to choose options through a menu driven interface. See Fig. 4.1 for an example of the route guidance system provided in Avis rental cars.

Drivers can request directions to a given street address, to a given intersection, or to specific tourist attractions. They can request routes with certain characteristics such as shortest time routes, scenic routes,

Fig. 4.1. Photograph of a route guidance system. Photograph used with permission from Avis.

and routes with or without freeways. The response from the GIS includes driving instructions, maps of designated routes with street intersections and landmarks, and the vehicle's location relative to the maps. Voice prompts assist the driver in making turns, and in the event of a wrong turn, the system generates a new route. The memory in the computer can store numerous routes to commonly visited destinations for easy access. Figure 4.2 shows some example screens from a route guidance system.

For tourists who do not know their way around a city or region, these systems can reduce frustration, delays and accidents which can mar a tourist's vacation. The systems are installed in some rental cars and their use is expected to grow in the future as more car manufacturers equip cars with on-board computers. Taxis and tour buses also use route guidance systems to help drivers navigate the most appropriate routes, whether it be the fastest or the most scenic route.

4.2.2 Traveller Information Systems

In-vehicle computer systems also provide on-line, real-time information on road conditions in the region for drivers. Dynamic details of

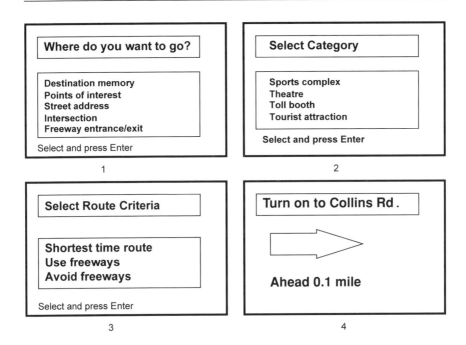

Fig. 4.2. Sample screens from a route guidance system. Source: Avis.

congested streets, accident locations and parking lot availability are examples of such information. The information is received at a central monitoring location from video cameras and other sensing devices. It is then transmitted to vehicles either with satellite communication or ground communication systems. A system in use in Japan called Vehicle Information and Communication System (VICS) was launched by the Japanese government in 1996 in selected areas of Japan. It provides travellers with road and traffic information to facilitate their journeys. VICS collects real-time information on road conditions from the Japan Road Traffic Information Centre and other traffic authorities, edits and processes it and then transmits it to roadside devices. These devices use infra-red beacons, radio-wave beacons and FM radio transmission to emit signals to the computer in the vehicle. The government provides the service free to drivers but the receiving device in the vehicle must be purchased by the owner (Anon, 1996). Figure 4.3 shows how VICS works. When combined with route guidance systems, traveller information systems can be used to generate alternative routes to bypass congestion, thereby empowering drivers to avoid long delays and reach their destination easily.

Drivers also need information on the status of their vehicle to drive safely. Certain key pieces of information such as their speed, the

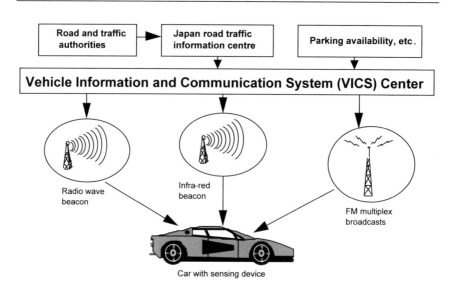

Fig. 4.3. VICS traveller information system. Source: New Breeze, Spring 1996, p. 11.

status of their turn signal, lights, fuel, water and oil indicators are typically displayed on dials in the dashboard. The lag time that it takes for a driver's eyes to refocus on the road after viewing the dashboard displays can be a safety problem. Avis Car Rental Company has introduced a windshield display of this information so that drivers can see it without looking down and having to refocus their eyes. These systems, called 'head-up' displays, were first used in aircraft and later in boats, so pilots could view the information while keeping their eyes on the environment. The digital display appears to float above the car's front bumper, can be adjusted in position and is visible at all times. Studies of drivers who have used head-up displays have shown that 82% of respondents feel safer driving cars with a head-up display (Avis, 1996).

4.2.3 Automated Vehicle Location Systems

Equipment to monitor the location of a vehicle is another component of an ITS. This technology called Automated Vehicle Location (AVL) is relatively simple and yet holds many potential advantages. The vehicle is equipped with sensors which communicate with a Global Positioning System (GPS) to determine the position of the vehicle. This technology was previously used by ocean vessels and aircraft to determine their exact location, and uses approximately 25 GPS satellites in orbit to identify the vehicle's location. Signals from three satellites are needed to position the sensor, and hence the vehicle, with the exact latitude and longitude coordinates. This information can then be superimposed on a street map in a GIS to determine the exact location of the vehicle.

Other AVL systems use a different technology to identify the location of a vehicle. In Sydney, Australia, for example, taxis and buses are fitted with a tag which communicates by radio waves with interrogators at numerous key intersections in the city. By identifying taxi locations, travel times can be computed and users can be informed of potential waiting times. They are also being used by bus companies to provide information about the precise position of the bus along its route (ITS, 1996). AVL systems used by taxi companies can inform fleet operators of the location of each vehicle. Based on this information, the company can give travellers an estimated time of arrival at a given location. AVL systems also have advantages for public transportation vehicles. Real-time schedule information on public transportation vehicles can be passed on to the public in two ways. First, information displays on board public vehicles can advise passengers of the expected time of arrival at their destination. Second, information can be displayed at terminals or stops to advise passengers of how long they have to wait for the next vehicle.

AVL systems have also been found to increase tourist safety in situations where travellers may be stranded due to vehicle problems, criminal activities or inclement weather. Information on the exact location of the tourist's vehicle can be immediately communicated to the police department or other emergency agency. Knowing their exact location enables the agency to dispatch assistance immediately. For travellers driving in areas of high crime, this can be a very comforting feature. Cellular phones, now included in some rental cars, can also be used to bring rapid aid to emergency situations.

Individual or group tourists in the outdoors with or without vehicles can also benefit substantially from carrying GPS sensors (Hogenauer, 1996). Hikers, mountaineers and sailors can use hand-held GPS units instead of compasses to navigate, and as a locator in cases of emergency (Bartlett, 1996). The addition of a cellular phone provides the outdoor tourist with an increased sense of safety.

4.2.4 Fleet Management Systems

ITSs present various technologies to assist tour bus companies and taxi companies in managing their fleets of vehicles. The combination of these technologies is called a fleet management system. AVL systems provide information on the location of each vehicle in the fleet, and route guidance systems help drivers navigate the best routes. Both of these technologies together can increase revenue by maximizing the use of each vehicle. In addition, computer-aided dispatching connects vehicles with passengers much more quickly, leading again to higher utilization of vehicles and drivers, and to increased passenger service. Automatic passenger counting devices on board vehicles can be used to track the volume of passengers on certain bus routes, and thereby increase the information available to make decisions to improve the efficiency of their operations.

4.2.5 Automated Traffic Management Systems

Automated traffic management systems (ATMSs) help to manage the flow of road traffic using a variety of technologies including AVL discussed above. Two other technologies are ramp meters which smooth the flow of traffic onto freeways, and electronic toll booths which shorten the time to cross a toll. Electronic message signs at the roadside are another component of ATMSs. They inform drivers of delays, congestion, roadwork and accidents, and recommend speed limits depending on road conditions. These signs receive their information through closed circuit TV systems which monitor traffic flows or from intelligent sensing devices on the roadside. Public transportation vehicles can be given faster journeys by ensuring automatic green lights when they arrive at an intersection. A device inside the vehicle identifies it as a bus, tram or other public vehicle and communicates with a roadside device via radio waves. The signal automatically changes to green as the vehicle approaches, allowing it through without delays.

ITSs are currently being implemented in numerous locations around the world but as yet they are developing on a piecemeal basis. Increases in safety and decreases in congestion are already reported in areas where these technologies have been used. On-time performance of public transportation has been significantly improved (by over 20%) with the use of such systems (Intelligent Transportation Society of America, 1995). As the number of travellers increases and areas become more congested, these technologies will become increasingly important. Their success will depend on vehicles being equipped with on-board computers at costs which are marginal.

4.3 CAR RENTAL USE OF IT

This section will examine the use of IT by car rental companies in addition to the route guidance systems and automatic vehicle location systems discussed above. Car rental companies use IT to efficiently manage and market their companies. Because major car rental firms have offices and cars in numerous locations (some worldwide), like the airlines they need computer reservation networks to process bookings. Most chains operate a central computer system with databases on passenger reservations, rental agreements and car inventory. Some companies have their own hardware in-house, others contract out their reservation systems and IT needs, removing the need for their own hardware.

4.3.1 Reservation Systems

A customer reservation database stores information on customers, the type of car requested, the quoted rate, the drop-off and pick-up dates and times, and the source of the reservation (e.g. travel agent or free-phone call). Yield management systems similar to those used by airlines generate different car rates based on demand. The resulting rates are then incorporated into the computer reservation system. Frequent renter databases are used extensively by car rental companies to give frequent renters (often business travellers) special treatment and express booking procedures. Fast processing upon arrival (express check-in) and at departure are important service elements for the business traveller. By having frequent renter information on file in the frequent renter database (name, address, phone, credit card, insurance details, etc.), special services to reduce transaction times such as the following can be offered.

Frequent renters using express check-ins are driven from the airport terminal by a special bus. This bus takes them directly to the area where cars are parked without having to go to the rental counter. The customer inserts a credit card into a machine which processes the transaction and generates a rental agreement. The renter then goes immediately to the designated car where the keys are already located. Express returns are processed at the car return area using hand-held terminals to record the car mileage and to generate a receipt for the passenger. Again, presence at the rental counter is unnecessary – an important consideration for customers rushing to catch flights. As an additional service at drop-off, Avis connects its hand-held terminals to a database of flight departure time information to give to customers catching flights. The information is downloaded from the Official Airline Guide (OAG) computer.

Once a car is rented, the reservation record is moved into a separate database of active rental agreements. This is a centralized database which can be accessed from any office that is on-line, in the event that a renter needs assistance. A centralized database provides the capability for car drop-offs in locations other than the city where it was rented. Even though data on all company rentals are stored centrally, individual city offices can download records of their own rentals from the central database into their local area network. Activity reports can be analysed and used as a basis to improve their operations locally.

National and international car rental computer reservation systems usually consist of multiple mainframes (IBM and Unisys machines are common). These mainframes are connected through front end communication processors to data communication networks connecting rental and sales offices throughout the country or world to the central site. The TPF environment does not dominate the car rental reservation systems the same way it does the airlines. The application of client-server systems is being investigated by numerous car rental companies as a more efficient way of processing information and making it available to each location.

The reservation system mainframes must be connected to GDS to give travel agents the ability of making car reservations on-line with confirmations returned in seconds. The link also allows car type and rate information to be displayed and updated in the GDS. If the company does not have direct access links, ARINC and SITA connections may be used. Even if a car rental CRS has direct access links, ARINC and SITA connections may be used as backup for the direct lines, and for connections with smaller airline reservation systems. World Wide Web sites are now also used by many car rental firms to display car rental product and rate information directly to the consumer, and to take reservations.

4.3.2 Car Inventory Control

Another database used by car rental companies contains information on the vehicles themselves. It contains details on each individual vehicle, its classification, its features, rates, mileage and maintenance records. As an example, Alamo Car Rental uses an Integrated Vehicle System which orders cars, depreciates their value over time, and tracks their movement, maintenance and repair. Such information systems help to maximize the utilization of each vehicle and increase the company revenue. Inventory control of cars is often facilitated with the use of bar code technology. A sticker may be placed on the back window of the car, or the vehicle identification number may be optically read through the front window. This latter choice avoids identifying the car as a rental in areas where theft is likely to occur (Loane, 1996). Scanning of these codes keeps the database current on the status, the location, and the maintenance of specific cars.

The challenge to car rental companies is to match their supply of vehicles with customer demand. It is not an easy task to maximize revenue in a changing touristic environment. The applications discussed above help, but more sophisticated computer applications are needed to make strategic decisions. The use of Operations Research (OR) models, as used by the airlines, have been successful in assisting with car rental firms' decision-making. The case study at the end of this chapter examines some ways in which OR-based decision support models have been successfully applied to the car rental industry.

4.4 RAIL COMPANY USE OF IT

Rail travel is an important component of land transportation for travellers – more in some countries than others. Rail travel includes both surface rail systems and subway (or underground) systems. Surface rail travel has more needs for IT application than subway since it is likely to consist of longer journeys and more planning and reservations by travellers. Even so, the need for these systems is less than in air travel. Much rail travel is relatively short and only a small proportion is international in nature.

Rail companies therefore have less reliance on computer reservation systems but may still use them to manage the seat capacity on trains, and to ensure travellers of having a seat or berth. The rail CRSs need to be able to print tickets and itineraries and to be able to respond to passengers' requests for schedules and timetables. Some railroads in Europe are distributing schedule information on CD-ROM to consumers. Others are using the World Wide Web to display schedule and fare information. Some also have links to the GDS, so that schedules can be viewed and rail tickets can be purchased by travel agents for their clients.

Electronic ticketing is in use by surface rail and subway operators to monitor entry into vehicles or stations more efficiently. These tickets, which can be purchased from automatic ticket machines in stations, have magnetic strips on the back to encode the amount paid and the itinerary. Season tickets for residents or weekly tickets for tourists are also available. By using stored value payment cards for multiple journeys or season tickets, passengers receive discounts and no longer have to carry cash to purchase tickets. Electronic fare payment methods become important when cities or regions use intermodal transport tickets which can be used on all transportation services such as surface rail, subway and buses. The Chunnel, which has automated check-in 'gates', faced a particular challenge in automating its departure control and ticketing system since it involved integrating multiple systems in multiple countries. A systems integrator was used to accomplish the task more easily.

As with rental cars, railways must keep track of their engines and carriages. They need to know their location and their maintenance needs. This is done with the use of bar codes on the vehicles. Computer modelling is also used to determine the best route structures and the number of carriages to put on each train.

4.5 WATER TRANSPORTATION OPERATORS USE OF IT

Water transportation operators include passenger and car ferries which transport passengers and vehicles across stretches of water, and cruise ships which are used for vacations. The information needs of cruise lines are more comprehensive than ferry boats since the passengers are on board longer and the vessels have more facilities. Therefore most of this section will focus on cruise lines' application of IT.

Both cruise lines and ferry boats need computerized reservation systems. Individual cruise lines may have their own CRSs which store detailed information on their products and their passengers. Cruises are more complex products than airline seats and car rentals, meaning that the reservation databases need to be more comprehensive. CruiseMatch is a cruise CRS run by Royal Caribbean Cruise Lines and is connected to the GDS. Most GDSs have a cruise option where the travel agent can specify passenger requests and receive on-line information about products, prices and availability. Cruise bookings through GDS are, however, still small with only 10% of cruises being booked this way. Figure 4.4 shows one of at least four screens needed to book cruises through a GDS. First, a sailing needs to be chosen from an availability screen, then a rate code chosen from a rate screen. Next a cabin needs to be selected from a screen similar to Fig. 4.4, and finally the PNR must be created. This complexity is one reason for the small percentage of cruises booked electronically. Ferries which carry vehicles also need reservation systems. The database needs to store information on the length and type of car so that space can be reserved on the deck. Passenger information is also stored in the database.

Satellite communication of information plays a more important role in water transportation than any other transportation mode. Any

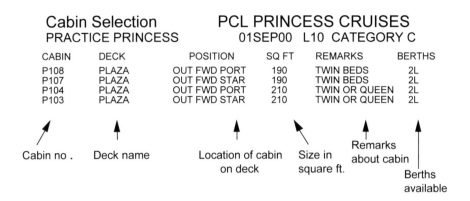

Fig. 4.4. A sample GDS screen to book a cruise. Source: Apollo Format User Guide, 1994.

communication between the vessel and land must occur this way. Global navigation systems on the bridge of the vessel use satellite communication to assist in navigation and use the same GPS technology as discussed above. More recent applications of satellite communication include Global Maritime Distress and Safety Systems (GMDSSs) which assist with medical emergencies at sea. Communication between a medical facility on land and the vessel in distress can provide on-line assistance with a medical emergency. Search and rescue operations at sea are enhanced by GMDSSs, and better treatment is provided for passengers who are injured as a result of distress situations or are suffering from general illnesses.

Satellite communication links from ship to shore also facilitate day-to-day business transactions on board ship. For example, credit card purchases made by passengers on board must be processed. Without satellite communication, the posting of a transaction to the credit card can take weeks. Communication links to on-shore processing centres enable transactions to be posted as quickly as if on shore. Guests may alternatively be given on-board charge cards which require only a one-time verification per passenger and a simple payment at the end of the cruise. Point-of-sale systems are also likely to be found on board ship in the shops and bars to track the sales of items. As most cruises include all meals in the price of the cruise, the restaurants do not need point-of-sale systems, except for the sale of alcoholic beverages.

Computers on board cruise ships are also used to monitor and control inventories of merchandise and supplies on board. This is especially important for long journeys between ports, requiring high levels of inventory of supplies on board. Ships that dock at ports regularly can use computers to determine what needs to be purchased at each port, and orders can be electronically communicated to shore before the ship arrives in the port. Figure 4.5 shows the various IT applications that can be found on board ship. The second case at the end of this chapter gives a description of how comprehensively Royal Caribbean Cruise Lines uses IT to improve its operations.

4.6 SUMMARY

Information technology is successfully being used to make land and water transportation more efficient and smooth for passengers and operators. As travellers increase in number, the need for efficient use of highways and waterways increases. Intelligent Transportation Systems are the framework for these developments. The individual companies in land transportation need to be aware of the various technologies discussed above to operate more efficiently. They will all need, over time, to install on-board computer systems as part of a more intelligent transportation system. Intermodal transportation is likely to become more prevalent in the future, and will make more demands on computer systems used by transportation companies. Intermodal reservations and ticketing will require more connectivity between

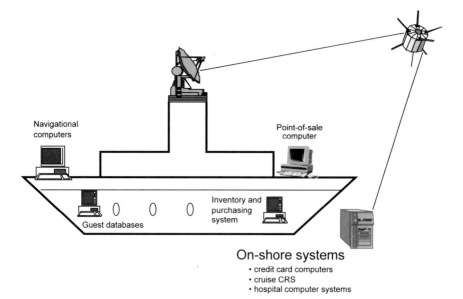

Fig. 4.5. IT applications to a cruise line.

individual companies' computer systems and standardization of documents and databases. All aspiring tourist destinations need to carefully examine the benefits provided by the systems discussed above. Ignoring these technologies can only produce more chaotic, congested, slow transportation systems, which many travellers will no longer tolerate. The success of a tourist destination depends heavily on the quality of its transportation system.

4.7 CASE 1 – NATIONAL CAR RENTAL

This case study describes briefly how National Car Rental used the design of new computer systems and Operations Research (OR) modelling to increase the company's profitability. Prior to the implementation of this system, National was facing possible liquidation by its parent company General Motors if profits were not increased significantly. To meet GM's demands, National Car Rental hired consultants to design new computer applications to better manage their information. It was ascertained that employees did not have adequate access to information about cars and rates, and that access to updated information for decision-making critical to the company's success was lacking. The new system incorporated pricing and reservations control to price car rentals better and thereby increase profitability. It also incorporated capacity management techniques.

National Car Rental's computer operations included four different systems at the time, wherein lay part of the problem. One system handled the daily activity on the rental lot, another handled customer reservations, another system provided rate information, and the fourth system fed information on their car rentals to the GDS. The new system had to tie together all of these systems so that a user could access information from the first three systems from one terminal. Another requirement was that data could easily be retrieved from each system and input into the computer OR models for decision-making on a timely basis.

A major problem that occurred in the design of the new system was the large volume of data needed to run the OR models. Typically, revenue management systems such as the one being designed, download data from the day's transactions and run overnight. Forecasting and optimization models are then performed using information gathered from the download. For

National's needs, the data had to be continuously downloaded on a transaction by transaction basis, because an overnight download would not allow the rate information from the OR models to be up and ready for the morning.

The system designers decided instead to use a completely centralized revenue management system, combining both pricing and inventory. This was an unusual approach, but it gave managers and operators access to all data elements in the system. In order to maximize revenues, information on car inventories was needed. This involved keeping track of the location of cars in the fleet. Capacity management techniques could then be applied to match car inventories to demand. Expected Marginal Seat Revenue models and other models, borrowed from the airline industry, were used to generate demand-based pricing systems for National Car Rental.

The system that was designed offered a comprehensive solution to National's revenue problems and performed the following functions:

- optimization of fleet utilization using capacity management models
- a pricing function based on consumers' price sensitivity
- rate levels linked with availability and booking activity
- a reservation and control function which maximized revenues by accepting or rejecting booking requests
- a function to optimize management of the car fleet using length-of-rent controls.

The system saved National Car Rental. It integrated both automated decision-making and decision support to give recommendations based on sound data and models. It enabled them to strategically decide on car rental rates rather than determining rates by following the competition.

Source: adapted from Greenfield, 1996.

CASE 2 – ROYAL CARIBBEAN CRUISE LINES

Royal Caribbean Cruise Lines' 74,000-ton *Grandeur of the Seas* (which carries 1950 guests and more than 750 crew) is a result of human ingenuity combined with computer technology. The vessel was designed with the aid of computers, the construction schedule was planned by computers, the plasma arc cutters which sliced the steel for its hull were guided by computers and its speed, location, safety equipment, engines, navigation and hotel systems are all monitored by computers. Not only do they make a ship's operation easier, safer and more economical, many systems would be impossible to operate without their use.

Computer assisted design (CAD) was used to create a suitable hull shape which would minimize drag and maximize fuel economy yet provide a comfortable ride. Drawings and revision were easily accomplished with the CAD system. Computers helped determine how much steel should be delivered on specific dates so that construction could proceed at a steady pace. The computerized blueprints were fed into computers which controlled plasma arc cutters that sliced the steel into precise large-scale duplicates of tiny drawings. From steel cutting to maiden voyage took less than 30 months, much faster than the four to five years with traditional methods.

On board are many computer systems. The theatre uses computer technology; most lighting cues, curtain cues and set changes are pre-programmed into a computer to be executed at precise moments during the show. The ship's navigation system links radar, gyrocompass, autopilot, the satellite navigation computer, voyage displays and docking information into one computer network and permits the ship's officers to program the ship to follow a designated route. The computers can even be connected to shore via a modem and satellite to update software, run diagnostics and remotely analyse a problem.

Inventory and maintenance systems are now overseen by computers and automatically notify the crew when parts, food supplies or other provisions need to be reordered. Guests' purchases are computerized which has allowed Royal Caribbean to create an on-board charge card system where purchases are registered with a guest cruise identification card, rendering cash unnecessary while on board.

Consumer Access to Travel Information Systems

5

5.1 INTRODUCTION

Electronic travel information and booking capabilities are now directly available to the consumer as never before. Leafing through brochures and talking to travel agents about trips are no longer the only options for travellers to plan their trips. This chapter examines the various technologies that give consumers this electronic access, and how they are being used by different parts of the travel industry. The ease with which technology is linking customers and suppliers is giving rise to new ways of doing business, restructuring the industry and causing new types of travel intermediary firms to emerge. These technologies are constantly developing and changing and, as the printed word is never able to capture the latest developments, undoubtedly new developments will have occurred since the publication of this book. The chapter will, however, give an indication of trends.

The use of the Internet and World Wide Web dominate most of the developments in the area of consumer access to travel databases. There are hundreds of thousands of home pages of suppliers and associations and many electronic bulletin boards, newsgroups and chat rooms designed for the travel and tourism community. In fact, tourism and travel home pages dominate the WWW. An overview of the Internet and its usage, in general and specifically for travel and tourism, will begin the chapter. Other applications of technologies that are available to the consumer will then be discussed. These include consumer access to GDS, automatic ticket machines, information kiosks in public locations, interactive TV, and videotext. All of these systems are giving the consumer more self-sufficiency in making travel choices but, of course, require both computer accessibility and some level of computer literacy on the part of the consumer. Despite the increase in general computer literacy, a significant portion of the world's population still does not have easy access to PCs and requires very user-friendly interfaces. This is an important issue for designers of these systems. Point-and-click graphical user interfaces, touch screens and more recently, voice input and voice recognition systems all make the human–machine interface easier to navigate. These will be discussed in the chapter. The chapter will end with a model of electronic travel distribution based on these systems. It will also examine new types of firms that are entering the electronic travel distribution system, and examines the Internet Travel Network (ITN) as a case example of such a firm.

5.2 THE INTERNET AND TOURISM

This section begins with an overall assessment of the coverage and usage of the Internet. It will then examine tourism and travel applications of the Internet. Consumer access to information in general, and particularly to travel information has burgeoned with the use of the Internet. The Internet began in the 1970s as a project of the US Defence Department called ARPAnet. The goal of the project was to create a communication network, in conjunction with some research universities, resilient enough to survive nuclear war. It subsequently evolved into a network for peacetime communication. From the late 1970s to the mid 1980s, the Internet was used almost exclusively by academic institutions as an adjunct to another parallel academic network, called BITNET. In the late 1980s high speed communication links were created between hubs of the Internet with the help of the National Science Foundation and academic usage continued to increase. At this time, a research university in Switzerland created standards for accessing text on different computers through linkages on the Internet. This was called Hyper Text Mark-up Language and was the basis for the World Wide Web. Subsequently, Web browsers (Mosaic and Netscape) were designed and the focus of the Internet became more commercial and recreational with firms and institutions using it as a medium to inform customers about their products and services. The travel industry quickly became an eager participant in creating home pages on the Web and is now the industry that uses it the most after the computer industry.

Consumers can access the Internet in one of three ways. First, via local access providers who charge a monthly fee to create the local link to an Internet node. Second, if a person is part of a large company, university or government agency their institution's internal network may be connected directly to the Internet giving direct access to all employees. Third, a consumer may connect via one of the on-line services such as America On-Line, CompuServe and Prodigy who charge a monthly fee and also provide additional value-added services.

A multitude of studies all point to a massive increase in users of the Internet with numbers in the range of 40 million. It has been estimated that if the growth of users increases at its current rate all of the world's population would be on-line by the year 2003. Many socio-economic conditions of course preclude this, and exact statistics are hard to come by and are soon outdated. One reason for the difficulty in measuring Internet usage is because people use the Internet from a variety of locations. It is not uncommon for a single user to access the Internet from home, office, cybercafes, schools, libraries and other people's homes, making it difficult to track individual usage.

Internet access was originally available only to upper socio-economic groups and to geographic areas of the world where PCs and data networks were readily available. Access is now possible for a broader range of consumers, however, usage is still predominantly North American with significant growth occurring in Europe (particularly in Scandinavia, Germany and UK) and in Asia. One in four sites on the Internet is registered in California, showing a strong regional dominance (Schonland, 1996). Although access is generally becoming more available, in some countries it is still controlled and requires some level of government permit or documentation (e.g. India, China). Numerous research companies regularly research Internet usage and the reader is referred to their home pages for statistical updates (e.g. Nielsen Research http://www.nielsenmedia.com/commercenet/exec.html). Recent studies of the demographics of Internet users show that in the US and Canada, 24% of the population (16 years or older) have access to the Internet, a 50% growth from six months earlier. The distribution of users is now reasonably well split between male and female (67% vs. 60%) whereas in the early days the Internet was decidedly male dominated. The majority of users (53%) are in the 30–40 age group, 31% are between ages 18–29, and the over 50s represent 13% of Internet users. The remaining 3% are under 18 (Millera, 1996).

Internet users have traditionally been classified into two groups – early users who came on-line in the early days, who tend to be heavier users, and the newer, lighter users. (This categorization does not accurately describe all users, but is a generalization.) Much of the growth in usage is from newer, lighter users who have a different profile than the traditional mould of the early users who were professionals, many being computer professionals. Long-time users have been shown to be more likely to make purchases on-line than newcomers. This is a group which should be of interest to the tourism suppliers wishing to sell their products on-line, and avoid paying commissions to travel agents.

Figure 5.1 shows the reasons people use the Internet. Not surprisingly, the most commonly used part of the Internet is the World Wide Web, followed by the electronic mail functions for communications. Downloading software from the Internet is the third most commonly used function. Discussions, both interactive in the form of chat rooms and non-interactive in the form of newsgroups and electronic bulletin boards, are the next most commonly used functions. Accessing data from another computer and using the Internet for real-time audio and video transmittal are both relatively small uses. In every type of usage, long-time users are heavier users of all functions.

The next sections will examine how different aspects of the Internet are being used to disseminate travel and tourism information. In particular, the World Wide Web and electronic bulletin boards, newsgroups and chat rooms will be discussed.

5.2.1 The World Wide Web

The World Wide Web (WWW) is the most rapidly growing part of the Internet. It is a distinctively different part of the Internet characterized by its multimedia information capabilities and by its hypertext links. With the click of a mouse on a blue underlined word or phrase, the user is connected via hypertext links to related information either on

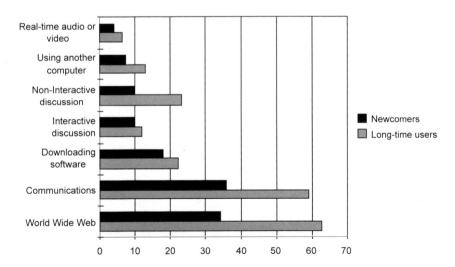

Fig. 5.1. Usage of the Internet. Source: Nielsen Web Page http://www.nielsenmedia.com/commercenet/exec.html, 1997.

the same company's server or to a related server anywhere in the world. That information can take the form of text, data, graphics, still images, videos and animation. The use of a Web browser is needed to navigate the Web.

Of the US and Canadian population 13% have used the WWW in the last six months versus only 8% three months prior. The WWW is used heavily for commercial applications as evidenced by the fact that the most common use of the WWW is for consumers to gather information about products in the marketplace. The next most common use is for suppliers to research their competitors' product information. Since information is more easily available it is creating a more perfectly competitive market place for consumers. Vendor support and customer service are two other uses for consumers who have purchased products from suppliers on the WWW. The smallest usage is to actually sell products, however, this is expected to grow in the future (Nielsen Web site, 1996). A limiting factor in the growth of this usage is the lack of security for financial transactions. Improvement in the encryption methods used is likely to remove this limitation. Figure 5.2 shows that for all functions of the Web, long-time users have higher levels of usage than newcomers to the Web.

The travel industry is very well represented on the WWW, and users will find a wealth of travel products. In fact, travel is the Internet's second largest commerce area after computer technology. All types of travel suppliers from destinations to airlines, hotels, car rentals, travel agencies, tour operators and attractions all over the world have home pages on the Web. Government tourism offices and visitors and convention bureaux also have their own home pages and

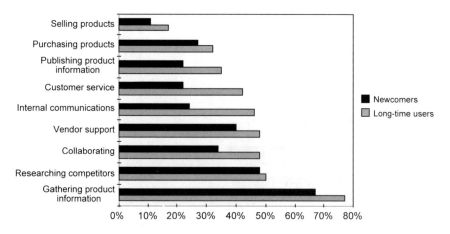

Fig. 5.2. Usage of the WWW. Source: Nielsen Web Page
http://www.nielsenmedia.com/commercenet/exec.html, 1997.

often serve as a central point for consumers researching a destination by providing hypertext links to suppliers' home pages. In addition, the generic search engines (Yahoo, InfoSeek, Magellan, Lycos and Excite) allow consumers to define searches and receive a selection of sites and URLs which match the search criteria. Some search engines have travel related categories in their directories which facilitate the searches even more. Figure 5.3 shows the possible ways to search for travel information on WWW.

In addition, there are numerous home pages of catalogues and indexes that consolidate information on a particular travel industry sector. Brymer *et al.* (1996) discuss the hotel-related sites and their features, and the restaurant industry's Web activity is discussed in Forrest *et al.* (1996). Examples of other travel-related indexes are:

- All the Hotels on the Web: www.all-hotels.com
- Hotel and Travel Index: www.travel.net/htio
- The Hotel Guide: www.hotelguide.ch
- New World Hotels: www.newworld-intl.com
- World Travel Events: www.world-travel-net.co.uk/world-travel-events
- World Travel Resource Registry: worldhotel.com
- Dr. Memory's Favorite Travel Pages: 204.148.98.169/select/trref.17.html

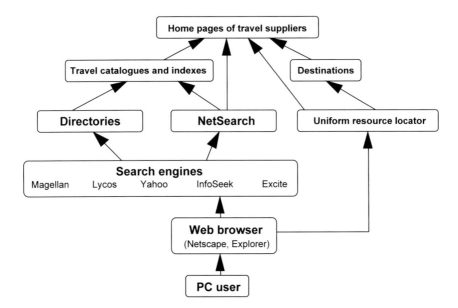

Fig. 5.3. Pathways to tourism information on the Web.

- CNN Travel Guide: www.cnn.com/TRAVEL
- International Travel Guide: www.iisys.com/www/travel/itg.htm
- World Travel Guide: www.wtg-online.com

There are many others which cover regional or destination specific topics, but they are too numerous to mention here.

Many travel industry associations and institutions are present on the WWW. These sites are valuable sources of information about particular sections of the industry. For example, the International Air Transport Association (IATA) plans to make its site the premier location on the Internet for aviation information. On-line education related to the airlines is offered on the Web page of Aeronautical Technology Centre in the UK (de Pommes, 1995). The Air Transport Association provides industry statistics, press releases and publications catalogues on their WWW site. The International Association of Amusement Parks and Attractions has a Web site that is rich in information on the attractions and theme park industry, and the Travel and Tourism Research Association uses their Web page to distribute information on its conferences, publications and events. These are only a sampling of the multitude of associations on the Web.

Booking travel on the Internet is happening slowly despite the many possibilities. Initial studies show that the minority of Web users make travel reservations this way. Recent statistics show that about 5% of business air tickets were booked on-line in 1995, and 2% of all travel transactions were booked on line in 1996. It is predicted that approximately 20% of air bookings will be made on-line by the year 2000. Since business travellers are more likely to book on-line than vacationers, and since air travel is the most likely travel product to be booked on-line, statistics for the rest of the industry are even slimmer. As credit card security improves, it is expected that consumers will feel easier about purchasing travel this way. Many suppliers, recognizing this limitation, are encouraging on-line consumer bookings by offering discounts of at least 5%. Since their commissions to travel intermediaries (10%) are eliminated, they can afford to do this. It is not uncommon for travellers to call a travel agency to complete the booking after they have researched the products themselves on-line. Bookings for travel products can be made on-line by e-mail, but travel suppliers are finding that the public availability of their e-mail address (as opposed to their Web page) is leading to large and unexpected volumes of general information queries from consumers. This deluge of messages must be responded to and the personnel costs to do so are a concern for some firms.

In addition to the plethora of commercial information on the WWW, the Internet provides non-commercial functions with information on travel and tourism. Numerous newsgroups, electronic bulletin boards, and chat rooms exist for travellers to exchange views, ideas, questions and answers about different aspects of travel and tourism. These will be discussed in the next section.

5.2.2 Travel Newsgroups, Electronic Bulletin Boards and Chat Rooms

Newsgroups, electronic bulletin boards (EBBs) and chat rooms are important services on the Internet that allow travellers to research travel products and destinations in a less formal medium. They tend to lack the commercial flavour of much of the information on the WWW. Most have a specific focus which matches a particular interest group. That focus might be a particular destination or a given type of travel such as ecotourism or culture tourism. Some focus on the interests of professionals, researchers, educators and students in the industry, others are for the general traveller. Almost all are text-based and do not have the multimedia capabilities of the WWW. Leshin (1997) describes some interesting sites for the tourism and hospitality field, focusing mostly on the students' needs. Newsgroups, EBBs and chat rooms each function somewhat differently and are described below.

Newsgroups are accessible through Usenet, a part of the Internet which links computers which house the information, called newsgroup servers, together. Newsgroups are 'virtual communities' where users interested in particular topics can store and share information and commentary. Special software is needed to participate in and view the discussions from any newsgroup server. The user must actively retrieve the newsgroup messages from one of the servers, as shown in Fig. 5.4. There are numerous categories of newsgroups, each with its own unique name, and there are hundreds of newsgroups in each category. The names of the categories start with certain prefixes such as *rec* (recreational), *alt* (alternative), and *soc* (social). Many newsgroups cover travel to specific destinations, all of which begin with the title rec.travel. For example, rec.travel.asia contains discussions on travel in and to Asia. Listings of the various newsgroups in all subjects including tourism can be accessed from the Web site: http://www.dejanews.com. A sampling of tourism-related newsgroups is shown in Table 5.1.

Electronic Bulletin Boards (EBBs) offer a similar service, however, the information is not replicated on different servers. Instead one central computer server sends the messages from the EBB to all subscribers' e-mail boxes. Each subscriber does not have to actively seek out the messages as is the case with newsgroups. The designated server can also archive all messages and other files for subscribers to

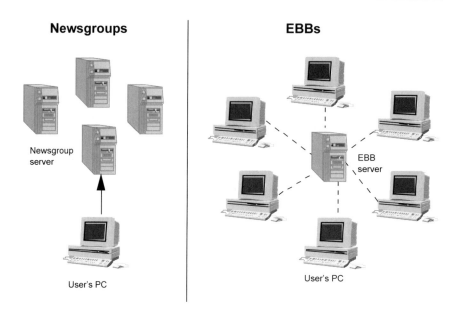

Fig. 5.4. Newsgroups and Electronic Bulletin Boards.

Table 5.1. A sample of tourism newsgroups.

rec.travel.africa	for those interested in travel to Africa
rec.travel.air	for those wishing to discuss air travel
rec.travel.asia	for those interested in travel to Asia
rec.travel.australia&nz	for those interested in travel to Australia and New Zealand
rec.travel.cruises	for those interested in cruises
rec.travel.europe	for those interested in travel to Europe
rec.travel.latin-america	for those interested in Latin-American travel
rec.travel.resorts.all-inclusive	for those interested in all-inclusive resorts
rec.skiing.resorts.europe	for those interested in skiing in Europe
rec.scuba.vacations	for those interested in scuba diving
rec.outdoors.rv-travel	for those interested in travelling by recreational vehicles

See http://www.dejanews.com for a full listing of newsgroups on the Internet.

access at a later date. Some EBBs are 'open', meaning that any Internet user who discovers the EBB address can automatically subscribe themselves and send and receive messages. This can lead to EBBs generating large volumes of trivial messages of little interest to anyone. To keep the message traffic clear of these inappropriate messages, EBBs are often moderated. The owner of the list receives each message, previews it, and if appropriate releases it to the EBB. Another way of keeping the EBB free of inappropriate messages is to make it 'closed' rather than 'open'. This requires a manager or gatekeeper to monitor access, and only users who meet certain criteria will be subscribed to the EBB. Various software packages are available for creating and managing EBBs. Three of the most commonly used are Listserv, Listproc and Majordomo. Table 5.2 shows a sampling of the travel and tourism EBBs available through the Internet and the action needed to subscribe to them.

Chat rooms differ from both newsgroups and EBBs because the information exchange is in real-time. When the user logs on to the chat room, real-time typed discussions take place with others logged on to the chat room at that time. Internet relay chat requires the use of 'chat' software which can be downloaded from the Internet. A directory of chat channels can be found at http://www.yahoo.com/ Computers_and_Internet/Internet/Chatting/IRC/Channels. Numerous travel chat rooms exist. For example, on America On-Line, experts on travel may be invited into chat rooms to share their subjective expertise on a given topic or destination. Users can then send requests to them and receive responses on-line – as if 'chatting'. The on-line nature of chat rooms is closer to personally interacting with people and often side conversations ensue of people with like interests.

General travellers using these services can expect the information gleaned from them to be more subjective and ad hoc, and yet valuable in its own way. It may be used to augment the information given by suppliers or travel agencies directly. A wide variety of travel and tourism topics is covered by these services. Some discuss topics such as market trends, customer reactions, employment information, safety and regulatory issues, issues of interest to the travel professional or educator, in addition to the discussions of destinations and travel products of interest to the general traveller.

5.3 CONSUMER ACCESS TO GDS

The GDSs have made various attempts to give consumers access to their huge databases. It has, of course, required that user-friendly interfaces be created since no consumer would take the time to learn the somewhat archaic formats needed to operate the GDS. While the technology has been possible for some time, concerns by the airlines about damaging relations with travel agents have been present, precluding major activity in this area. This section will discuss the ways in which consumers can now access GDS themselves and also

Table 5.2. Electronic bulletin boards in tourism.

Name	Topic	Address	Action
AAA_TRAVEL_ RELATED_WEB_SITES	Provides information about travel related Web Sites	WEBSCOUT@ WEBCOM/.COM	Send message *subscribe AAA_ Travel_Related_ Web_Sites*
FINANCENET	Allows participation in governmental financial issues in tourism	LISTPROC@ FINANCENET/. GOV	Send message *subscribe financenet <name>*
GREEN TRAVEL	For those interested in sustainable tourism	MAJORDOMO@ IGC.APC/.ORG	Send message *subscribe green-travel <name>*
HERITAGE EBB	For professional interpreters of heritage tourism sites	MAJORDOMO@ MASSEY.AC.NZ	Send message *subscribe heritage <name>*
HOTEL-L	A list for hotel and restaurant educators	LISTSERV@ MISSOU1/. MISSOURI.EDU	Send message *subscribe HOTEL-L*
HOTEL-L(2)	A list for hotel and restaurant professionals	LISTSERV@ CORNELL.EDU	Send message *subscribe HOTEL-L*
IIPT TRAVEL	EBB coordinated by International Institute for Peace through Tourism	MAJORDOMO@ IGC.ORG	Send message *subscribe iipt-travel <name>*
INFOTECH.TRAVEL	For those interested in information technology and travel	MAJORDOMO@ IGC.APC.ORG	Send message *subscribe infotech-travel <name>*
RTSNET-L	For those interested in geography of recreation and tourism	LISTSERV@ UNIVSCVM.CSD SCAROLINA.EDU	Send message *sub rtsnet-l <name>*
RTSTU-L	For undergraduate students of tourism programs	HILL@PLATTE. UNK.EDU	Send message requesting information
SPRENET-L	Supported by Society of Parks and Recreation Educators	LISTSERV@UGA. BITNET	Send message *sub sprenet-l <name>*

(Continued)

Table 5.2. Continued

Name	Topic	Address	Action
STICnet	For those interested in sports tourism	MAJORDOMO@ MCB.CO.UK	Send message *subscribe STIC \<name\>*
TRADESHOW	For tradeshow, convention, meeting industry	LISTPROC@ NEVADA.EDU	Send message *subscribe trade-show \<name\>*
TRAVABLE	Discussing travel for the disabled	LISTSERV@ SJUVM.STJOHNS. EDU	Send message *subscribe travable \<name\>*
TRAVEL-L	Discussing general travel experiences	LISTSERV@ TREARNPC.EGE. EDU.TR	Send message *subscribe travel-l \<name\>*
TRINET-L	For tourism researchers	TRINET@UHM TRAVEL.TIM. HAWAII.EDU	Send message requesting information

use automated GDS ticket machines for ticketing and information retrieval.

5.3.1 GDS On-Line

The first consumer access to airline databases was in the early 1980s when TWA's Travel Shopper and the Official Airline Guide were put on-line through CompuServe (Henderson, 1995). Menu-driven interfaces achieved through front-end software allow the consumer to access similar information to that available to travel agents. American Airlines placed Eaasy Sabre on-line in 1985 and it is now accessible through a variety of on-line services including CompuServe, America On-Line and Prodigy. In 1994 it was accessed 12 million times and more than one million bookings were made using it.

Today many airlines such as United Airlines, American Airlines, British Airways and USAir provide consumer access to their CRS or GDS in a different way. They do this by sending software discs to frequent fliers who can load it onto their own PC to research flight information and make reservations. In addition to flight schedules and fares they can view the flight's on-time performance, meal information and aircraft details without needing to subscribe to an on-line service.

United Airlines' product, called United Connection, is a set of discs giving access to the Apollo database. American Airlines has numerous consumer access products. Personal Access is Windows-based software that links the consumer to Sabre again without the need for an on-line service. Another product called 'Access via the Web' allows frequent fliers to make reservations and purchase tickets via the Web. Their third product, 'Corporate Access', is the version of public access designed specifically for corporate travellers. USAir has a similar system and expects that its use will significantly reduce their operating costs by up to $1 billion per year. Travel agent commissions which no longer have to be paid are a large part of these savings. SystemOne/Amadeus, Worldspan and Sabre have each made their databases accessible on the WWW requiring no distribution of discs.

5.3.2 Automated Ticket Machines

Automated ticket machines (ATMs) provide an additional method for consumers to access travel databases. ATMs are usually located in the check-in area of airports to be used for numerous functions such as accessing flight schedules, making seat reservations, printing itineraries, tickets and boarding cards, and giving or changing seat assignments. The terminals are connected directly into the mainframes of the airline's CRS. Travellers on single carrier, shorter flights, and particularly business travellers without check-in luggage on commuter flights find these machines useful. If the passenger is carrying check-in luggage, the normal check-in process cannot easily be bypassed. Lufthansa, as an example, has invested heavily in these ATMs in European airports, where there is much short-haul business travel. Terminals must be built to withstand heavy public use and so are expensive to install. Significant labour savings, however, can be incurred since fewer check-in agents are needed. Also passenger satisfaction is higher since the time taken to check-in is reduced.

5.4 INFORMATION KIOSKS

The technologies discussed above all provide the customer with pre-trip information retrieval and reservation capabilities. But tourists also require access to information once they arrive at the destination, and even though access to the Internet while travelling is possible, it is less convenient. Other destination-specific electronic information devices may be more appropriate to answer travellers' questions in a destination. Since many decisions about tourist activities are left until travellers arrive in the destination, the information needed to make choices there must be presented when they need it, in a suitable electronic format.

There are at least three ways in which this information can be made available electronically. First, a comprehensive database of the destination's facilities called a Destination Information System (DIS) can be created by the government tourism office (to be discussed in Chapter 8). This can be used by travel counsellors in tourist information offices throughout the destination. Sometimes public access terminals to the same database are installed. A second option for tourists to access information in the destination is by information kiosks in public places. A third option uses TV-based technologies to provide destination information in the hotel room or home.

Information kiosks retrieve the information from CD-ROM discs inside the kiosk. They are found in shopping malls, hotel lobbies and airports, and offer travellers access to product information to assist them in their activity choices. The data is stored on a CD-ROM disc and therefore is unable to provide dynamic information such as availabilities at hotels or to take reservations. The user interface is usually a touchscreen, since ease of operation is critical. Designs of the systems need careful attention. Long, tedious looping through menus can cause the consumer to abandon the search process since it is too time consuming. Since only one person (or travelling party) can use a kiosk at a time, speed of access to the information is important. Tourists' tolerance to wait in line to use a terminal is very low, since they could be enjoying themselves elsewhere. Information kiosks can be either privately or publicly operated. If the kiosks are government operated, the information should be comprehensive and unbiased. If they are created by commercial interests, product bias and a significant amount of promotional material are possible drawbacks.

Printers inside the kiosks can be used to print out maps and directions to the attractions. Some kiosks have live video connections to destination counsellors to answer questions that the CD-ROM disc cannot answer. This is a costly option, but removes much of the frustration tourists might feel when they are seeking information not available in the kiosks. In Europe, many of these kiosks are designed specifically to assist tourists in finding accommodation. The CD-ROM provides the usual video and textual information on the accommodations, but the addition of telephone equipment to the kiosk gives the traveller immediate access to each facility so they can find out if rooms are available. The telephone calls are free to the traveller and allow them to book a hotel or guest house directly, overcoming the static nature of CD-ROMs. All of these kiosks are alternative information sources to the traditional print media and to visits to tourist information offices.

5.5 TV-BASED TOURISM INFORMATION RETRIEVAL AND BOOKING

The television set, which is more accessible to a larger population than any other technology, can also be used for consumers to access travel information. Since TVs are found in most houses and most hotel rooms, this is an important information retrieval device for travellers both in the destination and at home prior to travelling. This section examines different aspects of TV usage for travel information retrieval and booking, including videotext and interactive TV.

5.5.1 Videotext System

Videotext has been used for decades in Europe and Asia to provide information access to masses of people at home inexpensively. Some videotext systems use the TV set in the home, office or hotel room to display 'pages' of information. Others such as the Minitel system in France require the use of a special monitor. One in four citizens in France uses Minitel, with terminals distributed by the government. If ordinary TV sets are used, they must be equipped with a special encoding box to receive videotext signals, which are transmitted over broadcast networks (along with TV signals) or via data networks. The user selects topics from a menu on the TV screen with the use of a remote control device or with keyword searching. Access may be slow as pages must be cycled through until the selected page appears on the screen.

Information pages are formatted by suppliers with special page creation software. Once created, the pages are sent to the host video-text computer. This is usually operated by a government TV station or telecommunication company which is also responsible for transmitting the signals to the homes. Figure 5.5 shows a typical videotext network. Information providers usually pay to put their information on the system, but the costs tend to be low compared to other media. There is no cost for consumers to access information this way. Systems can either be based on one-way communication called 'teletext' systems which allow information retrieval only, or they can provide both information retrieval and transaction processing, known as 'videotext' systems, based on two-way communications. If transactions are to be made, booking requests are first received by the central videotext computer which then forwards the reservation to the suppliers' CRS for processing.

The travel industry has been an avid user of videotext technology in some countries. Examples of travel information to be found on

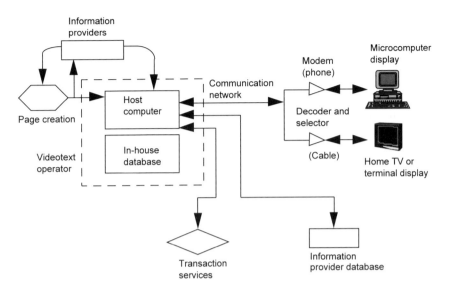

Fig. 5.5. A sample videotext network.

videotext systems are train timetables, airport arrival and departure information, information on tour packages, and weather and currency information. England, Germany, France and Taiwan all use their videotext networks extensively for travel information. The UK system called Prestel is dominated by travel information and was the major method for travel agents to make bookings and view product information before the arrival of GDS terminals. The French Minitel system which was introduced to the French public in 1984 is used extensively for travel applications such as schedule consultation and booking of air, rail and ocean transport. It also provides on-line banking, shopping and electronic directory services. The system operated by the Taiwanese government has all of these features and also includes information on tourist attractions, cultural events, hotels and restaurants in Taiwan. The US has not readily adopted videotext technology although there have been a few regional efforts. There are numerous reasons for this. First, the US is too large to realistically have a national system. Second, telecommunications in the US are privatized, whereas in countries where videotext has been successful, the telecommunication networks are nationalized. A third reason could be that PC technology is more ubiquitous in the US than elsewhere and so a larger proportion of the population uses computers and computer networks to access the information required. In countries where videotext systems have succeeded, the proportion of the population with their own PCs tends to be less.

Videotext systems are likely to be outmoded and phased out in the near future as more countries have larger proportions of their populations on-line to the Internet. To avoid this obsolescence, videotext networks can adopt the protocols of the Internet and become a part of it. Indeed, the same issue for videotext networks as for GDSs must be considered. That is, how can they make information exchangeable between the two networks, allowing them to become part of the Internet trend instead of being consumed by it. As an example of this integration, Minitel emulation software for PCs is now available, providing French citizens with e-mail, Internet access and newswire access.

5.5.2 Interactive TV

Interactive television is another possible media for consumers to access travel information and databases. It is a relative of videotext, except that the communication links are faster and able to handle multimedia information which is not the case with videotext. Cable television, already installed in millions of homes, can be a path to bring interactive TV signals into the home. They have broadband capacity and can be used as fast data communication networks, turning the TV into an information and transaction processing device. In order to do this, cable subscribers must have addressability, which allows consumers to order specific channels on demand via a special converter box. A service called Interactive Video and Data Service is also needed. This provides a two-way wireless control channel so that programmers can offer on-line transaction services such as the ability to order goods and services, to play video games, to view stock market reports, weather reports, timetables and other travel information.

Interactive TV systems are still in the developmental phase, but offer significant potential for the travel industry. Thomas Cook, in conjunction with British Telecom (BT), for example, has test-marketed an interactive multimedia television service called BT Interactive TV to promote their holiday packages, flights, foreign exchange, guidebooks and destination videos (Bennett, 1993). Also, InfoTravel, which is an interactive city guide operated by Bell Atlantic, is available in hotel rooms with a particular in-room movie system. Hotel guests use their TV remote controls to retrieve information on the destination's facilities. Maps and discount coupons can be printed out at the front desk.

The merging of television technologies and computers continues, both at the functional level and the corporate level. The recent sale of America On-Line to the owner of MTV, a cable network, is a significant development which points to the merging of TV, cable companies, and personal computers to bring a diversity of signals into the home. Further development is expected in this area, particularly as TV technology expands into high definition TV making the TV image more alive. Travel industry suppliers, whose products lend themselves well to visual display, may want to consider these technologies as they plan their future strategies.

5.6 VOICE INPUT AND RECOGNITION SYSTEMS

Consumer access to computer systems needs to become increasingly easy, so that larger proportions of the public feel comfortable using it. The graphical user interfaces and touch screens are a vast improvement over typed interfaces, but voice input and recognition is the next step in making communication with a computer easier. Systems which understand voice commands and respond accordingly are already in place, however, they are limited since the voice tone and pronunciation of the message must be exact for the computer to understand. This limits their usefulness, but research is pushing the field forward so that less precision is required. Voice recognition via telephone can be used by consumers to request information rather than using the telephone key pad. In 1993, AT&T introduced voice recognition technology into its networks, allowing recognition of a limited number of simple words and phrases. This is the beginning of an infrastructure that travel firms can use. An example of voice recognition being applied to the travel reservation domain is a system called Galaxy which uses recent advances in conversational systems to provide a spoken language interface for on-line information retrieval. Galaxy servers provide access to various information sources such as airline schedules, telephone yellow pages, metropolitan maps and weather forecasts. Further developments in voice recognition technology will certainly receive an enthusiastic reception by the tourism industry.

5.7 A MODEL OF ELECTRONIC CONSUMER ACCESS

The travel distribution system is undergoing huge changes as a result of all the technologies mentioned above. The traditional travel distribution channels as shown in Fig. 5.6 used phone, fax and GDS terminals as the main communication media between suppliers and consumers. As consumers gain electronic access to travel data, a new Electronic Travel Distribution System is now replacing the traditional one. The vast array of travel information that can be accessed by the consumer electronically is shown in Fig. 5.7. It is clear from the

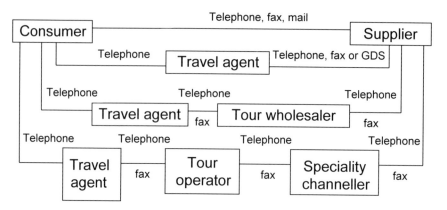

Fig. 5.6. Traditional travel distribution channels.

diagram that the Internet is the central hub of all accessibility, creating a link between the consumer's PC and a plethora of travel data. The traveller can access GDS information, travel intermediaries, suppliers' home pages and specialized travel databases such as TravelFile and OAG. Through these channels, consumers now have access to almost everything that the travel agent does, as never before.

Before projections can be made about how rapidly the traditional channels will give way to the electronic ones, the advantages and disadvantages to consumers, travel intermediaries, and travel suppliers of each option must be analysed (Sheldon, 1995). These advantages and disadvantages are displayed in the matrix in Table 5.3. For consumers, surprisingly, the analysis shows that they have the potential to experience more disadvantages than advantages by using on-line services. The advantages to the consumer include control of the search for information. This allows consumers to feel sure that all of the available options for their trip have been investigated. This has great value to many travellers. If the Internet is used, other benefits are the travel discounts, and the avoidance of travel agents' fees for cancellations, changes or even bookings. Potential disadvantages to the consumer are the time needed to be on-line to perform the research, and the subscription and on-line costs to do so. In addition, the consumer will not have access to travel agent negotiated rates and the expertise and advice given by travel agents usually at no cost. The very volume of data available to consumers may be overwhelming, causing them to seek out a travel professional.

For travel agents, the major disadvantage of consumers using on-line systems is the loss of their commissions. But since many consumers

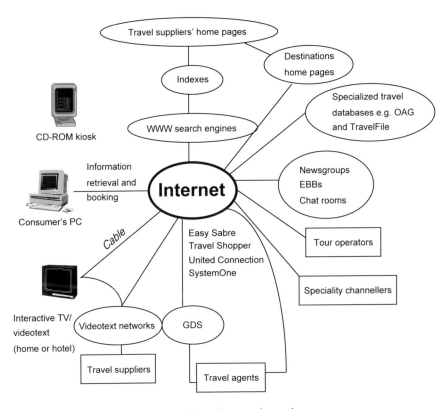

Fig. 5.7. Model of electronic travel distribution channels.

Table 5.3. Advantages and disadvantages of electronic travel distribution.

For:	Advantages	Disadvantages
Consumers	• Control over the search • On-line discounts • Avoidance of travel agent fee	• Time needed to research • Subscription and on-line costs • no access to travel agent negotiated discounts • No travel agent expertise and advice • Data overwhelm
Travel Agents	• Can focus on value-added products	•. Loss of commissions
Suppliers	• Avoid payment of commissions • Effective distribution tool • Easy to update information electronically	• May lose intermediary relationships

who research their own trips still use a travel agent to ticket them, means that some commissions are retained. The travel agent also has more free time to create value-added products. This is a particularly important direction for agencies if they wish to increase their profitability. New travel intermediaries housed on the Internet are entering the marketplace and traditional ones are either disappearing or needing to redefine themselves. Many of the new ones are creating value-added products and services on the Internet. A discussion of the Internet as a marketing tool for travel agents can be found in Walle (1996).

For travel suppliers, there are major advantages to be gained by bypassing the travel agent. Commissions do not have to be paid (although discounts to consumers may be given), and it is easy and relatively inexpensive to distribute information on the Internet and in particular to keep it updated. A danger for travel suppliers if they pursue direct-to-consumer distribution channels is that they may lose their relationships with travel agents when the traditional distribution system needs to be used. Electronic pathways are proving to be cost effective and profitable for many suppliers, but they must examine the best mix of media for their information and booking channels.

The reader is left to adjudicate the balance between the advantages and disadvantages for each player, and the choices made by each as a consequence. Over time, trends will certainly emerge. At the present time, the proportion of travellers using electronic channels is currently in the minority. However fast the growth, it seems there will always be a significant proportion who continue to choose to use travel agents.

5.8 SUMMARY

This chapter has examined the different electronic technologies that give consumers direct access to travel information. The sweeping impact of the Internet was discussed, and the services it offers. In particular, the WWW for its commercial applications and the electronic bulletin boards, newsgroups and chat rooms for more informal information on travel and tourism were presented. Other methods such as interactive TV technologies, videotext, GDS access and information kiosks which are all growing in use were discussed. An evaluation of the forces acting on the industry to shift from traditional to electronic distribution is also presented in the chapter.

5.9 CASE – INTERNET TRAVEL NETWORK

The Internet provides many opportunities for consumers to access travel databases. The Internet Travel Network (ITN) is one company which has been a major force in this area and was one of the first to sell travel to Internet users. They have subsequently helped to redefine the role of travel intermediaries in the electronic marketplace. ITN, whose WWW home page address is http://www.itn.net was founded in 1994 by a team of computer scientists and a travel agency owner with the goal of providing the first plain language, user-friendly, WWW-based reservation system for consumer access. ITN has its headquarters in Palo Alto, California with a staff of over 35. Their philosophy as stated by Chief Executive, Ken Swanton, is 'For technology to succeed in travel it should make the task of travel planning as simple and effective as possible or it is worthless.'

ITN provides travel information and booking capabilities to Internet users through their WWW home page. Rather than posing a threat to the travel agent community, ITN facilitates the interaction between the consumer and the travel agent, and so is supporting the continued existence of travel agents. In fact it provides electronic reservations to over 10,000 member travel agencies in 45 countries. Travel agents are charged a flat transaction fee of US$3 for every US Internet booking received from ITN, and $4 per booking for bookings made by international agencies via ITN. Travel agents are not charged registration fees or monthly subscription fees to become part of ITN.

Consumers can use ITN to access real-time, last seat availability and pricing for airline, car and hotel products in the same way that travel agents can. When the Internet user is ready to book, the reservation goes to one of the travel agents who are registered with ITN chosen by the user. ITN's seamless interface with the four major GDSs (Apollo, Sabre, SystemOne and Worldspan) allows the consumer booking to be automatically forwarded to the agent's terminal over the agency's native GDS network where it then shows up on their screen in a queue to be processed. Most trips booked through ITN are domestic business air trips with an average price of approximately US$375. Incentives for travel agents to use ITN are lower labour costs per ticket since they do not have to do the research for the trip they are booking. Also their clientele is expanded geographically and their agency becomes a 24-hour operation. It requires no knowledge of the Internet on the part of the travel agent to join ITN.

ITN has continued to develop more products and services which provide easier and more user-friendly travel booking opportunities to Internet users. In August 1996, it launched a product called Internet Travel Manager which is designed for the business traveller and large corporations. It handles rates for air, car and hotel bookings which the corporation or traveller has previously negotiated with the supplier. It also makes sure that all bookings are made in compliance with corporate policies, a function that had previously not been possible for Internet travel bookings. Both of these features are important for corporate bookings, and were previously only available through corporate travel agencies who had specialized software.

A Java-based product called 'Low Fare Ticker' is another innovative product of ITN. It automatically displays on the Internet user's screen the lowest fares available to a selection of top airports around the world. The user can leave the ITN Web site, detach from the main Web browser and continue to monitor the fares as they change throughout the day in a small Web window on their desktop computer. When the right price shows in the window, a click of the mouse books the fare immediately.

A second new feature designed to help the user obtain the lowest fares is the product called 'Fare Mail'. This requires consumers to register to use this service and as part of the registration, the user completes a survey form entering a list of destinations and the prices they are willing to pay. Once registered, 'Fare Mail' provides e-mail notification to registrants when fares have dropped to the price point specified by the user. The value of this service is that the user does not have to initiate the fare check, but instead just reads their e-mail in the normal way to receive the information.

ITN has also become a hub for Internet travel bookings in the sense that it develops private Internet booking sites for over 150 other travel companies. Companies such as American Express, Choice Travel Systems and Ticket Master all use ITN for their WWW presence. The product they use to do this is called Private Label and with it ITN brands and customizes the ITN product, giving it a look and feel to match the travel agency's own Web page, if they have one.

The services provided by ITN are relatively unique in the travel industry and represent a different kind of travel intermediary that has no counterpart in the traditional distribution system. The future undoubtedly holds more developments and more innovation in providing consumer access to travel information, as the Internet increases in scope and usage.

Hospitality Information 6
Systems

6.1 INTRODUCTION

The hospitality sector of the travel industry includes lodging operations (hotels, motels, guest houses, campsites,etc.) and food and beverage operations. Each of these components consists of a diverse array of
types of operations – some small independent operations, some large
multinational chain operations; some very specialized, some catering
to the mass market.

A strong focus in hotel and restaurant management has always
been the maximization of guest satisfaction and personal service. The
use of IT has sometimes seemed incompatible with that goal, and so
the hospitality sector has tended to lag other sectors in applying IT to
its operations. Indeed, IT has often been viewed as an impediment to
personal service by creating a cold, impersonal, mechanical atmos-
phere. A shift in this belief was necessary before widespread use of
computer applications in the hospitality sector could occur. That shift
is now happening and many hospitality operations see that 'high tech'
and 'high touch' are not mutually exclusive, but together can bring
efficiency, reduced costs and the potential for higher levels of personal
service.

This chapter examines ways in which computer technology is now
being applied to hospitality operations. Applications in accommodation firms will be discussed first. This includes property management
systems (PMS), their hardware and software platforms, their functionality, and issues in their purchase, installation and operation.
Computer systems commonly interfaced to the PMS such as point-of-
sale systems, telephone systems, safety and security systems, guest
room technology, executive information systems, will also be discussed. The role and impact of telecommunications on the hotel
industry including teleconferencing and the electronic distribution of

hotel rooms is an important section of the chapter. The last section of the chapter will investigate computer applications to the food service industry. The chapter ends with a case of a hotel chain which is using IT innovatively.

6.2 COMPUTER APPLICATIONS IN THE ACCOMMODATIONS SECTOR

The hotel industry's first experience with information technology was not inspiring. The first hotel computer was installed in 1963 in the New York Hilton (Sayles, 1963; Alvarez *et al.*, 1983). It was an IBM minicomputer with software written to automate guest room management. The technology at the time, however, was inappropriate for the task, requiring front-desk clerks to use key-punch cards for data entry which were then batch processed. The resulting time delays caused such long lines at the front desk that the system was removed soon after its installation. Almost a decade passed before more appropriate on-line systems were available and successfully installed in numerous large hotels first in the US and then in the rest of the world.

In 1994, a survey of lodging properties in the US revealed that 95.3% were using some computer technology, whereas in 1980 a similar survey showed that fewer than 10% were computerized (Van Hoof *et al.*, 1996). Large hotels have always perceived more benefits from automation than smaller properties; they are also more easily able to finance the necessary expenditures. As Table 6.1 shows, the majority (57.4%) of managers of large hotels (more than 300 rooms) rate their overall technology needs as 'high' or 'very high' whereas only 28.9% of managers of smaller properties (less than 100 rooms) do so (Van Hoof *et al.*, 1996).

Two factors other than size affect the use of IT in an accommodation establishment. They are the type of clientele and the complexity of operations. Consideration of the type of clientele and how their experience will be affected by technology will help to determine the correct level of automation in a hotel. Business travellers often value efficiency and speed of service, and appreciate more technology in the hotel. Other types of guests prefer hotels where technology (even a TV) does not intrude into their vacation experience. The complexity of the hotel operation also impacts upon the number of computer applications. Large resort properties with many activities and amenities (such as multiple restaurants, tennis and golf, health spa and convenience stores) gain more benefit from IT applications. The complexity of their operations generates higher volumes of information to be processed, transferred and stored. Bearing in mind these differences, the next

Table 6.1. IT usage by different sized hotels.

Hotel size	% using IT	% high IT needs	% agreeing 'IT enhances guest satisfaction'*
Less than 100 rooms	89.4	28.9	70.2
101 to 300 rooms	96.7	43.6	83.2
Over 300 rooms	97.2	57.4	86.1

* Percentage responding to 'high' and 'very high' on a five point scale
Source: data adapted from Van Hoof *et al.*, 1995.

section discusses the most common hotel IT applications. Not all hotels use all of these systems, however, they represent the trend of hotel applications of information technology.

6.2.1 Property Management Systems

Property Management System (PMS) is the name given to the central computer which handles the core functions of a hotel's information processing (or motel, guest house, campsite, condominium or other property). This includes reservations, front office operations, some back office operations and some managerial functions, in addition to being the hub for all interconnectivity with other systems in the hotel. A PMS can run on different hardware platforms and software environments depending on the size and type of hotel, and the requirements of the installation. The next section discusses some hardware and software issues of relevance to a hotel's computer installation.

Hardware and software issues

The type of hardware used to run a PMS varies depending on the size of the hotel and the applications for which it is being used. For a very small hotel or guest house a single microcomputer may be enough to store and process guest and room data and to generate management reports. For a medium size hotel (between 100 and 300 rooms), a local area network with workstations in different departments is appropriate. A file server to house all the software and files allows multiple users to perform multiple tasks such as check-in and check-out concurrently. For large properties (over 500 rooms), mini or even mainframe computers may be needed for the heavy volume of transactions. Figure 6.1 shows the type of hardware configurations in use a few years ago in US hotels. Standalone PCs represented the largest installation, with networks of small and large systems as the least common.

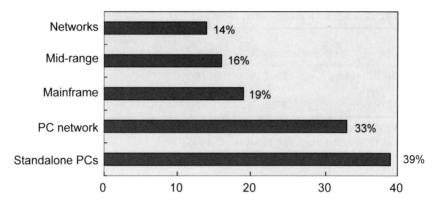

Fig. 6.1. Hardware configurations in hotels. Source: Rowe, 1990.

More recently, networks of small and large systems are becoming increasingly common.

A hotel's PMS may be a turnkey system (including hardware, software, training support and maintenance) or in unique cases the PMS may be designed in-house. The latter only occurs for either very specialized or very large companies. Hyatt Hotels, for example, designed their own system in-house to be used by all properties in the chain. The size of its operation justified the cost of in-house development. The more common turnkey PMS are written by program developers in vendor companies, and modified as necessary for individual applications. Languages such as Basic or 'C' were traditionally used to write PMS applications. These generated PMS with menu-driven interfaces, which had the advantage of ease-of-use for employees with low computer skills, and the disadvantage of slow movement between screens. Many PMS now have graphical user interfaces and multi-tasking terminals which increase the productivity and efficiency of PMS operators. UNIX-based systems and SQL (Standard Query Language) databases are popular environments for modem PMS because they provide more universal access to data and more portability.

The large number (over 100) of vendors of turnkey systems makes the task of choosing a system difficult. Some of these vendors are international and provide their software in multiple languages. Others are country specific, particularly in Asia where the character sets are different. To identify the best vendor for a particular hotel, research must be done including attending tradeshows, and reading trade magazines. Industry publications such as the *CKC Report* frequently publish updated lists of PMS vendors. The hotel may also choose to hire a consultant to assist with this choice process.

Kasavana and Cahill (1992) give a thorough description of issues involved in the choice of a system and the subsequent agreements with vendors. They also suggest an evaluation method to choose between vendors and systems. This matrix method weights the various desired functions and gives scores to each vendor's product. Once a system is chosen, it can be either purchased or leased. Purchasing is more common, but leasing removes some concern about the technology becoming outdated and also may be easier on a hotel's cash flow. The hotel's hardware choice is determined with considerable input from the PMS vendor. Each vendor works with different hardware companies and is likely to recommend a particular hardware platform.

When chosen, the implementation and installation of the system require careful planning (Ford *et al.*, 1995). The installation of the system is the responsibility of the vendor in cooperation with the hotel's management, and requires the initialization of many parameters, such as room types, rates and other codes before it can become operational. Adequate training and consideration of the computer system's impact on employees is an important part of implementation and is well covered in Peacock (1995). Indeed, a study of the impact of the system on the hotel's personnel is recommended prior to installation to detect any resistance from employees (Collins, 1990). Ongoing training after the initial training is important to ensure maximum effectiveness and job satisfaction for employees. Whether the new installation is replacing a manual system or an old computerized system, care must be taken to ensure a transitory phase for the conversion. Parallel conversion in which the old and new systems run together for a while is recommended over the more risky direct cut-over conversion in which the old system is turned off when the new one is turned on.

The failure of a hotel's computer system can create havoc. Therefore, consideration must be given to prevent computer hardware malfunctions. One solution is to have redundant PMS hardware in which two identical machines run side by side. One runs the PMS while the other is used for less critical tasks such as back office applications. If the first computer fails, the other automatically switches over to run the PMS. Alternatively, the redundancy may be contained within one hardware system as with systems using RISC technology where each component chip or circuit is redundant. Another important action to ensure 24-hour, seven-day performance is the use of an uninterrupted power supply (UPS) or backup generator. Surge protectors are also strongly recommended. Critical data and programs can also be saved and stored off-site so that they are recoverable in the event of a hotel fire, flood or other disaster.

PMS functionality

The PMS is the hub of information processing in a hotel. PMS have many levels of functionality, some basic and some more specialized. A detailed coverage of PMS capabilities can be found in Kasavana and Cahill (1992). The purpose of this section is to highlight the major functions and discuss trends and developments in each. Figure 6.2 shows a typical PMS installation for a hotel. This includes a reservations module, check-in, check-out, guest accounting, guest history and rooms management. Each of the functions will be discussed below.

The reservations module

The PMS handles reservations at the property level. Property reservations come to the hotel in the form of letters, phone calls, faxes, e-mail from the hotel's Website, or bookings from a GDS. In each case, the reservations must be entered into the PMS. If the hotel is part of a chain or other central reservation agency, reservations may be received on-line directly from the central CRS into the interfaced PMS. A recent trend for hotel chains is to incorporate their central computer reservation system with each property's PMS, into a system called an Integrated Property System (IPS). In addition to seamless connectivity between the CRS and the PMS, this configuration provides the ability for guests in one property to make reservations in other hotels in the chain.

The reservation module of a PMS (or IPS) records and stores details of the guest reservation, their preferred room type and special

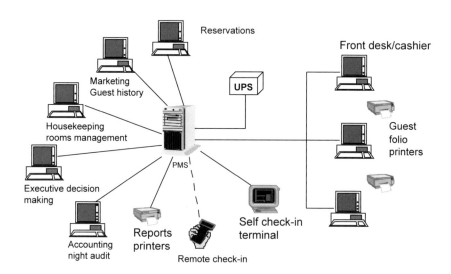

Fig. 6.2. A typical PMS installation.

requests, dates of stay, deposit information, details about their booking agent (if any) and generates confirmation notices. Group reservations modules which assist in the handling and checking-in of groups are also needed by many properties. This module is more complex since home rooms, preassigned room rates, and block bookings must be dealt with. Data in the reservations module is an important input to forecasting modules of room occupancy and revenue.

Electronic pathways for hotel reservations are increasingly common, particularly for hotels which are part of a chain (Hickey, 1988). Hotel CRS receive reservation requests either through tollfree calls from consumers and travel agents, on-line bookings through GDS terminals of travel agents or through the Internet. Of all hotel bookings made by US travel agent, 61% are done electronically through a GDS terminal. In other countries the percentage is less, but increasing. Hotel chain CRS store and process reservations for all of their affiliated properties and then forward each reservation to the specific property either on-line (in the case of IPS or off-line. The chain CRS contains a proportion of rooms from all properties in the chain. Often only a limited selection of room types and rates are stored, since each individual property needs to keep control of some of its inventory for directly booked business and walk-in business. The local property may update the CRS host with room availability information either by fax, phone or more efficiently by being on-line with the system. Best Western Hotels, for example, has a satellite communications network which enables instant updating of rates and room availabilities by the individual properties. This allows faster processing of reservation requests by reservation agents. Reservation agents can also see photographs of properties and maps of the locations of hotels with the new CRS. Other hotel chains are also on-line so that their individual properties can upload information easily and quickly.

If the property is not affiliated with a chain it can subscribe to a non-affiliate computer reservation system to become on-line to the global electronic marketplace. Such non-affiliate systems are operated by independent companies such as UTELL, or sometimes other hotel chains such as Best Western Hotels offer space on their computer systems for fees. Another option for both independent and chain hotels is to use the World Wide Web to receive electronic hotel reservations. The creation of TravelWeb has significantly increased Web hotel bookings (to be discussed in Chapter 9). TravelWeb is a computer switch connecting Internet users to hotel CRS.

To facilitate the message transfer between the various GDSs and chain hotel CRSs, a computer switch called Ultraswitch was created by THISCO (The Hotel Industry Switching Company). THISCO is a consortium of major hotel chains who pooled their resources to facilitate electronic reservations of hotels. Ultraswitch formats the GDS request into the language of the hotel CRS and transmits it to the CRS directly. More recently, the same organization provides Internet access for hotels in the form of TravelWeb. The various electronic pathways for all types of hotel reservations are shown in Figure 6.3. It can begin with either the direct consumer or the travel agent. Each can use the Internet to make bookings; the travel agent can also use the GDS. The reservation is then sent to the chain CRS or the independent PMS either on-line or off-line. The data communication links which permit electronic hotel bookings on all levels are discussed in detail in Chapter 9. CD-ROMs of hotel facilities are also distributed by numerous organizations and publishers. These multimedia images of hotel facilities can be easily viewed by consumers and travel agents on PCs with CD-ROM drives, and are a supplement to the electronic pathways discussed above.

Check-in, check-out and guest accounting

The process of checking-in a guest can be made more efficient with IT. The check-in process brings the guest's reservation file into an active in-house file and a guest folio is opened. If a guest does not have a reservation upon check-in, then a file is created at the time of check-in. Most PMS menus have a 'walk-in' option to handle this occurrence. Interfaces between the PMS and credit card verification systems in banks are used to ensure adequate funds for the length of the guest's stay. After the guest has provided necessary registration and payment documentation, a room is assigned and a key given.

Self check-in machines in hotel lobbies allow guests to bypass check-in lines and quickly check themselves in. These terminals are

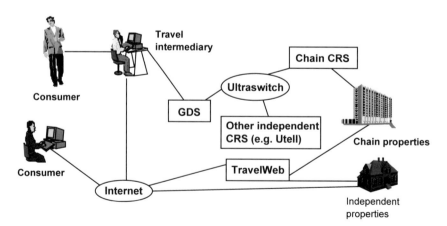

Fig. 6.3. Electronic hotel reservation channels.

connected to the PMS, and are activated by the swipe of a credit card or by motion detectors which detect the approach of a guest. They greet the guest, guide them through the check-in procedure, assign a room, generate keys and give the guest directions to their room. They can also be programmed to activate the energy management system, the phone, and voice mail for the room. The self check-in machines can be used by a guest with a reservation or a walk-in guest. They may be touch screen or keyboard driven. Hand-held, remote, wireless check-in terminals can also be used for remote check-in, for example, at the airport or in the limousine or taxi driving to the hotel.

Once the guest folio is initialized at check-in, all guest charges throughout the stay are posted to this folio either manually or electronically. Manual postings done by clerks are prone to time delays and errors. Electronic postings done through hardware and software interfaces are completed rapidly and without error. This removes the possibility of bad debts incurred by guests not reporting last minute charges before check-out. The night audit function is another major beneficiary of automation. All financial transactions are posted and consolidated into reports in a fraction of the time that a manual night audit would take.

The check-out procedure in automated hotels does not require the guest to pay at the front desk. Automated funds transfer via credit cards allows automated express check-out, in which the guest's folio is presented under the door, and the credit card is automatically billed if there are no discrepancies. Alternatively, electronic presentation of the bill on the guest room TV is possible if the PMS is interfaced to the TV system. The TV monitor in the guest room can display the guest folio allowing guests to view and resolve any billing discrepancies in the privacy of their room. Check-out is completed using the remote control pad. Some TVs also have printers to print out the guest folio and some rooms have in-room faxes which can be used for that purpose. PMS software to translate the bill into numerous languages is used by hotels with a large international clientele.

Guest history

Guest history databases are part of many PMSs and are a powerful marketing tool. Their implementation and value to a hotel are discussed in detail in Bieber (1989). After check-out, guest information can be placed into a guest history database in the PMS. Details of guests' consumption patterns and preferences during their stay are recorded for three purposes. First, to enhance future marketing activities such as direct mail marketing. Second, to facilitate future reservations by not requiring the data entry of information such as address, credit card number, etc. at the time of reservation. Third, and perhaps most importantly, the guest history file can be used to customize guests' future visits. This is done by generating reports from the database alerting staff in different departments to guests' needs and preferences. For example, the housekeeping department can be informed to provide a guest with extra pillows.

Examples of fields in the guest history database are: preferred room type and/or room number, address, phone, credit card number, travel agent, services requested during the last stay (such as extra pillows or newspaper delivery) and other personal information. In some instances only guests with high spending or other distinguishing features are entered into the database to limit its size. The extra disc space required by a guest history module is significant.

Guest history systems at the property level are increasingly common and are a critical tool for the hotel to remain competitive. Hotel chains are now developing guest history databases at the chain level so that a guest who has visited one property can be given the same personalized service when they arrive at another property in the same chain. Guest history databases represent a very tangible example of how IT can improve and enhance the quality of personal service given to guests.

Rooms management

Another important component of the PMS is the rooms management module which tracks the status of rooms and assists the housekeeping department with their duties. The hotel room master in the PMS contains data on each room such as room number, room type, room features (bed types and amenities), room rates, locations and the status of each room. Typical room statuses in a PMS, are 'occupied', 'vacant', 'dirty', 'clean', 'inspected' and 'uninspected'. With each check-in and check-out, the room status changes. Updated knowledge of these changes is important so that rooms can be sold as soon as they are available – an important consideration for hotels running at high occupancy levels. Room status updates can be accomplished manually by the housekeeping staff calling the front desk or sending periodic reports. They can also be done electronically via PMS terminals in the housekeeping department. Even more rapid updates can be made via the telephone in the room or via the electronic lock if these systems are interfaced with the PMS. Staff productivity can also be tracked with these systems, since they require staff to punch in and out as they begin and end cleaning. These interfaces will be discussed later in the chapter.

Other functions of the PMS

A PMS can include many other specialized modules depending on the needs of the accommodation unit. Some of these features are travel agent accounting, function room scheduling, golf, tennis and other amenity scheduling, and condominium or time-share management. Each will be discussed briefly below.

Travel Agent Accounting: For hotels which receive a large proportion of bookings through travel agents, detailed accounts of commissions due to each travel agent must be kept. This is a tedious task to perform manually. The PMS can track commissions by capturing the information at the time of reservation. Cheques can then be automatically generated at the end of each month or week for prompt payment of commissions and better relationships with agents. To assist hotels with the generation of commission cheques to multiple travel agents, a central computerized clearing house has been established by THISCO called Hotel Clearing Centre (HCC).

Function Room Scheduling: For hotels with numerous function rooms and banquet rooms used for conventions, meetings, seminars and social events, details of upcoming functions and activities must be stored and processed. Reservations for each room, the room set-ups, the equipment needs, and any food and beverage needs must be coordinated and recorded. Such software used by hotels needs to consider the systems used by meeting and convention planners as discussed in Chapter 3.

Golf, Tennis and Other Amenity Management: For hotels which have sports and other amenities, the PMS needs additional capabilities. Golf and tennis courts need to track tee times and court scheduling. In addition, they need to process fees and transmit them to the guest folios in the PMS. Special modules to perform these functions can be purchased.

Condominium and Time-Share Management: Accommodation units owned by different parties require modified property management systems to include details on the separate owners, and to track the payments. There are PMS modules to account for this.

6.2.2 Management Applications of a PMS

The PMS database provides management with a wealth of real-time information to better understand their operations. On-line insight into critical statistics can give management a better sense of control over their operations and more power to make decisions. Occupancy percentage, average room rate, gross operating profit and room sales were rated the top four statistics desired by hotel executives (Geller, 1985). Many other standard reports can be generated from the PMS for management analysis. Examples are marketing reports, arrivals and departure reports, and night audit reports. Ideally the PMS has a report generator which prints specialized, ad hoc reports from the variables in the database as needed. PMS data can also be downloaded into spreadsheet or graphics packages on managers' PCs for them to analyse and manipulate on screen. This requires computer competency by managers, something which is being fostered by executive seminars (Parker, 1984).

An ongoing challenge for executives is to glean from the information overload the critical information for effective decision-making. Expert Information Systems (EISs) and Decision Support Systems (DSSs) in the form of revenue management or yield management are making their way into the hotel environment. These systems allow managers to determine what rates to charge for different rooms, when to overbook and what rates will maximize yield or revenue. Forecasting modules are a critical component to revenue management systems. They use historical data from the PMS to analyse demand for various products, examine market conditions and generate forecasting modules to predict demand. Predicted demand is then compared with inventory and availability (either actual or projected) and room rates are generated to go into the PMS or reservation system. Yield and revenue management packages usually run on separate PC hardware but the ability to download historical data from the PMS to the PC is important as is the need to upload the generated rates.

6.2.3 Back Office Applications

Information technology in the back-of-the-house operations is common. It is here where volumes of information must be processed and aggregated and reports generated. Back office applications include payroll and employee information, accounts payable and receivable, inventory and purchasing, and other data which does not directly relate to the front desk. The same PMS hardware may process this data, but for some properties a separate back office system interfaced with the PMS is common. An interface between the two systems is necessary so that data can be downloaded as required.

6.2.4 Interfaces between PMS and Other Hotel Computer Systems

Many specialized computer systems exist to enhance hotel information processing other than those mentioned above. Connectivity between these systems and the PMS brings significant benefits, particularly in the area of guest accounting (Rowe, 1990). Information can be transferred rapidly to the PMS from the interfaced system without the need for manual input, thereby significantly reducing labour costs (no need for entry clerks), increasing accuracy and timeliness of the data transferred, and minimizing the number of unpaid guest bills due to slow information transfer prior to check-out. For example, the point-of-sale systems in restaurants which store and track sales can be interfaced with the PMS to instantly post restaurant charges to guest folios. The electronic locking system used to enhance security can become more efficient if there is an interface to the PMS. Interfaces with guest room electronic devices, hotel telephone systems, energy management systems, back office systems, credit card verification systems, and executive PCs are other examples of valuable interfaces with the PMS (CKC, 1993).

Interfaces also bring technical complexity to the hotel. Compatible hardware and software must be installed, in addition to communication hardware, software and cabling to accomplish the interfaces. Each interface represents a cost, not only for the hardware itself, but also for the connection. A separate interface processor is needed to make the connection to the PMS from the various systems. Also a higher skill level is required of the MIS (Management Information System) staff in the hotel to manage day-to-day running for the interfaces. Cooperation between the vendors of the PMS and the system to be interfaced is also a prerequisite to smooth operations, particularly in the event of data transfer problems. When the hotel has to deal with multiple vendors, complexities and complications can occur. Corporate mergers between vendors of PMS and other hotel systems have recently occurred, simplifying things for the MIS department by having fewer vendors to work with. Figure 6.4 shows the variety of systems that can be interfaced to a PMS, and Fig. 6.5 shows an actual hotel's computer installation with many of the interfaces discussed below. The hotel is the Sheraton Waikiki Hotel in Hawaii which was one of the first to install computers in the US. The next sections examine, one by one, some of these systems.

6.2.5 Guest Room Technology

The level of comfort, enjoyment, and security of the guest room can be significantly enhanced by IT applications. Not all accommodation units will find every technology to be appropriate to their guest rooms. A key to success with choosing these IT applications is to focus on the appropriateness of the technologies to the hotel's clientele. City hotels with a significant proportion of business travellers will make different decisions about appropriate technologies than will smaller properties or luxury resort properties. Guest room technologies include electronic

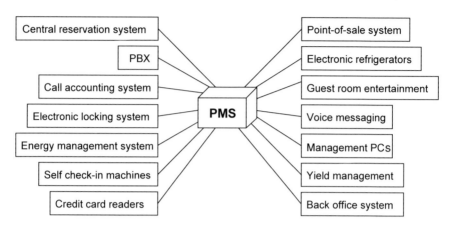

Fig. 6.4. PMS interfaces.

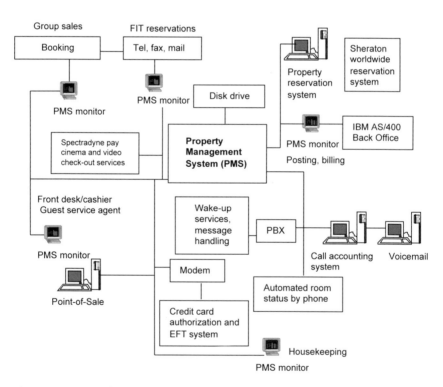

Fig. 6.5. PMS interfaces in a Sheraton Hotel. Source: Sheraton Hotels, Hawaii.

locking Systems, guest entertainment and information systems, and guest service technology such as electronic refrigerators and guest room offices. Applications in each of these categories are discussed below.

Electronic locks

Electronic locking systems increase the safety and security of guests, by removing the possibility of illegal entry and the illegal duplication of keys. Indeed, many meeting planners, government travellers and corporations require hotels to be equipped with electronic locks before they consider booking with the hotel. Electronic locking systems can have different designs and configurations. In each case they consist of a central computer console, a key-making device, and keys which are recoded for each new guest. The central computer stores codes which are placed together with pertinent guest information onto the electronic key. Magnetic strip technology or punched holes in a paper or plastic card are the most common encoding methods. When the key is inserted in the door lock, if it matches the door code, the door is unlocked. Inside the door, a solenoid for the magnetic keys, and light beams for the punched keys, check the accuracy of the code. The computer also monitors all entries and exits into each room (both guest rooms and other spaces) so that security breaches can be easily tracked.

Electronic locking systems can be either microfitted or hardwired, each using a different technique to ensure the lock and key have the same code before the door is opened. Microfitted systems require a microprocessor in the door lock to store a sequence of entry codes. The door lock progresses onto the next code when a new guest checks in, so that previous guests cannot enter the room. Hardwired systems require cabling or radio transmission between the door lock and the computer so that the code can be transmitted to the door via Group Controller Units (GCUs) from the key-making device at the front desk. In addition to guest room use, keys may also be used in selected areas of the hotel such as the spa or health facility, library or other places intended for guest use only. Cleaners and other service people are given their own keys permitting them access to the rooms their job requires. Figure 6.6 shows a diagram of the hardware for a hardwired electronic locking system.

Electronic locking systems provide numerous additional benefits. They can be used as point-of-sale verification in hotel restaurants, to ensure that guests are valid in-house guests before meals are billed to their room. Hardwired systems can also be used as a method of updating room status. After the staff have cleaned the room, they can use their key in the door lock to transmit information on the room status change to the PMS. Electronic locking systems can also work in conjunction

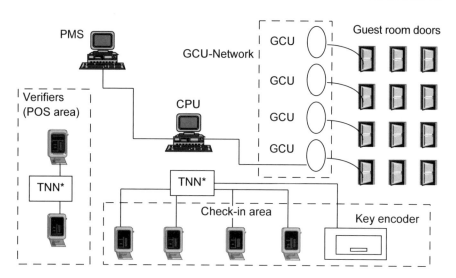

Fig. 6.6. Electronic locking system. Source: Vingcard International.
* TNN = Terminal Network Node.

with the energy management system. The locking system computer
knows when the guest is in the room and so the power (air conditioning, light, heating) can be adjusted accordingly. With some energy
management systems, guests must insert the card key into a slot in the
room to activate electrical power. When they leave the room, all power
is cut off or reduced to a background level. Other integrated guest room
management systems provide bedside control panels for lights, TV, air
conditioning, 'do not disturb' signs, heating and the movement of the
drapes. Hotels can also expect to pay significantly lower insurance
premiums when electronic locks are installed, since fewer claims are
expected.

New methods of ensuring security without cards are being investigated. The use of the guest's credit card for door entry is one method.
The code is taken from the credit card and put into the computer and
the door lock. Systems, however, must be able to account for multiple
occupancies in a room, and this may be a problem with credit cards as
keys. Biological methods of identifying the guest are also being considered. For example, finger printing and eye retina identification are
possible ways of enhancing security. Despite their technical availability, these systems may not be appropriate for the hospitality environment. Additional safety for guests' property can be provided in the
form of electronic safes in the guest room. These allow guests to store
their valuables in a safe which is locked with their own code.

Guest information and entertainment devices

Enhanced TV sets which are on-line to numerous devices can provide a range of entertainment and information services to guests in their room. With the attachment of an electronic selector box and appropriate hardware and cabling, the in-room TV can receive signals from different programming sources. Some of the services that can be received in the guest room are satellite programming (if the hotel has an earth station on site), on-demand videos and movies, and video games. A central computer system monitors the signals to the room and automatically bills guests for the services they choose through an interface with the PMS.

The TV can also act as a computer monitor allowing guests to retrieve information from the PMS and other computers. Guests can review their folios and check themselves out of their rooms with the remote control pad of the TV. They can also complete customer satisfaction surveys, order room service or bellman service, and view voice mail messages on screen, all through the TV set. Developments in TV technology are producing TVs with high speed modems and Internet connections. These applications require the use of a wireless keyboard and/or a mouse. The TV screen itself is also improving. Flat screen TVs (one inch thick) can be hung on the wall, and their superior image resolution will encourage their use for all applications. It may also justify their installation in public areas such as bars and lobbies. When guests can use the TV interactively to access other databases, they have options such as on-line shopping, and information retrieval. Figure 6.7 displays the different hardware needed for a hotel to provide a comprehensive entertainment and information system. The guest room TV is rapidly becoming the central information and entertainment device, and the merging of TV, computer and phone technology is already occurring in the guest room.

Guest services technology

Services to the guest that would otherwise require hotel employees' time can now be provided electronically. Three examples of this are: the provision of refreshments in the hotel room, the provision of business services offered in the form of a guest room office, and concierge services.

The provision of refreshments in a hotel room refrigerator is a service offered for the convenience of guests and to minimize small room service orders. The consumption of items from the refrigerator must be monitored daily and billed to the guest folio. This has traditionally been done by either hotel staff entering the room and checking the contents of the refrigerator or by the honour system in which the hotel relies on the guest to report the items consumed. Both of these methods

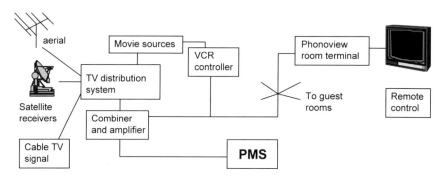

Fig. 6.7. Guest room technology system.

are inefficient. The first method is labour intensive and/or intrusive to guests, and the second method relies on guest honesty which is likely to lead to some bad debts.

IT brings efficiency to this process in the form of in-room electronic refreshment centres. These refrigerators contain an electronic sensor below each bottle or can, a microprocessor to store data, and a connection to a central computer. The refrigerator is usually divided into different refrigerated compartments for different drinks, and the microprocessor stores price and inventory information for each compartment. When the bottle or can is removed, the sensor notifies the microprocessor of the items consumed and their prices. This information is then transmitted either via radio waves or cable to the central computer which in turn communicates it to the guest folio in the PMS. The storage of sales information for all guest room usage is valuable to the hotel in analysing consumer demand for the various products. The system also tracks the inventory of items in the refrigerators so that replenishment can be done efficiently, and ordering is facilitated.

A second example of increased guest service in the room is the guest room business office. Hotels with a large business clientele need to provide equipment for business travellers to use while travelling. Some provide separate business centres on one floor of the hotel with computers, modems and faxes. Guests who use the facility are billed for their use on an hourly basis. As a way to differentiate themselves through better amenities, some hotels provide a business office in the guest room and charge the guest a premium room rate. In-room computers with data jacks and modems, printers, in-room fax machines and larger working spaces constitute most guest room offices. They provide more privacy for guests' electronic transactions, and interfaces between guest room computers and the PMS allow the guest folio to be printed in-room. The hotel must carefully determine how many guest rooms to equip with a business office to ensure maximum usage. Unlike other guest room technologies, it is unlikely that guest room offices will be installed in all rooms in a hotel in the near future. The case at the end of this chapter discusses one hotel chain's approach to 'guest offices'.

Concierge functions in a hotel are also being somewhat automated, although it is difficult to imagine complete automation of this complex function. Destination information retrieval from in-room TV sets is one attempt to reduce demands on concierge personnel, and databases accessible by concierge staff can speed information inquiries. Expert system technology finds a natural application in concierge functions and can tolerate the vagueness of many requests (Cho *et al.*, 1996).

The infiltration of technology into the guest room must be monitored with great care. The enhancement of the guest experience must always be the overriding concern when deciding what to install. Additional concerns are the increase in efficiency, ease of guest room maintenance, and reduction of labour costs for the hotel. Decisions based on a consideration of all of these will lead to successful installations. The next section will discuss developments in telephone and telecommunications technology which are affecting all levels of hotel operations including the guest room phone.

6.2.6 Telecommunications in a Hotel

Telecommunication needs in the accommodation sector are increasing in complexity. They include the transmission of voice, data and images both within the hotel and with the outside world. Specialized equipment and cabling are necessary to ensure that all telecommunication services can be offered to guests (Moore and Wilkinson, 1993). This includes computerized telephone switches, or private branch exchanges, multiple function phones (including cellular phones), cabling that can accommodate voice, data and image transmission, and two lines (one for voice and one for data) per guest room. Fibre optic cabling with its higher bandwidth and speed is especially important for hotels to consider installing if they wish to host videoconferences. This section discusses the computer systems that facilitate voice and data communications in a hotel. Private branch exchanges, call accounting systems and equipment to host teleconferencing are the most important considerations. The chapter also examines the impact of teleconferencing on the hotel and travel industries.

Private branch exchange (PBX)

Call switching between hotel guests, hotel employees and with the outside world is an important function which used to be done with a mechanical device often referred to as a 'spaghetti board'. The operator used to insert a plug into the socket connecting the caller to the party being called. For an outside line the connection would be made to the telephone company operator. 'Spaghetti boards' were soon replaced by private branch exchanges (PBXs) which control the connections of telephone calls in the hotel and to the outside world for guests and employees. There are two types of PBXs: the electro-mechanical (analogue) PBX and the electronic (digital) PBX.

They provide similar basic functions, but digital PBXs provide additional features over analogue PBXs. Voice mail, automatic wake-up calls, room status updates through the phone, and guest name recognition are some of these features. Voice mail provides a more efficient way for callers to leave messages, and is a particular benefit for hotels with significant international or conference clientele. Messages can be picked up in the caller's language and significant reductions in telephone operator staff are possible. Automatic wake-up calls can be handled by a digital PBX so that operators do not have to dial the calls or even receive the requests. The guest's wake-up call details can be entered through the telephone by the guest, and are stored in the PBX until the time of the call. When the call is made, pre-recorded information constitutes the message the guest hears. Both of these features reduce labour costs in the telephone department.

Some digital PBXs also provide the guest name recognition feature. This displays the name of the guest who is calling the telephone operator or hotel staff on an LCD display on their phone. The information is pulled from the PMS, permitting the hotel staff to personalize the response and call the guest by name. Automated room status updates by staff from the guest room phone to the PMS are also possible when a digital PBX is interfaced with the PMS. An interface with the PMS is important for many other reasons. A digital PBX can be used for data communication between the PMS terminals and PCs. A PBX can also provide Internet access, and can be expanded to provide both voice and data lines to each room. More intelligent telephones in guest rooms are in competition with TVs as the information hub. Cellular phones are also offered by some hotels to their guests.

Call accounting systems (CASs)

Tracking guest calls and billing them to the guest folio in a timely way is necessary in a hotel environment. Call Accounting Systems (CASs) allow the hotel to route and track calls without the outside help of the telephone company. Using a CAS, hotel telephone departments can substantially increase their revenues, since they need no longer pay the telephone company for their charge tracking services. An analysis of the factors involved in selecting a suitable CAS are presented in Engel and Ives (1982). Tollfree, credit card and collect calls are also a source of revenue for the hotel. CAS functions are now being integrated into some PBXs, reducing the number of systems and vendors that have to be dealt with.

CASs track call activity with a feature known as Station Message Detail Recording (SMDR). This feature records the duration of the call, the number called, the extension dialled from and the cost of the call. It does this in one of two ways. Either the 'time-out' method, in which the number is dialled and a certain time elapses (30–90 seconds) before the CAS commences billing (whether or not the connection is made). This method produces incorrect billing if the phone rings for more than the set time without being answered, and guests receive bills for calls they did not make. The second and more preferable method, called 'answer detection', suppresses SMDR when calls are not answered, meaning that only answered calls are recorded. Call information is forwarded directly to the guest folios through a PMS interface, and can also be used by management to analyse administrative phone usage. Another feature of a CAS is Least Cost Routing (LCR). This is worthwhile when numerous long distance carriers can be used for phone calls. By storing cost information for a selection of long distance carriers, the LCR feature routes each call over the least expensive line. Figure 6.8 displays a sample telephone system configuration for a hotel or other accommodation operation.

Teleconferencing

Teleconferencing is the interconnection of two or more locations electronically using telecommunication links such as fibre optic links, microwave or satellite transmission. The signals sent on these links can be audio, video or a combination of the two, each requiring different equipment. The signals may be transmitted two-ways, or one site may be the major transmitting site with multiple receiving sites. The first type of teleconference is referred to as point-to-point and the second as point-to-multipoint teleconference. Point-to-multipoint videoconferencing occurs in many examples such as news conferences and training sessions. By adding teleconference equipment to their properties, hotels can provide services required by many business travellers and meeting planners. Hotels affiliated with chains lend themselves well to multi-site videoconferences. This section will examine the use of teleconferencing in the hotel and travel industries.

The first use of videoconferencing in hotels was by Holiday Inns in 1979 when it created its own teleconferencing network called

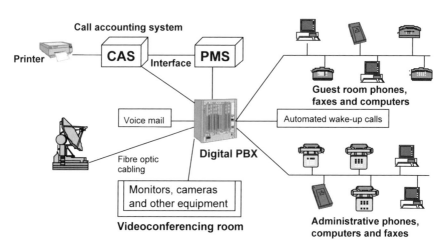

Fig. 6.8. Hotel telecommunication system.

HINET. This network connected together a number of Holiday Inn Hotels and could be used for in-company purposes or be leased for use by clients. Since that time costs have declined by a factor of six, and many more hotels have installed equipment (Coopers and Lybrand, 1995), although there are still some which choose not to use this technology. Hotels with teleconferencing equipment can increase their revenues from the rental of the teleconference facilities and from additional food, beverage and room rental business generated by the attendees at the teleconferences. The various types of equipment needed to host teleconferences are discussed below.

The connection of multiple sites with audio signals is the simplest and least expensive form of teleconferencing. Guest room phones installed with microphones and speakers and the ability to connect to numerous sites simultaneously can be provided for audio conference calls. The addition of fax machines and/or electronic drawing surfaces add graphic information and are referred to as audiographic conference calls. Equipment can be installed either in the guest room or in specially equipped conference rooms which are leased separately. For both audio conferencing and audiographic conferencing, data can be transmitted via voice grade phone lines, and so no extra cabling is required.

Videoconferencing can take one of two forms: slow-scan videoconferencing or full motion videoconferencing. Slow-scan (or freeze frame) videoconferencing adds a frequently-refreshed still image to the audio signal. The combined signal can be transmitted using voice grade phone lines since the volume of data is less in comparison to full motion videoconferencing and only requires a camera and encoding device as extra equipment. Slow-scan videoconferencing is often used in situations where cost is an issue. Full motion videoconferencing requires higher bandwidth transmission devices to transmit the larger volume of data in a reasonable amount of time. Compressed video techniques permit more video information to be transmitted via voice grade phone lines.

Full motion videoconferences place much higher equipment demands on the hotel and are more expensive than the other types. They typically require rooms equipped with cameras, screens and transmission technology, in addition to an earth station on-site to receive the satellite transmissions. This equipment may be permanently set up in a dedicated room or it can be mobile. The technology is developing rapidly and now desktop videoconferencing is possible on the guest room PC.

The overall impact of teleconferencing on the travel industry is yet to be determined although certain trends are emerging. It presents both a potential opportunity and a potential threat – a potential complement and a potential substitute to travel. The business travel sector is most likely to substitute teleconferencing for travel, and so companies serving that sector are likely to receive the most impact (Coddington, 1993). As telecommunication costs decrease over time, and the technology becomes more available and easier to use, the choice to travel versus to meet electronically may increasingly conclude in a decision to use teleconferencing. Research has shown that videoconferencing is expected to decrease the demand for domestic air travel in the US by 12–16% by 2030. A European study estimates similar trip reductions of 13–23%. Hotels with videoconferencing equipment are also considering the family reunion market as a way to increase the usage of their videoconferencing equipment, thereby also affecting the pleasure travel market.

Teleconferencing, however good, is unlikely to replace all business meetings for numerous reasons. First, many employees like the travel opportunity that business trips and conferences provide. Second, business trips often accomplish more than one goal such as attending a conference and visiting a client in one trip, making teleconferencing an unlikely substitute for this type of travel. Third, the personal contact and networking provided by face to face meetings is invaluable in many business situations, and videoconferencing can never provide it. On the other hand, teleconferencing does permit more people in a company to participate in a meeting or conference, and it can significantly reduce travel costs for a corporation. One company estimated it would save $365,000 a month on air travel if it installed videoconferencing in its 72 locations. Firms in the tourism industry who choose to provide teleconferencing services (such as hotels and travel intermediaries) can mitigate the substitution effects and actually benefit from serving the market segments that value it. The case example at the end of the chapter discusses a hotel chain which has installed videoconferencing equipment.

This concludes the discussion of hotel applications of information technology, which is indicative of some of the developments and trends. The reader is referred to Chervenak (1993) for more insight into hotel technology trends. The next section covers the use of computer technology in the food service industry. Research has shown that of all hotel departments, food and beverage operations are the third most likely to be automated after front office and back office applications (Van Hoof *et al.*, 1996).

6.3 COMPUTER APPLICATIONS IN THE FOOD SERVICE SECTOR

Food service operations, whether they be independent or part of a hotel or club, quick service or table service, commercial or institutional, have specific IT needs. This section will describe the applications common to most food service establishments. Point-of-sale systems are by far the most common applications and are used to increase the efficiency of food delivery, and to track and analyse sales. Restaurant management systems, another common application, are back office systems which assist in the control, monitoring and analysis of food production.

6.3.1 Point-of-Sale Systems

A point-of-sale (POS) system improves the efficiency of food delivery from kitchen to table and assists in analysing sales of menu items (Kasavana, 1987; Collins, 1991). The hardware of a POS system consists of a fileserver which houses the software and the database, and a network of order-entry terminals, cashier stations, manager workstations, and printers. There may also be modem connections for credit card authorization and uploading of sales data to a central location. An example POS configuration is shown in Figure 6.9. For many years POS hardware was uniquely designed for the food service environment with specialized designs and the systems were proprietary. Now, POS systems run on PC-based hardware with open operating systems, increasing their ease of use.

Order-entry terminals can be either micromotion keyboards,

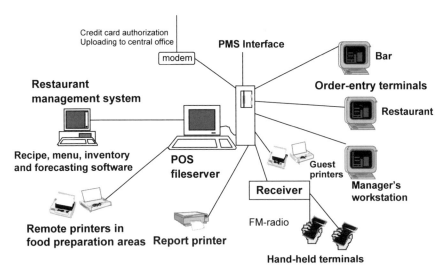

Fig. 6.9. Food service computer applications.

touchscreen terminals, or hand-held terminals. Hand-held terminals connect to the processing unit via radio waves and a receiver, and are particularly useful where the installation of an order entry terminal is not possible, such as poolside or patio dining. The keys (or positions), called present keys, on the order-entry terminal are programmed with menu items, their prices and the appropriate workstation printer that the order must be sent to. Modifier keys allow the order to be customized (e.g. well done, medium, rare; large, small). Settlement keys and other function keys serve a variety of functions such as changing the menu from lunch to dinner, handling coupons, and serving as time and attendance modules for employees. To improve the food delivery system, a POS network must include remote printers (or video screens) in the food preparation areas. These workstation printers deliver orders electronically to the kitchen without delay, in readable form, and without staff needing to enter the kitchen. Printers are also needed for guest bill printing and report printing. There are instances of guest-operated touchscreen point-of-sale terminals, where guests input their own food order at the table. Automated beverage control systems can also be installed to control the dispensing of beverages and to analyse sales.

Software for POS systems often provides numerous abilities such as sales analysis, forecasting and precosting. Menu engineering is one example of software which analyses the sales data in the POS system for decision-making purposes. This menu analysis helps a restaurant to determine whether or not a particular item should remain on the menu, and what is an optimum price for each item based on an analysis of sales and food cost. Frequent diner tracking is also a possible module of the POS software. For hotel restaurants, a PMS interface provides the immediate posting of a guest's restaurant charges to their folio. It also allows the hotel restaurant to check that the guest is resident (by using the electronic key) before billing the meal to their room.

6.3.2 Restaurant Management Systems

There are many other functions to be automated in the operation and management of a food service establishment. These include, the purchasing and inventory control of food items, menu and recipe control, and food costing. Purchasing and inventory control systems track the items on order, details of suppliers, inventory on-hand, and minimum par level so that ordering can be automated. On-line connections to suppliers via modem can be used to transmit standard orders electronically. Menu and recipe management software, which creates files for each recipe and menu item permit an analysis of the impacts of changes of ingredient costs, ingredient quantities and price changes. Food cost percentages can be calculated with these systems, which then form the basis for the precosting of menus and events.

Separate systems called restaurant management systems handle these functions. They are usually PC-based systems, which can be interfaced with the POS system for maximum benefit. Such an interface allows perpetual inventory of food ingredients to be kept in the following way. When the POS system registers the sale of an item, its component ingredients can be calculated and transmitted to the restaurant management system where the food inventory amount is subtracted from the quantity on hand. Multi-unit restaurants require additional hardware and software so that data can be shared between units, and from each unit to the head office. Data communication between units permit the sharing of databases of suppliers, recipes, employees and other critical information so that each unit can benefit from the other's experience. Data communications between each unit and the chain's headquarters allow for on-line consolidation of sales and financial reports, as well as centralized ordering from suppliers.

6.4 SUMMARY

This chapter has examined the use of information technology in the hospitality sector. Their initial lag behind other travel sectors in using

IT is being overcome. But hospitality remains essentially a 'high touch' service-based industry requiring the judicious use of technology. Experience to date has shown, however, that the appropriate use of technology can provide an increase in efficiency and reduction in costs so that more human and financial resources can be funnelled into personal service. In fact, hospitality operators are demonstrating that technology can augment personal service when used carefully.

Since hospitality managers are challenged to implement technology in many areas of their properties, the appointment of a talented information systems professional and staff is important. The information systems director must work with the various vendors of systems to ensure problem-free interfacing, and to plan for the installation of upgrades and new systems. As more hotel technology vendors are merging with other vendors, the task of the IT professional will be simplified.

Hospitality technology is increasingly keeping pace with the general world of computer technology. The systems are less closed and are written in environments that users outside of the industry are familiar with. This facilitates training for new employees and makes the systems easier to upkeep and maintain. It also has the potential to reduce costs. Many of the PMS and POS applications are being written in Windows or UNIX environments, and the movement to client-server architecture is also a trend. The hospitality sector, often faced with human resource challenges, is currently investigating whether robotics technology fits into their industry. Numerous applications have already proven to be successful and will be discussed in Chapter 10.

As technology becomes more commonplace in hotels and restaurants, it no longer represents a competitive advantage. Instead, it is going to require managers to creatively use and apply the technology and the information it provides rather than simply purchasing new systems. This is currently evident with guest history systems. The richness of the data in those databases must be massaged and analysed and turned into real knowledge to improve decision-making capabilities and customer satisfaction. Hospitality operators with that vision are likely to be the ones to succeed in the future.

6.5 CASE – SWISSÔTEL

Swissôtel is an example of an international hotel company using information technology creatively to improve the efficiency of its operations and to improve guest satisfaction. Swissôtel is a fully owned subsidiary of Swissair with thirteen hotels, four in North America, four in Europe, and five in Asia. Half of the hotels are owned by Swissair and half are under management contract. All are deluxe hotels targeting the high end business traveller. A leading goal of Swissôtel is to use information technology creatively to differentiate itself from its competitors by offering the image of Swiss efficiency and traditional hospitality valued so highly, particularly by business travellers. According to Oliver Bernet, Director of New Technologies: 'Nowadays there is hardly any activity that is not at least recorded in a computer system, if not completed by a computer'.

Swissôtel has two different focuses in its use of information technology. First, to provide an optimal array of guest services for its customers, and second to increase efficiency by centralizing and simplifying its operational processes. The technologies implemented to meet each of those strategic directions are discussed below.

6.5.1 Guest Service Technologies

Swissôtel has many guest service technologies in place. Self check-in machines in the lobby and remote check-in from locations outside the hotel reduce the check-in time for business travellers. Once in the room, guest interaction with in-room computer systems to perform functions such as making reservations, reporting repairs, and ordering room service, are all possible. The provision of low cost connectivity to worldwide computer systems from all guest rooms is perceived as an important goal for the future. This could include Internet access through portable devices (either provided by the hotel or the guest's own devices). Internet connectivity from the guest room TV sets is another project being considered. Connectivity with Swissair's reservation system to provide travellers with one stop booking services is another goal of Swissôtel.

The business traveller is a definite target market for Swissôtel and so many guest technologies are focused on their needs.

'Business Advantage Rooms' represent 20% of Swissôtel rooms and truly cater to the business traveller by providing the latest in telecommunications technology. These guest rooms are equipped with state-of-the-art business office equipment including cellular phones with confidential access numbers, two phone lines – one for voice and one for data connections for laptops, a fax machine, a printer and large screen TVs.

Another product for business travellers is the videoconferencing facilities that have been available to guests at Swissôtel since the beginning of 1996. Portable videoconferencing units can be moved to the desired locations in the hotel to receive incoming and outgoing videoconferencing signals transmitted via ISDN lines. An analysis of return on investment of videoconferencing equipment showed it to be a feasible investment for Swissôtel even if the videoconferencing equipment was used only for in-company use. For example, Swissôtel's sales managers meet regularly using the videoconferencing facilities in the hotels. With more business travellers looking to use videoconferencing, it is expected to be a profitable venture.

For business travellers who need meeting facilities in the hotel, another product called Swissoffice is available. Swissoffice is a business centre found in all Swissôtel's properties fully equipped for business meetings with TVs, videos, screens, overhead projection equipment, PCs, some with high speed Internet access and, in addition, four board rooms off each Swissoffice centre for meetings. These facilities are available for hotel guests for 2 hours at no charge and can be used for longer or by non-guests for a charge.

6.5.2 Improved Efficiency Through Centralization

A second major focus of Swissôtel's use of information technology is to centralize and simplify its operational processes and thereby improve efficiency. Part of this goal is to build a company-wide data communications network to connect units in geographically separated places with data communications. This wide area network (WAN) allows a central database of guest information to be rapidly downloaded to individual properties so that guests staying in different hotels in the chain can receive the same level of personalized service. The frequent guest program is located on the same database. With this network in place, the centralization of accounting and purchasing procedures (including decisions on computer systems) will provide worthwhile efficiencies. Swissôtel also expects centralization to facilitate the reorganization of hotel operating procedures when needed and thereby bring about change in the corporation more easily and quickly.

Another significant venture to increase efficiencies through the use of information technology is the Virtual Sales Organization which was implemented in 1995. An analysis of sales force activities showed that too much time was being spent by the sales staff in the office writing proposals and other documents, and not enough time working directly with clients. The Virtual Sales Organization concept was designed to take sales managers out of the hotels and put them closer to the clients in virtual offices (their homes, their client's offices, or on the road). In order to do this, they are provided with the latest technology in the form of notebook computers, modems, faxes and cellular phones. With this technology they can electronically access information and book directly into the individual hotels' Fidelio property management systems, sales and catering systems and the yield management system. They also have access to on-line availability and rates to provide immediately to prospective customers. The notebook computers also house an interactive presentation tool to show clients details of guest and meeting rooms, layout options, equipment and banquet menus. They can also play video clips of each hotel's products on-screen. Delays in providing clients with relevant, correct, updated information are almost completely eliminated, ensuring a higher percentage of sales.

6.5.3 Summary

This case has shown numerous ways in which a hotel company has used technology to accomplish its goals of improved guest satisfaction and increased efficiency of operations. In its eager adoption of these many new technologies, Swissôtel has also made it a point to remain sensitive to the cultures of each hotel location and to not allow modern technologies to overshadow tradition. This approach of 'high tech/high touch' is exemplary in an industry where service is, and will always be paramount to success.

IT Applications in   7
Attractions and
Entertainment

7.1 INTRODUCTION

Attractions, entertainment and recreation firms constitute an important sector of the travel industry. Most leisure travellers are interested in participating in some level of entertainment or education offered by such firms. This varied sector includes theme parks, national parks, museums and exhibitions, zoos, aquariums, theatre and cultural events, sports events, skiing and gaming. Some of the firms which run these attractions are large, such as theme parks, ski resorts and gaming operations and have high needs for IT to control their operations. Smaller operators, including small museums, zoos and cultural events may also use computer technology but to a lesser degree.

The usage of IT in the attractions and entertainment sector falls into three categories. First, IT is used to monitor and control the usage and activity of the attraction. This takes the form of electronic ticketing and entrance control systems used by parks, theatres, sporting events and others. Second, IT applications help to create or enhance the experience of the attraction. As successive generations have come to expect dynamic, multimedia entertainment, the attractions industry has responded with a similar level of technological sophistication, particularly in the area of themed entertainment. Third, IT is used to assist in marketing and management decision-making at the attraction by all types of entertainment operators.

This chapter will address these main areas of usage in three different specialized attractions operations. These are theme parks and theme attractions, gaming operations and ski resorts. The chapter will focus mostly on these three environments since they are more on the leading edge of IT applications, but sporting and other parts of the attractions industry, such as museums, theatres, zoos, aquariums and cultural events will be mentioned throughout. The chapter will end with a case study of a cultural theme park which has used IT effectively in its operations even though culture and humanity are the focus of the park.

7.2 TICKETING, ENTRANCE CONTROL AND USAGE MONITORING SYSTEMS

Most paid attractions and entertainment facilities can benefit from automated ticketing and entrance control, and in some cases systems which also monitor usage. Computerized ticketing systems store information on the attraction or event, generate tickets and process payments. The database contains information on events, times and prices (of which there may be many), and reservations including group bookings. It must also be able to generate tickets immediately for customers arriving at the event and to handle commissions. Ticketing systems for theatres, concert halls and other attractions with numbered, designated seating need more detailed reservation systems. Seating plans showing occupied and unoccupied seats need to be viewable on screen, and tickets must, of course, show the seat numbers. Attractions and events often use centralized ticketing agencies who manage ticketing for multiple events. These agencies have huge databases of many events.

Some attractions such as national parks, museums, sporting events, theatres and some theme parks require only one general entrance fee which is paid upon arrival. Others, particularly theme parks, may require payment for individual rides, events or experiences once inside the park creating needs for more complex systems. Smart cards and tickets with magnetic strip cards are particularly helpful to monitor entrance into an entertainment facility with multiple experiences since they store payment information. They remove the need for payment at each point and the inconvenience thus created for visitors. Turnstiles requiring the insertion of a smart card or ticket can control entry into many types of events and attractions such as sporting events and outdoor concerts. Portable ticket collection stations are another option for use when access to the facility's power and cabling is not possible. These are particularly useful in large outdoor national parks, zoos or other natural attractions. Admission tickets can also be barcoded allowing the information from the ticket to be sent to a computer system running ticket collection software. This software automatically cancels used tickets, notifies ticket collection operators of counterfeit tickets, prevents admission fraud by employees and provides other revenue control functions.

Some attractions such as museums and parks may use IT for

signage to guide visitors around the attraction for the best experience and to provide information on exhibits. The signage may be in the form of audio-visual electronic media which can easily be changed as necessary. Kiosks or information pillars with CD-ROM players inside have a significant contribution to make to help guide visitors around the attraction. They are also used to give the visitor multimedia information on exhibits.

7.3 THEME PARKS AND THEMED ATTRACTIONS

Themed entertainment involves the creation of experiences of other places, times or events (real or fictitious) for the purposes of entertainment or education. The industry is currently experiencing significant growth in popularity and large financial investments are being made by operators of many of these firms. Traditional amusement parks with rides focusing on thrill-seekers are part of this industry as are theme parks such as Disneyland (US), DisneyWorld (US), Alton Towers (UK) and EuroDisney (France). But there are many others, each with its own special niche or theme and it is here that much creativity is being shown in the application of IT.

In 1995 in the US, attendance at theme parks and amusement parks increased by 5.2% over the previous year (US Travel Data Centre, 1995). In general, families on vacation seek out these attractions to entertain the children. But the theme parks industry is changing as themed attractions are being located, not only in parks set aside for that purpose only, but in hotel lobbies, restaurants and shopping malls. For example, hotels in Las Vegas incorporate themes into their design. This is possible due to technological developments which create the themed environment. This section will examine those technological developments.

7.3.1 IT in the Production of Experiences

Visitors to theme parks expect to experience some form of altered reality, either in a purely entertainment mode or in an educational or 'edu-tainment' mode. This can be accomplished mechanically as, for example, in the various rides and roller coasters of amusement parks. It is also possible to create an altered experience for a visitor using both mechanics and electronics together. But the electronic creation of more sophisticated altered experiences is now common. An advantage of electronically created experiences is that they can be more easily changed than mechanical or electro-mechanical experiences.

Modifications in the software allow the experience to be changed without a large cost. To change a mechanical 'ride' requires significant investment and so is not done often. This is an important consideration since theme parks with new attractions tend to be the most popular. They also are able to attract repeat visitors to a destination, making them more favoured by operators and destinations.

Equipment to electronically create the experiences comes in a variety of forms varying from high quality audio and visual equipment all the way to virtual reality 'pods'. There is a whole industry of companies selling such technology to theme parks and attractions, competing in their ability to produce the most stimulating visitor experiences. Audio and visual equipment in the form of videos and movies is used to create the experience. This may be in IMAX format, with very large screen images or even 360° wrap-around images. Stereophonic sound and computer-generated acoustics, together with images create an experience for the visitor to become immersed in. One theme park noted that the technology when used successfully 'makes either fantasies seem more real or reality seem more fantastic' (P. Scanlon, BRC Imagination Arts, October 1996, telephone communication).

Computer generated motion simulators give the audience the feeling of moving in a different reality and can be part of many different rides. Many water theme parks use computer technology to generate ocean-like waves for surfing and to provide appropriate environments for other water sports. Futuristic theme parks such as the Space Park in Bremen, Germany, which plans to open in 1999 uses combinations of these technologies to make unknown experiences more real. This particular theme park will give the visitor the experience of the G force, zero gravity, a simulated experience of being on the surface of Mars, in an asteroid belt, or to witness the Big Bang. Other types of theme park experiences can be found in Stipanuk (1993).

The concept of virtual reality, wherein the visitor is immersed completely in a computer simulated interactive environment called a 'pod', is available in many attractions. A 'pod' consists of stereovision goggles, stereo sound earphones, sensory inputs through body suits to stimulate the skin, motion simulators and other electronic devices. The users immerse themselves in altered realities by wearing a helmet and body suit or sitting in a capsule. The pod can be designed for two or more users, so that the altered reality can be shared. An example of such a pod can be seen in Fig. 7.1. Pods such as these are now found in shopping centres, airports, museums and casinos as well as theme parks. They are much more accessible in public areas than in amusement parks. They take up less space, can augment other activities in an area, and may be less costly to the user. Virtual theme parks look

Fig. 7.1. Photograph of a virtual reality pod. Photograph permission of Virtual World, Montreal, Canada.

quite different from the traditional ones, and Fig. 7.2 shows what Virtual World, a theme park in Montreal, Canada, looks like. It can be seen that the park is much smaller than its traditional counterparts. Another interesting application of virtual reality is a virtual brewery in a museum in Tokyo, Japan. This allows the visitor to see, feel and experience the art of beer making and the history of Sapporo, Japan, which they would not otherwise experience (see WWW site http://vr-atlantis.com/lbe_guide/82.html). Most applications of virtual reality pods seem to have more of an entertainment value than an educational one.

Technology is also used extensively in the safety measures required of theme parks and amusement parks. Many rides pose significant safety concerns. Computers are used to measure and determine the weight, speed and strength of the rides. This enhances visitor security and safety and such systems are an integral part of many

Fig. 7.2. Photograph of a virtual theme park. Photograph permission of Virtual World, Montreal, Canada.

amusement park and theme park rides. Firms specialize in the production and installation of these systems.

Museums, aquariums and zoos also use information technologies to give visitors simulated experiences at the border between entertainment and education. Science museums were the first museums to use technology to bring their exhibits to life. Since they are curators of 'concepts and ideas' in addition to 'things' (as aquariums, natural history museums and zoos are) they have had to be more creative in bringing their museums to life. To successfully give the visitor an experience of a 'concept', electronic and interactive exhibits have been used extensively. Themed 'walk-throughs' of exhibits that are enlivened by movies, sound and direct interactive experience are common today in museum exhibits of all types.

7.4 GAMING

Gaming is another growing sector of the attractions and entertainment industry. As governments around the world continue to legalize gaming activities, more establishments are opening their doors to those wishing to gamble. These establishments may be part of hotels and cruise ships, or they may be standalone casinos. Gambling is an established attraction in Europe (e.g. Monaco and Nice, France), in Asia (Macau), in all but two states in the US, in the Caribbean and Rio de Janeiro, Brazil. In the US, gaming occurs in a diverse array of locations. Many Native American reservations are using gaming to attract tourists and revenues and are building state-of-the-art casinos with computerized slot machines and table games. Gambling on the Internet, available through home and hotel room computer systems, is a gaming environment requiring information technology. It poses particular legal problems, since anyone with a credit card can play, whatever their age. Gaming on board ship to avoid legislation on land is occurring in many locations also – some on riverboats, some on cruise ships. On-board gambling requires data networks for ship-to-shore communication with on-shore banks. Las Vegas, Nevada, is the mecca of gaming with very sophisticated computerized systems to track and monitor play.

Casinos of all types use computer technology to efficiently manage and control the facilities and to give maximum benefits to their players. The functions of these systems can be categorized into slot machine maintenance and accounting, table games, player tracking and marketing, cage management, and staff systems. The mathematical calculations to determine payouts in gambling casinos, the probabilities and the models of gaming are all generated by computer systems. Once the probabilities are calculated using payout algorithms and random number generators (RNGs), and they meet minimum payout standards imposed by governments, they are then implemented into the hardware in the casinos. It is possible to run such a gaming management system on a PC network but some of the larger casinos use minicomputers. Each of the functions will be discussed separately.

7.4.1 Slot Machine Maintenance and Accounting

Automated slot machines, the most common form of gambling, convert random numbers from a RNG into the various symbols displayed on the video screen of the slot machine (Kasavana, 1996). They also have microchips inside to record all of the machine activity, including the amount of money or chips inserted, the amount of payouts and the number of players playing that machine. If a player has a frequent player card, the card can be inserted into the slot machine and play is recorded. The programming of automated machines ensures that payouts are occurring at the minimum level and compares the actual payouts (or yields) with the theoretical ones calculated by the computer.

Slot machines can also be on-line to a central computer, so that the gaming activity is not only stored in the machine but also in the central database. This central database has numerous uses. It can be used to analyse player activity and to forecast future activity. It is also used to generate reports by machine, by area, by type of machine, by position of the machine, or for the entire casino. The central computer aggregates payout data on a weekly, monthly or yearly basis. Numerous on-line slot machines can be connected together throughout an entire town or location and tracked in a central database. This central database calculates the amount of the jackpot for the entire grouping of machines and communicates the jackpot amount to each machine which displays it electronically.

7.4.2 Table Games

In a casino, card or dice games are played around a table. The tables are usually in an area called a 'pit' and each pit has a pit boss and certain staff to oversee the activities. Computerized systems are less evident here than in the slot machine areas, but are becoming more evident. Data on player activity can be collected using hand-held units used by the staff, or from terminals in the pit. Touch screen terminals placed in the pit allow floor supervisors to rate players by capturing information such as: the player's buy-in of cash and chips, their average bet, changes in their betting behaviour, and their movement between tables and seats. Customers give their card to the pit boss who scans it into the computer. The player is then given a ticket with the play information on it. This is tracked by the pit boss to capture the way the customer is playing, the time played and the number of chips used. Tracking on non-carded players is done by staff who observe the play and input their observations into the terminals. One development in table games is the ability for players to insert their credit card into a slot in the table, removing the need for them to buy chips, and consequently perhaps, causing them to gamble more.

7.4.3 Player Tracking and Marketing

Automated casinos track players' activities as they move throughout the casino playing different games. This allows a computerized rating system to give management a clear picture of the player's true worth and identify frequent players and high rollers. This tracking can be done in numerous ways. First, by giving each player an identifying customer number and/or card to use when playing the various games. Slot machines, for example, have a reader in which the card is inserted, and the time played, the money spent and the payouts given are all tracked. The systems track and store information not only on each play but also on multiple visits to the casino per customer.

The resulting database is used to rate the player's value to the casino and based on the rating, the player is given incentives. These incentives typically include complimentary meals, hotel rooms or entertainment such as shows. The higher the rating the more the player receives in the way of incentives. Interfaces from the central database to the point-of-sale systems in the restaurants and to the hotel property management systems are important so that information on complimentary items can be sent immediately to the restaurant or hotel front desk. Direct mail campaigns to the high spenders, which again include incentives to encourage more play, are also generated from this frequent player database.

7.4.4 Cage Management Systems

All financial transactions (cash, credit and chips) in a casino are centralized in a cage for security purposes. The cage activities can be computerized in the same way as a banking system to permit credit and cash checking functions. Both employees and customers use the cage. Employees use it to obtain the necessary cash and chips to operate their table games, and also to receive their wages. Customers use it to purchase chips, to open credit lines and to obtain their winnings. Customer credit lines are calculated based on the player tracking information discussed above. Credit lines are often shared between casinos' computer systems as a security device against uncollectable debts. To improve security the cage computer systems may store the picture or signature of customers so that fraud is minimized. Interfaces to central credit computers are also advisable to check customers' credit card balances and to process payments. The computerized cage system can generate important reports for management to analyse the cash flow and finances in a casino.

7.4.5 Staff Functions

Casino computer systems also assist in the management of the employees. Employee badges with bar codes or magnetic strips can be used for clocking in and out. The systems can also be interfaced directly with the human resource systems which contain additional information on employees. Since security is paramount in a casino, security guards are hired to track activities. Their observations of players can be discreetly recorded in hand-held computer terminals which are then transmitted to the security manager.

The diversity and level of sophistication of computer equipment is high in a casino. Much of it, as discussed above, is used to improve the controls. Figure 7.3 shows the various applications that can be found in a fully automated gambling casino.

7.5 SPORTS AND SKIING

Sports activities and events (either participative or observer) constitute a significant portion of the attractions and entertainment industry. The Olympic Games (summer and winter), various team games such as football, baseball, hockey and basketball, and individual sports such as marathons, skiing, tennis and golf are all enjoyed by tourists. Computer systems are used throughout these activities to control entry to the events as discussed above. Computers are also used to track details of the play in the form of electronic score boards. The ticketing and marketing of these events also relies heavily on the use of computer databases. One of these sports in particular, skiing, is using information technology in interesting and specialized ways. This

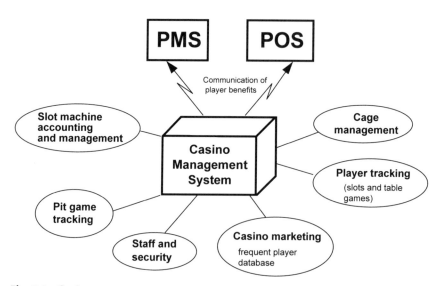

Fig. 7.3. Casino management system.

section focuses on the applications in ski resorts exclusively, and focuses on computer applications on the ski slopes and skiers' use of IT.

7.5.1 Information Technology on the Slopes

Ski resorts use information technologies to monitor and control the quality of the snow, and to design and plan their resorts. This section focuses on these two uses. Skiers today find higher quality snow available for longer seasons, and better designed slopes than in the past. This is due mostly to IT. To improve the condition of the snow, sophisticated snow grooming machines called 'snow cats' travel the slopes nightly to detect the condition of the snow and to immaculately groom each slope to the corduroy-like quality that skiers prefer. Drivers of the snow cats input data into the on-board computer system to record which trails have been groomed and the prior conditions of the trails. Computerized snow production can also occur if the snow falls are not adequate. Sophisticated sprinkler systems laid throughout the slopes generate a perfectly designed mist that will create high quality snow. In addition to improving the skiing experience, these technologies also serve to extend the skiing season and to maximize the revenue of the resorts by making the slopes skiable for more days during the year.

Snow fall and quality is important for skiers to know before arriving at the resort. On the mountain tops 360° cameras can record conditions on the slopes and transmit the images to TV channels or to the ski resort's World Wide Web site. Prospective skiers can thereby check on conditions before deciding whether to ski and which resort to go to. Once at the resort, they can again check conditions on the various slopes by viewing monitors which display the same information.

The terrain of ski mountains and resorts is often planned using computer systems which image and analyse the terrain prior to its construction. Such systems use both geographic information systems (GISs) and computer assisted design (CAD) systems to give 3D models of ski slopes and features. The best locations for the lift towers can be determined based on the particular terrain, as can the cable sag and the best location for resort buildings. The most suitable locations for trees and the type of trees best suited for the terrain and the altitude can also be viewed and determined in these systems. View shed analysis systems allow planners to go into a resort and view all of its aspects at any angle to determine the aesthetics prior to construction. Extremely high telephoto and wide angle lenses allow close-up and distant views of the facilities. Another aspect of ski slope design is solar shedding, which identifies locations which are in sunlight or shade at different times of the day. This is also calculated by the systems as an important component of the skiers' experience and the success of a ski resort.

The manufacturers of ski lifts are incorporating IT into their designs to maximize the performance and maintenance of the lifts. Electronic eye sensors at critical locations on the lift count the number of skiers using the lift, the number of times the chairs have travelled the lift, and the occupancies of the chairs. This is important information, along with weather information and temperature readings, for management to know when the lifts and chairs need maintenance. The electronic eyes which count the skiers on the lifts at different times provide information into a database which is transmitted on-line to a manager's office. This database allows managers to study the skier traffic patterns for future decision-making purposes.

IT is also being used to create artificial ski slopes in locations where there are none. There is one in Japan about 20 km from downtown Tokyo, which provides access to skiing for residents of Tokyo who otherwise would not be able to ski due to time or financial constraints. The facility consists of a slope (500m long, 100m wide, 100m high), a mechanical room for snow making equipment and refrigeration equipment, and restaurants, sauna pool, etc. The internal environment of the ski slope resembles that of a real slope with lifts and trees.

7.5.2 Skiers' Use of Information Technology

IT is also being used to monitor and control the lift tickets and skiers' activity, to improve the messaging systems in ski resorts, and to facilitate visitor purchases in the resort areas off the slopes. This section will examine these three applications of computers. Lift tickets control the access to the lifts and represent the major source of revenue for ski resorts. Ticketing systems which monitor the payment for and usage of ski lifts can be computerized. The computer database must be able to handle multiple types of tickets, since many skiers purchase season tickets, while others buy individual tickets. The transfer of unused rides on season tickets to other skiers can be a problem and so many resorts are putting photographs on the tickets to minimize abuse. Traditionally tickets are shown to personnel at access points to the slopes, or they are inserted into a turnstile to allow access. The problem with both of these methods is that they require skiers to keep their tickets accessible, and this is sometimes a problem in very cold temperatures when skiers are wearing thick gloves.

Computer technology helps to streamline these procedures. Tickets in the form of smart cards can be read by entry devices when the card is in the skier's pocket, making entry onto the lift much more convenient. An even newer technology stores ticket and payment information in a watch which the skier wears on the wrist. The watch also contains a sensor ring which communicates to the ski lift or cable car. Skiers point their arm in the direction of the gate and the gate registers the signal and opens automatically (Fig. 7.4). As the skier passes

Fig. 7.4. Automated ski lift entry point which communicates with Swatch watches.

through the gates and goes to the lifts, the watch is debited for the amount of the ride. The skier can view on the watch details about their skiing activity such as the last lift used and when they used it, and how much credit remains in the watch. When the credit is all used up, the watch can be reprogrammed and used at any resort which has this technology. The watches can also be used to receive and view messages transferred from people on the slopes. Hundreds of ski resorts, use these watches. They were created by a joint venture of Swatch from Switzerland and SkiData in Austria. They have subsequently been used by the city of Salzburg, Austria, to give tourists access to various tourist attractions.

Skier purchases in shops and restaurants in the resort can also be tracked with smart cards. They are convenient for skiers since they do not have to carry money and wallets. Resort managers can examine traffic and buying patterns based on the information from these cards.

The ski industry is changing with the introduction of many new sports such as snow boarding, bicycling on snow, and the various sports offered in the summer when the lifts are not in operation. Therefore, ticketing and information systems must be flexible enough to accommodate the diversity of activities. Some ski resorts offer accommodation and so property management systems in the hotels are also important.

7.6 SUMMARY

The attractions and entertainment industry is changing rapidly to provide visitors with ever more enjoyable, thrilling, educational and diverse experiences. Whilst technology is not leading the way, it is providing more options for the development of entertainment and educational experiences. Virtual reality technologies are likely to increase and become more and more refined so that visitors can experience changes in time and place at will. Operators are using IT to efficiently track their operations and to control access to their facilities. They can also use IT to market their activities. Decision support systems can be used to help determine pricing strategies based on market research. Many now have homepages on the Web and are marketing themselves electronically in numerous ways, such as on the GDS (Dreistadt and Gardens, 1996). It is possible for travel agents around the world, for example, to book tickets for shows in London through the GDS. GDS distribution is only an appropriate option for higher priced attractions since transaction fees tend to be high. Marketing of attractions, as with other travel firms, can be done more efficiently with the use of customer databases. Such databases track customers and allow promotional mailing to inform them of future events.

7.7 CASE – POLYNESIAN CULTURAL CENTRE

There are many different types of theme parks around the world, but the Polynesian Cultural Centre (PCC) on the north shore of Oahu in the Hawaiian Islands is quite unique. It is a non-profit, business/educational entity dedicated to helping preserve the cultural heritage of Polynesia. It does this by providing jobs and scholarships for hundreds of students (from Polynesia) at the adjoining Brigham Young University campus who work their way through college at PCC. Students demonstrate to visitors their way of living in a very authentic way. It was founded in 1963, and since 1977 has become Hawaii's top paying visitor attraction.

PCC includes seven Polynesian villages (Samoa, New Zealand, Fiji, Hawaii, Tahiti, the Marquesas and Tonga) each having its own location with houses, vegetation and other things unique to that culture. This is all housed in a 42-acre setting. In addition, there is a canoe pageant show on the freshwater lagoon in the Centre, and an evening show in a 2770 seat auditorium. An IMAX theatre with vibrant shows of Polynesia was added recently to diversify the attraction for repeat visitors.

To put on their shows, to service their guests and to market their centre, PCC is an avid user of information technology with an MIS department of 8 full-time staff. PCC's own computer network consists of 120 Macs, 60 terminals and 48 PCs connected via a fibre optic network throughout the Centre. Concentrators, repeaters, bridges and terminal servers constitute a very sophisticated network. Some of the successful applications run on this network are discussed below.

PCC pioneered the development of a full-scale ticket reservation system for museums and attractions. PCC's system is one of the largest and most complex museum/attraction reservations systems in the world. This is due to their multiple venues, packages, promotions and reserved seating needs. There are over 400 ticket types stored in the system. The system accepts reservations, displays seating plans and generates bar-coded tickets. These tickets can be used at different locations around the centre to study time and usage by visitors of different venues. The ticket reservation system is interfaced with PCC's accounting and payroll systems and also supports their frequent guest card which tracks users' activities and provides incentives. The possibility of having guests access the reservation system via the Internet is being investigated. This would allow guests to see their seats, reduce the need to pay commissions, allow payment with a credit card and get a confirmation number without human intervention.

The Internet is already being used creatively by PCC in a number of ways. Their externally accessible Internet site provides detailed information such as travel agent information, convention/incentive travel planners, their souvenir catalogue and on-line surveys. An on-line, virtual tour of PCC and a discussion forum for Internet users is also part of PCC's Internet presence.

A second application of the Internet is with a secured PCC Intranet site which is password protected and accessible by management, and marketing and sales staff only. It provides on-line access to various critical company information such as their strategic plan, operational plans for every department, sales training, information about PCC's customers, travel industry trends, and specifics of the marketing plan. The use of this Intranet site is expected to reduce paperwork, improve planning and coordination, and share company objectives among staff. Links to statistical and economic sites that are of interest to staff are also part of the PCC Intranet site.

Another IT application that PCC is using to increase efficiency and decrease storage space, is digital imaging. All invoices, purchase orders and human resource paperwork is scanned into the computer and stored there for easy retrieval. Computerized forms for personnel action, travel authorization and on-line job applications, for example, reduce their need for secretarial services and storage space.

Communication with travel agents is also significantly automated. A CD-ROM of the Business Yellow Pages is used to mail out to travel agents information on tariffs, special events and reservations procedures. Travel agents can also access on-line versions of the above information via a tollfree fax and voice mail system. PCC finds that this eliminates many nuisance calls that take up personnel time.

Lastly, PCC is installing laser disc kiosks at the site and in Waikiki at their sales desks to provide a walk-through of each of their many packages and products. The disc is multilingual in Japanese, Korean, Spanish, German and Chinese. It is an important tool to assist the customer in choosing which of the many products to purchase. Figure 7.5 shows the IT configuration in place at PCC.

So a theme park which focuses on people and cultures finds many ways to use information technology to do a better job of providing the visitor with a superior experience.

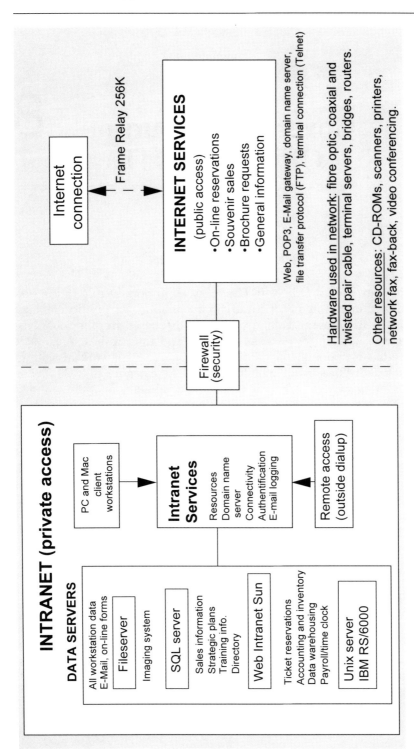

Fig. 7.5. PCC's network infrastructure.

Government Tourism   8
Office Use of IT

8.1 INTRODUCTION

Government Tourist Offices (GTOs) play an important role in the promotion and management of a tourism destination. As public agencies, their focus is different from applications discussed in other chapters. It is one of service to both the industry and the tourists. A country usually has a national tourist office (NTO) and a network of state or local tourist offices all of which fall into the category of a GTO. The NTO is often part of a federal government ministry or agency and is funded to market the destination to the rest of the world in conjunction with the private sector, and to assess the size and economic significance of tourism in the destination. To accomplish their marketing goal, GTOs are usually active in a variety of tasks (Pearce, 1992). Some of the most important of these tasks are: information provision to potential travellers, travellers and travel intermediaries; promotion and marketing activities; and collection and analysis of tourism statistics. All of these functions can be improved and made more efficient with the use of information technology.

This chapter will discuss the application of information technology to these three functional areas of information provision, marketing and promotion, and collection and analysis of statistics. It will examine the hardware and software applications within a GTO and the ways in which a GTO communicates electronically with tourists and firms in the rest of the world. The chapter will end with a discussion of management issues that must be addressed by tourism offices implementing IT. A case example of the experience of a particular national tourism office (Finnish Tourist Board) in implementing IT concludes the chapter.

8.2 INFORMATION PROVISION

This section will examine the ways in which GTOs disseminate destination information. It will first describe the traditional (i.e. non-electronic) methods used, followed by the various electronic distribution methods of information provision and transmittal.

8.2.1 Traditional Methods

Destination information is available from many sources – from private suppliers, from publications, from the media and by word of mouth. But when comprehensive, objective information on a destination's facilities is sought, the GTO is often considered to be the most unbiased and therefore the best provider. The GTO is the source of destination information used by the general public, by many travel agents and by convention, meeting and incentive travel planners. Traditionally GTOs have distributed information by mailing printed materials and brochures in response to mail, fax and phone inquiries, or by answering simple requests directly by phone. Postal charges and timelags in mailing (particularly for foreign mail) and the generic nature of the brochures can make this a less than efficient way of disseminating information.

Many GTOs also provide more detailed information to tourists in the destination via a network of visitor information offices (VIOs) throughout the country, and to potential tourists through offices in the country's major markets. These offices, which are in direct communication with the home office, provide potential visitors with destination information for planning purposes before they leave home. They are staffed by residents of the destination who assist customers in making travel plans and reservations.

Traditionally, each of these offices has relied on printed brochures and the verbal expertise of staff to disseminate information. Brochures quickly become dated and the knowledge base of the staff can be sporadic and reduced when an employee leaves. These limitations were evident in a study of US and Canadian State Tourist Offices which revealed automation of visitor information provision to be one of their most desired applications (Sheldon, 1987). Information technology provides a way for the GTO to improve the accessibility, the accuracy, the comprehensiveness, the timeliness and the quality of information on the destination's facilities and thereby improve the quality of service provided.

8.2.2 Electronic Methods

GTOs have numerous options to disseminate destination information electronically. The most comprehensive option is to design and implement a Destination Information System (DIS). A DIS is a database of the destination's facilities which can be accessed by travel counsellors in the destination's visitor information offices in response to tourist inquiries, or by travellers themselves. Other electronic methods are available to distribute destination information. The World Wide Web is an increasingly common way to provide destination information directly to the traveller. The distribution of destination information to travel agents and other travel intermediaries is still heavily dominated by the GDS. CD-ROM discs can augment the above methods by providing static destination information to travel intermediaries and travellers. These various electronic information channels are shown in Fig. 8.1 and are discussed separately below.

Destination information systems
Recognizing the limited nature of current electronic media to provide comprehensive, on-line destination information, many GTOs are creating Destination Information Systems (DISs) (otherwise known as Destination Management Systems or Destination Marketing Systems (Haines, 1994)) to fill the gap left by other electronic media.

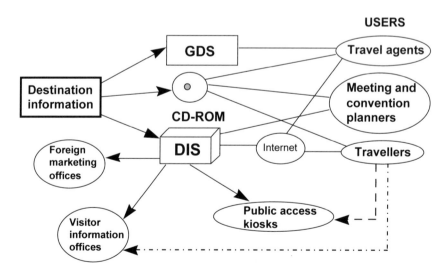

Fig. 8.1. Electronic distribution of destination information.

A Destination Information System is a comprehensive electronic database of a destination's facilities that can be accessed by travel counsellors and/or travellers themselves, either in the destination or in the origin region.

A DIS can replace or augment the traditional methods of information provision discussed above, and can better represent a destination in the electronic marketplace. It is capable of handling both pre-trip and post-arrival information requests from either the marketing offices in foreign countries or visitor information offices (VIOs) in the destination country. The use of DIS terminals in VIOs and in marketing offices abroad improves the efficiency of information distribution on many levels. Customers receive accurate detailed information more easily and travel counsellors in tourism offices have an efficient tool to help them answer questions. It can also be accessed over the WWW if designed correctly. The DIS may also have a reservation capability for accommodations and other facilities in the destination (Wayne, 1991).

A DIS fills a large gap left by the GDS in the electronic distribution of destination information. GDSs tend to favour large, chain companies with high price products. Smaller, independent travel suppliers of travel products tend not to be listed on a GDS because of the cost. A travel agent wishing to book a vacation in youth hostels or small inns, which includes lots of outdoor activities, would find it difficult to do on a GDS. A DIS fills that gap because it includes all types of travel products – large or small. It also includes public sector facilities such as museums, parks and beaches, and charges little or nothing for the firm to be listed. Table 8.1 shows the differences between the two systems in detail. While GDSs emphasize the type of products in the first column, DISs include these and the ones listed in the right hand column also. Studies have shown that the use of a DIS can significantly improve the competitiveness of a destination, in particular its small and medium sized enterprises (Vlitos-Rowe, 1992, Archdale, 1993, Sheldon, 1993, Buhalis, 1995, Buhalis, 1996) by giving them more market access.

Many issues must be considered by GTOs as they design their DIS. Its organizational structure, its economic structure, the typologies of information included, the technology used and its interfaces with other systems, are all variable factors and are discussed below. These factors are affected by issues such as: the geography of the destination, the nature of tourism to that area (independent or group); the preferred mode(s) of travel (air, public transportation or private automobile); the political environment of the GTO; the various sources of funding; and the existence of other travel information and reservation systems in the country or region.

Table 8.1. Characteristics of travel products listed on GDSs and DISs.

GDS	DIS
Chain companies	Independent companies
Large companies	Small and medium companies
Homogeneous products	Heterogeneous products
Business travel products	Leisure travel products
High price products	Low price products
International market	Domestic market
Products that are booked in advance	Products that are booked at time of use
Products with cross-border payment procedures	Products that do not necessarily have crossborder payment procedures
Standard travel	Customized travel
Travel with an air component	Independent travel by private automobile

Organizational structure

A DIS can be implemented at the national, regional or local level. A national DIS has a centralized database of the entire country's facilities, whereas a regional system covers only one part of a country. The nationally centralized system is likely if the funding and initiative come from the national level, if the country is small, and if the NTO has a close affiliation with the local and state tourism offices. Otherwise, regional or local DISs are likely to be created.

There are numerous advantages to the nationally centralized DIS. First, information on tourist facilities in all parts of the country can be accessed by any location with a terminal connection. This is especially important for countries that experience independent touring and multi-destinational travel, requiring tourists to access information on their next destination in their current destination. Second, it gives all visitor information offices and foreign market offices access to the central DIS database over telecommunication links. Third, it facilitates the interface with other travel industry systems such as GDSs. Disadvantages of the centralized system are that telecommunication costs can make this configuration more costly and prone to technical problems, and keeping a centralized database of the entire country's tourism facilities updated can be a challenge.

The Danish Tourist Board is one of many NTOs which uses a nationally centralized system. The DIS is called Dandata and is shown in Fig. 8.2. Dandata consists of a product database of over 15,000 tourist facilities throughout the country. As the diagram shows, travel counsellors in the Copenhagen office, in the visitor information offices in Denmark and the marketing offices abroad are all on-line to the system. The significant task of keeping the large central database updated

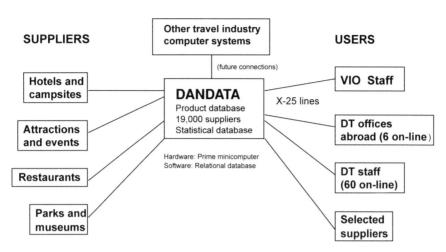

Fig. 8.2. DANDATA: Danish Tourish Board's DIS. DT – Danmarks Turistrad – the Danish Tourist Board.

is done with help from the local tourist information offices who coordinate the information transfer between facilities and Dandata. Some larger suppliers are on-line and can make their own updates. The success of Dandata is partly due to its commitment to keeping the database complete and current and using it as the sole information source. It also contains a market database of details on the major tourism generating countries. Information on economics, distribution channels and other trends are used by Dandata for marketing. Other nationally centralized DISs currently in operation include those in Singapore, Ireland and Finland.

An alternative design for a DIS is to distribute the database at the state or local level. This is likely in large countries such as the United States and Australia, where the central collection of data at the national level is too overwhelming. This design is also more likely to occur when the initiative, development and financing come from the local level, and where the regional and local tourist offices have autonomy. It is particularly appropriate when each region is significantly different from the others in the nature of its tourism facilities (city, country, ocean, mountain) since each requires a different design of the database structure. Updating distributed databases can be easier because the local staff have more contact with the local industry, and fewer telecommunication links are needed.

A successful DIS developed at the regional level is the Tyrol Information System (TIS) (Ebner, 1994). The Tyrol, a famous Alpine skiing resort in the west region of Austria, receives the largest percentage of tourists to Austria. Its tourism facilities differ significantly from those in the rest of the country. High information needs of travellers to the Tyrol was the impetus for the development of TIS. Funding for the development and operation of TIS came from both the national and regional levels. Other successful regional systems can be found in the US, Canada and Australia. An example of a DIS for a specific city (Glasgow, Scotland) can be found in Hardman (1989).

Financial structure

Financial considerations of a DIS include development and operational costs and revenues generated by the system (if any). System development funds usually come solely from the GTO's budget. In some cases, funds may also be generated from private industry if perceived benefits from the system are obvious. Once the DIS has been developed, operational costs include the maintenance and updating of the system. Updating is labour intensive but essential to the quality of the DIS.

Few immediate revenues are usually expected from the DIS. Most DISs list suppliers at no cost and finance all operating costs as a service to the suppliers and the destination, knowing that increased tourism will ensue. In some cases, suppliers are charged a nominal annual fee to be listed. If suppliers are required to pay, then willingness-to-pay is the determining factor of who is listed and this again favours larger, more financially strong companies. If payment is not required or is minimal, all suppliers in the region have the opportunity to be listed, including public facilities such as parks, museums, and environmental conditions such as traffic and weather. A fully comprehensive system can only occur if no payment is required. If the DIS includes the reservation function, suppliers may be charged a commission per booking received through the DIS, making a contribution to operating costs. Transaction costs incurred in processing the reservation must also be offset.

Information content and sources

In the design of electronic marketplaces, time sensitivity and product complexity can create a challenge to the designers (Malone *et al.*, 1987), and the tourism product has both of these characteristics. The success of a DIS is highly dependent on the detail, accuracy and currency of its information. This is challenging, since rates, schedules, events and opening hours change with the days, weeks, months and seasons. If the reservation function is also part of the DIS, availability information requires even more frequent updates. Also, many tourism products require detailed descriptions to portray each product to the potential buyers. Multiple fields in the database are needed for each type of product and its description.

Timely information collection on the various tourism products is essential to the DIS. It is usually delegated to the local tourist offices where there is a greater knowledge of, and communication with, the facilities. Product information is obtained from suppliers by questionnaires sent out periodically by the GTO, with more frequent updates coming through fax, phone or on-line as necessary. On-line updates are preferable but require suppliers to have terminals and modems – an option not yet feasible for some smaller tourism firms.

Quality control of the information in the DIS is extremely important. If the data are found to be false or misleading, there is a danger of the entire DIS losing its credibility. An evaluation or classification system administered by the GTO or other agency can assist in ensuring quality control of product information. In some destinations, the Chamber of Commerce, the hotel association, or the automobile club establish a classification system for accommodation units and other facilities which can be used in the DIS. The GTO may do its own checking of the accuracy of the information to be entered into the DIS or it may choose to trust each supplier's information.

Hardware and software

Appropriate hardware and software for a DIS depends somewhat on the organizational structure discussed above. For centralized systems, which must provide on-line access to the database for hundreds of terminals, a minicomputer may be best. Network controllers for incoming and outgoing data lines may be necessary. For regional systems with smaller databases, a high end microcomputer can serve as the fileserver in an office with networked terminals.

The most common software used for the creation of the database is relational database software, which allows querying and searching of the database and customized reporting. Some systems use text-based searching, with the advantage that the information does not have to be formatted into a database structure but can be scanned directly from text into the computer. An additional advantage is that the DIS can be more easily accessed through the WWW if it is text-based. Public access terminals to a DIS can be found outside tourist offices and in other public places for use when the office is closed or when staff are busy. Such terminals must be designed for consumer access and have touchscreen and/or menu driven user interfaces.

In countries where videotext systems are in place and used by the resident population, DIS information can also be made available this way. The GTO uploads the pages of information onto the public videotext network to be stored on the national videotext computer. Page creation software is used to create the pages of information that will appear on the user's screen. Communication costs are less than using data lines, and the information is accessible to residential videotext users in their homes or to tourists in hotel rooms. When a destination has a significant amount of domestic tourism, videotext can be an important information medium.

An important technical consideration in the design of DISs is the potential for connections with other travel industry computer systems. This allows the inclusion of data already collected by other agencies. Connections to GDSs also give travel agents on-line access to comprehensive destination information. A nationally centralized DIS rather than numerous regional ones will facilitate this interface. The GTO then will be the sole agency responsible for negotiations with the GDS (Haines, 1991). DISs can be accessed through videotext gateways which connect suppliers to millions of potential tourists in their homes. Numerous DISs also have interfaces with other computer systems such as national weather computer systems, traffic systems and hotel databases to provide information that is important to travellers. More connectivity between DISs and other tourism information systems is likely in the future.

Destination information on the Internet

Many destinations are distributing information through the Internet and the World Wide Web (WWW). Destinations (at the country, state and city level) have home pages on the WWW which describe their tourist facilities. Such home pages are text-based with some photographs and graphics and often provide hypertext links to the home pages of suppliers in the destination. The tourist office may have its own computer which is a WWW server, or it may rent space on another Web server. If the GTO has its own, suppliers in the destination can place their home page on it. Text-based DISs can be accessed through the WWW more easily than those based on relational databases.

Users can use e-mail to contact the GTO to request additional brochures. Independent companies on the WWW offer brochure fulfilment services to tourist offices which place their destination information on the WWW. The Internet also provides user groups where people can discuss certain travel destinations. The Internet and WWW are important tools for GTOs to disseminate information to both travellers and travel intermediaries and are discussed further in Chapter 5. The use of the Intranet to provide information to employees within the GTO is another important use of the Internet.

Destination information on the GDS

Since travel agents do not yet have access to most DISs, nor do they use the Internet as their major research tool, GTOs must make their information accessible on GDSs. Each GDS has a section of its database which stores destination information provided by the GTOs (Travel Guide in Apollo and Direct Reference System in Sabre, for example). The primary purpose of this is to allow travel agents access to destination information needed by a client once they have chosen a destination. GTOs which choose to list information this way pay a fee to do so, and a limited number of countries (28) have chosen to include their information in the GDS. The categories of information for all destinations to be found on a GDS are similar and are shown in Box 8.1 for a sample destination (Australia). The information is mostly general (customs, drinking age, geography, etc.) with some private sector information (airlines, car rentals, etc.). The information on the destinations' facilities is not complete and is not intended to impact upon a destination choice decision, but to provide travellers to a destination with relevant information for their trip. Information on a country's border controls can be accessed by travel agents through their GDS terminals. The database is called TIMATIC and contains information on entry requirements such as visas and passports, health requirements, departure taxes, and customs information.

TravelFile is another database of destination information accessible through the GDS (and more recently through the Internet). This is

Box 8.1. Types of information on GDS (sample country: Australia).

Airline service	Geography
Airport information	Holidays
Bank hours	Hotel tax
Capital	Language
Car rental	Major attractions
Clothing	Pet importation
Credit card/currency	Postal service information
Customs (entry)	Shopping
Departure tax	Sports
Drinking age	Telephone area code
Driving age	Time zone
Electricity	Tipping
Embassy	Tourist bureaux
Entry requirements	Transportation
Gambling	Weather

an independently operated database containing thousands of destination facilities in hundreds of destinations worldwide. It is directly linked to the GDS and so can be searched by travel agents from their GDS terminals. The database can be queried by destination and by type of attraction or facility required. Box 8.2 shows the types of information that is kept in TravelFile. The database is hierarchical with subcategories in each section as shown. Costs are involved to list information in TravelFile, and so some destinations choose not to do so or may choose to list only selected information. Facilities can also be booked through TravelFile.

CD-ROM discs

CD-ROM discs can store multimedia information with colour photographs, sound and video clips, which is more user-friendly than the textual information found on the GDS. It is a good medium for static information but inappropriate for dynamic information. Technological developments, however, are making it easier to imprint information onto a CD and in the future it may be possible to download updates onto a CD more easily. The creation and distribution of destination CD-ROMs by GTOs has become a popular and inexpensive way of distributing destination information to the travelagent, travel intermediary and travellers. As more travel agents and homes own PCs with CD-ROM drives, this medium is increasing in usage. Some GTOs provide CDs free to travel agents, and at low cost to travellers. Another important use of CD-ROMs for GTOs is in public access kiosks that can be located throughout a city or region. These CDs store easily accessible information on the destination's facilities, and are discussed further in Chapter 5.

Box 8.2. TravelFile information.

- TYPES OF FACILITIES – Accommodations, Attractions/Entertainment, Boating, Campground, Cuisine, Guides, Information Offices, Meeting Facilities, Recreation Lands, Shopping, Ski Conditions, Sports, Tour Operators, Tour and Packages, Transportation, Travel Service
- ACTIVITIES – Air Sport, Attractions, Camping, Culture, Entertainment, Fishing, Fitness, Food and Drink, Golf, Hunting, Motor Sports, Nature, Outdoor Activities, Racqet Sports, Science/Education
- SERVICES – Amenities, Business Services, Food Services, Reservations, Order Brochure, Personal Services, Recreation Services, Transportation, Travel Services
- DESTINATIONS – Africa, Arctic/Antarctic, Asia, Caribbean, Europe, North America, South America, South Pacific

---

8.3 MARKETING AND PROMOTION

Perhaps the most important mandate given to a GTO is to effectively market the destination. This includes information provision as discussed above, but understanding the customers' needs is equally important. This section will describe two ways in which IT is assisting with this function – with customer databases and market databases.

8.3.1 Customer Databases

A destination can improve its marketing efforts by creating a detailed database of its customers (Burke, 1986). A database of travellers and potential travellers typically includes details of their demographics, travel preferences and activities. It can be created when an individual contacts the GTO for information on the destination by phone, fax, mail or e-mail. Many GTOs are now using tollfree numbers with automated voice response systems to prompt the caller for information about themselves. This digital information is then added into the database. Customer databases can also be created through media campaigns (TV and print) which require the reader or viewer to provide information about themselves in return for destination information. For example, the state of Alaska, in its print media, requires consumers to fill out a vacation-travel profile in order to receive information on the state. This information is then put into their customer database (Jones, 1993).

The benefits of creating a customer database are multi-fold. First, the database can be searched to generate lists of customers with specific desires and travel habits. Some tourism offices give or sell that list to suppliers in the destination for direct marketing. For example, if a hotel with a golf course tends to have low occupancy rates in September, it may be interested in a list of potential travellers who play golf and prefer to vacation in September. Second, the GTO could match the customer's preferences with the products in the DIS and print a customized list of products that interest the customer. This can then be mailed directly to the customer for their trip planning. Similar brochures can be sent to customers in the database who have not yet visited the destination, but only inquired. Once a customer shows interest in a destination, the GTO can follow up with information to entice them to come. Such direct database marketing is more cost effective than media promotions and mass marketing. The customer database can also be used to encourage repeat visitation to a destination. Mailing of forthcoming events or promotions can be sent selectively to visitors with particular interests. For example, the French

GTO invites customers in the database (of previous visitors to France) to join a club. Membership in the club provides them with a newsletter about attractions and events in France, thereby encouraging repeat visitation (Jones, 1993).

Travel intermediaries also need destination information from the GTO and represent a different type of customer for the GTO. They may be speciality travel agents, tour operators, meeting and convention planners, or incentive travel planners wishing to bring clients and groups to the destination. Their information needs are different from free and independent travellers, requiring different information fields in the database. The additional information includes profiles of each travel intermediary including their previous booking and any future bookings they might have. Details of the groups, their size, their accommodation needs and other facilities are needed. Contact names and information for each company are also needed. Some DISs contain details on banquet rooms and meeting room facilities for all properties in the destination so they can advise meeting planners.

8.3.2 Market Databases

Another aspect of GTO marketing is to understand the underlying trends in the countries or regions that generate their tourists. For example, if the major markets of a particular destination are Japan and Germany, the more the suppliers in the destination know about Japanese and German outbound tourism trends, the easier it will be to market their products there. Information on economic trends, outbound travel behaviours and patterns, spending patterns, media information (magazines, TV, radio, etc.) and information on the types of travel intermediaries and outbound distribution channels is needed. This information can be collected by the GTO and included in the DIS (as Finland and Denmark have done). The marketing offices in the major markets are ideal sources to collect this data. The staff working there can locate the information and forward it to the GTO electronically for inclusion in the database. Suppliers in the destination are then able to access this database and gather information that will help them plan their marketing and promotion strategies to various markets.

8.4 MARKET RESEARCH

Research is an important function for most GTOs. This involves the collection and analysis of statistics on the tourist industry. Examples of these statistics are number of arrivals, party size, length of stay,

mode of transport, daily expenditure, economic, social and environmental impacts, satisfaction with the destination experience, and
other traveller demographics. This section examines how IT is being
applied to improve this otherwise labour intensive function.

8.4.1 Data Collection

Data collection for tourism statistics is most commonly done using
surveys. Surveys may be administered at entry points into the destination such as airports and seaports, or for land travel at border control
points. Surveys may be administered either by having the tourist fill
out the survey themselves or, more commonly, by research staff interviewing the tourist and recording the responses. The data may be
recorded on paper or electronically. If the responses are recorded on
paper, they must then be manually key-punched into a computer for
analysis. Alternatively, if the survey form is designed appropriately,
the responses may be scanned directly into a database. This saves
large amounts of labour since data entry clerks are no longer needed
and increases the accuracy of input. It does require, however, that
respondents take care in completing the form. Scannable survey forms
formerly required the respondent to use a specific type of pencil, but
can now be filled out with any writing instrument. Such forms may be
completed by the public themselves or by an interviewer. An example
of such a form is used by Hawaii Visitors and Convention Bureau to
collect data on incoming tourists and is distributed to passengers on
incoming flights to the state of Hawaii.

Another way of electronically capturing survey data is to have the
respondent or the interviewer place the responses directly into the
computer. As soon as the interview is completed, the data can be sent
via modem to a central database ready for analysis. When surveys
involve multiple researchers in the field collecting data this allows
rapid consolidation of results. Research done with computers has been
found to be less costly since it also removes the need for couriers to
collect completed surveys from interview sites and take them to the
central collection point (Jones, 1996). Hand-held computers such as
the Apple Newton or the Microsoft Personal Digital Assistant work
well for this type of interviewing and input is usually done with a pen
rather than a keyboard. Figure 8.3 shows such a hand-held terminal.
Laptop computers may also be used, but are slower since data entry is
via a keyboard. Special software is needed for data collection directly
into the computer. It must display the questions and response options
on the screen and be able to deal with both single and multiple
response questions. Possible answers to multiple choice questions

must be rotated to ensure more accurate responses. Software can also be programmed to automatically skip questions which the respondent need not answer. In addition, the software can do data verification checks to minimize the data entry errors. Open ended questions requiring text input are often part of tourist surveys. With hand-held computers which have no keyboard, a digital keyboard on screen can be touched with a pen to enter text. Such systems have been used for example by Disneyland to administer entry and exit surveys at the gate.

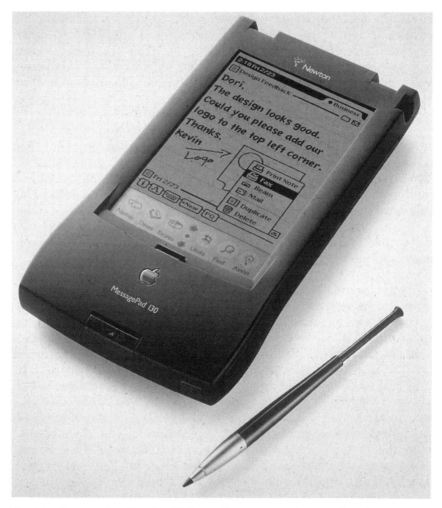

Fig. 8.3. Photograph of hand-held data collection unit. Photograph with permission of Apple Computer.

Tourists can also respond to questions directly into a computer terminal. Standalone kiosks located in airports, visitor information offices or other locations can be used for direct responses. It is important, however, that they be placed in locations where tourists have time to respond. There also needs to be some motivation for tourists to complete the survey. One example of a successful location for survey kiosks is at conferences and conventions where responses can be spread out over a two or three day period, and the sample is a closed population. Kiosks are not suitable for long surveys or for surveys where the sample of respondents must be carefully controlled.

A third way of capturing survey data electronically is by using electronic mail on the Internet or by posting surveys on the World Wide Web. There are appropriate techniques for surveying tourists after they return home or before they leave on their trip. In-trip surveying is not best accomplished this way. The electronic mail address of tourists must be known before the survey can be sent to them for completion. Responses can be e-mailed back and tend to be received more quickly than mailed surveys. Also, with e-mail surveys, it is easy to control the sample. This is not the case with WWW surveys, where the survey is posted on a Web site and any Web user can respond to the survey, making it difficult to control the sample of respondents. Instead of the respondent being sought out by the researchers, the respondent self-selects. Surveys which attempt to assess tourists' satisfaction with a destination and those which try to determine travellers' future plans lend themselves well to these two types of electronic surveys. They also tend to be cheaper than traditional survey methods. Internet surveys have also been used by destinations to gather input from residents to ensure sustainable tourism development (Bond *et al.*, 1996).

One example of a travel research survey on the Web is called the Net Traveller Survey administered by CIC Research and can be found on the www.ten-io site. Any Web user can complete the questionnaire, which asks respondents to report on their travel patterns and preferences (Schonland, 1996). Over 17,000 respondents complete the survey every year. Results include demographics of respondents, their travel frequency and reasons for choosing their destinations and travel products, for both business and pleasure travel. The survey also asks about airport preferences, frequent traveller programmes, and travel expenditures. Questions are also included on the respondent's use of the Internet. With surveys such as this, however, the sample cannot be controlled. A discussion of the Internet for tourism research purposes can be found in Williams *et al.* (1996).

The most important feature of these methods is the direct capture of the data into a computer file for analysis. Key-punching and scanning time is eliminated as the data goes directly into a database requiring no further data entry. Computer aided telephone interviewing also facilitates phone data collection. Computers use random number generators to generate phone numbers for easier telephone sampling and interviewing. In the future, data entry systems which incorporate voice recognition systems will make the data capture process quicker and easier.

8.4.2 Data Analysis

Once the data have been collected and input into a computer, they must be analysed into meaningful statistics and reports. Statistical software programs such as Statistical Package for the Social Sciences (SPSS) or Statistical Analysis System (SAS) are two of the most comprehensive and commonly used packages in GTOs. These packages generate frequencies and histograms of the responses. In addition to tabulation of the data, they also perform hypothesis testing so that researchers can investigate the responses more thoroughly. Multivariate analyses such as perceptual mapping and factor analysis can give deeper interpretation of the data and are possible using SAS or SPSS. Graphical representation of the results is also possible using these software packages. Trend analysis of tourist arrivals and other variables can be performed as well as forecasts for future time periods.

Once the analysis is complete, reports must be printed or made available electronically. Desktop publishing software provides GTOs with the possibility of producing their own reports and cutting printing costs. The reports are then sold, or made available to interested parties on-line. Many destinations now put their survey data on the Web, sometimes with a protected password to ensure some level of payment for the service.

As an example of a higher level application of data analysis software, the Austrian Tourist Office in conjunction with the University of Vienna has created a decision support system called TourMIS. This system incorporates statistical analysis and other decision-making tools with key market data. The system has a user interface that allows various analyses of data to be produced which help with decision-making for the tourism industry (Wober, 1994).

8.5 MANAGEMENT ISSUES

The implementation of IT to a GTO's operation should ideally be viewed by management as a strategic tool to position and promote the destination. Management support and commitment are essential for the most beneficial impact of IT on the GTO. A long-term strategic plan for the purchase, implementation, staffing and maintenance of the IT applications is necessary. An appropriate budget, not just for the initial purchase but for future upgrades and the hiring and training of human resources to operate the systems, is required. Destinations unwilling to make this investment in IT will find themselves left behind by the competition.

A Director of Information Systems to implement, maintain and coordinate the various systems is essential, even if some of the IT applications are outsourced as is quite common. A GTO needs a local area network to provide employees with applications such as word processing, electronic mail, spreadsheets, accounting packages, desktop publishing, and database software, in addition to the applications discussed above. The Director's responsibility will also be to oversee systems not only within the head office but also systems in regional and foreign offices and the data networks needed to link them together.

GTOs may choose to outsource some IT applications. It is common to contract with an outside computer consulting firm to assist in the design and programming of a DIS if the expertise is not available within the GTO. It is also common to use consulting firms for some of the data collection and analysis functions. Even when outsourcing occurs, there are numerous in-house IT applications that need day-to-day overseeing.

Another important strategic focus for management is the interaction with the private sector in the destination. First, in order to act as an information resource representing suppliers in the destination, communication and cooperation must be fostered. Data on the facilities must be collected and in issues such as standardization of information, formats must be addressed. Second, the GTO can take the lead by helping the private sector use IT for marketing their products. They may offer advice, formal education or simply serve as a role model for what can be done. For example, the Canadian Tourism Office has taken the lead in this area and has made research on IT and travel marketing available to its suppliers. It also offers seminars for travel suppliers in Canada to learn about various methods of electronic marketing. The Finnish Tourist Board has also assumed this role (to be discussed in the case at the end of the chapter). A GTO can also share their hardware and software with suppliers. For example, the sharing of a Web server so that suppliers can be represented on the World Wide Web can be helpful. The management of the GTO may also need to become involved in national and international telecommunication regulatory policy as interconnectivity issues are addressed.

8.6 SUMMARY

This chapter examines the role of IT in the three major functions of a GTO: information provision, promotion, and data collection and analysis. It also addresses the implications for management when computerizing their operations. The use of IT can make the destination more competitive and provide much needed distribution channels to reach travellers and travel intermediaries. Well-designed DISs will be important in the future as the traveller looks for and expects more customized vacations. A product database with details on each product and a consumer database with details on consumers' preferences ensure a more ideal product–market match. Tourist offices who successfully implement these systems may place themselves in direct competition with travel agents, particularly if they also take reservations.

Two features are likely to be incorporated into GTO information systems in the future. One is the inclusion of expert systems and artificial intelligence into the DIS, permitting higher level advice-giving to the traveller. The second is the investigation of IT applications to the earlier stages in the travellers' decision-making process. DISs and GDSs are currently designed to assist tourists in decision processes that are relatively mature, i.e. they have already decided on the destination and are looking for places to stay and things to do. There is also a need for the development of systems that assist in the embryonic stages of the decision process (Peroni, 1991). Information presented on the Internet is contributing to this as consumers can investigate many destinations in one easy location.

8.7 CASE – FINNISH TOURIST BOARD

The Finnish Tourist Board (FTB) is the publicly funded marketing organization for tourism in and to Finland. Its mission is to help promote pleasure travel, special interest travel, and meetings, conventions and incentive travel to Finland. FTB employs about 60 people, of which 25 are in the head office in Helsinki, the remainder in the marketing offices in 12 countries (Sweden, Norway, Estonia, Netherlands, UK, Spain, Italy, Switzerland, USA, Canada, Japan and France).

In 1992, FTB realized that it was not operating at peak efficiency and needed to investigate the application of IT to its operations. Without IT they found it was no longer possible to process, distribute and organize information with accuracy, speed and reliability. Elimination of duplication of tasks, and improved quality of operation were other goals. They also wanted to communicate better within the company and externally with clients in Finland and abroad. Another reason to invest in IT was for FTB to be a model for other travel companies in the country to apply IT to their marketing activities.

To accomplish these ends, they set up an information system workgroup called MAVI whose responsibility was to draft guidelines for information systems used by FTB and the Finnish travel business. A survey was conducted within the organization to determine its needs. The functions they decided to automate are discussed in the next section. For the software application, it was decided that a multinationally known IT product was needed so that their twelve foreign offices could be supported. The software selected was Lotus Notes, which is a multifaceted program to facilitate electronic communications in workgroups. One person per unit was trained as a support person to oversee the application and in addition, one person was trained as the expert for each subsystem. All applications were coordinated in Helsinki for all twelve marketing units. FTB has a network of 60 PCs using Notes Mail and Windows for Workgroups on an OS/2.1 server platform. The protocols being used are TCP/IP and the Token Ring network protocol. Currently data communication to the twelve foreign units is through dial-up lines but there are plans to move to packet-switching networks soon.

Using this hardware and software environment, FTB has developed two additional applications to assist with their handling of product and market information. In 1995 they implemented Marketing Information System (MIS) – a market database which holds information on their major markets. They also implemented a Destination Information System called Professional Marketing Information System (PROMIS). Each of these systems will be discussed in detail below.

8.7.1 Marketing Information System (MIS)

MIS assists in the national and international marketing of the FTB. It ensures that all travel organizations including multinational travel organizations are provided with all the information needed. MIS includes statistical information on tourism to Finland, and information to assist suppliers in the production of basic marketing tools. Specifically it includes the following applications:

- Tourism statistics for Finland – arrivals, expenditures, travel patterns, etc.
- Company profiles of tour operators and travel agents in 40 countries
- Profiles of various media in each of the major markets
- FTB's marketing strategy and plans for each country
- Information to assist in events and conference management
- Annual reports of the FTB
- A library of books, articles and journals on Finland and tourism that can be accessed on-line from the 12 market countries
- MEKKALA – an electronic bulletin board and suggestion box to be used by all employees of FTB.

The architecture for MIS is represented in Fig. 8.4. It shows how travel agents and other resellers and producers have access into MIS. It also shows the plan to have travellers and small producers gaining access through networks such as videotext networks (Telesampo and Infotel) and the Internet.

8.7.2 Professional Marketing Information System (PROMIS)

PROMIS is FTB's Destination Information System which went on-line in September 1995. It contains tourism product data for

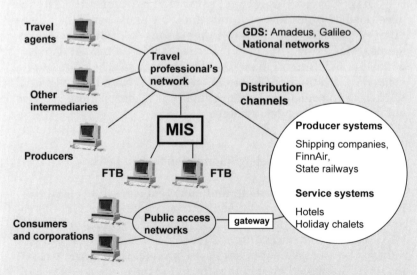

Fig. 8.4. Finnish Tourist Board's IT installation. FTB – Finnish Tourist Board.

the whole of Finland and general information on the country. Information for PROMIS comes from the suppliers and the regional tourism organizations and updating of the data is the responsibility of each supplier. The data is not only used to service client requests but also to produce brochures to be sent out in response to requests. More specifically, PROMIS contains information on the following:

- Country information – 'Finland in a Nutshell'
  travel facts
  points of interest
- Suppliers' profiles and contact persons
- Package tours and excursions – details of tour components, dates, etc.
- Accommodations: hotels, hostels, farmhouses, camping sites, B&Bs, VIP cottages
- Transportation: charter flights, domestic flights, lake and coastal traffic, motor coach services, rail and water transportation
- Conference and meeting facilities
- Events and attractions
- Equipment hire

This is an example of a comprehensive, nationally centralized DIS that can be used to answer questions on any tourism product in Finland.

8.7.3 Benefits

The above IT applications have improved FTB's image and have provided them with more time to interact with their customers. They also feel more connected as a company – employees know each other better because of improved communications. Automation has also standardized many of their procedures. They feel that the centralized approach to their IT application saved both money and time for the twelve foreign units. In general they feel that they are more effective, provide more quality and need less paper, fewer phone calls and faxes.

In the future, FTB plans to have PROMIS interfaced with the Amadeus GDS and the Internet. They are also planning some multimedia products and a third application called RELIS (Research and Library Information Service). This will be a common database for statistics and survey results on tourism to Finland.

The International Web   9
of Travel Networks

9.1 INTRODUCTION

So far this book has examined the use of computer technology within different sectors of the travel industry. While efficient operation and enhanced service provided by such technologies are important, the interconnectivity of the vast diversity of travel computers throughout the world is equally critical. This connectivity is important to enable information, reservations and documentation to flow between travellers, suppliers and destinations. Both data and voice networks are required, and both weave a complex web upon which today's travel industry rests. They are necessary to allow firms to communicate internally, to connect with clients, with travel intermediaries and with other firms worldwide. The data communications networks used to accomplish these tasks represent some of the largest data communication networks in the world. New communication technologies are constantly being implemented, providing networks able to carry higher volumes of information more rapidly and less expensively than ever before.

This chapter discusses and explains the electronic threads tying the travel industry together, and is structured as follows. It first discusses the data communication networks linking travel firms in different sectors together. It then discusses specialized computer switches which have been put in place to link computers and networks together, and specialized hardware required by travel firms to connect to these networks. The chapter will then examine data and voice communication needs and options within a travel company focusing on local area networks (LANs), wide area networks (WANs) and Computer–Telephone Integration (CTI). The final section examines the concept of electronic document interchange (EDI) and its acceptance and relevance in today's tourism industry.

9.2 INTER-COMPANY DATA COMMUNICATION LINKS

The most challenging data communication needs in the travel industry today involve networks which connect together the computer systems of travel firms in different sectors. Data must be able to flow, for example, between the computer systems of the airlines and the hotel chains, between travel agents and airlines, and between airline GDSs and car rental companies. The need of travel agents to make bookings in different industry sectors (e.g. car, hotel and cruise-line) from one terminal creates a major challenge. Part of this challenge is that travel industry computer systems tend to use different operating systems, different programs, different formats and different communication standards and protocols, and are often located in different parts of the world. All of these factors create significant challenges in the design of these networks. These issues will be addressed later in the section but first, the two major data networks which connect the travel industry together will be discussed.

9.2.1 Travel Specific Networks

The telecommunication needs of the travel industry were recognized early on by the airlines, and communication networks were formed to help transmit airline industry messages around the world. In fact, the airlines were one of the first industries in the world to form a closed user group for telecommunication services. Aeronautical Radio Incorporated (ARINC) was the first network to be developed in 1929 predominantly for US communications, followed by Société Internationale Télécommunications Aéronautique (SITA) in 1949 which had more international coverage. Both networks have grown substantially and provide a vast array of data communication services and value-added services to travel firms and others. They both claim to be among the largest private data networks in the world today.

ARINC

ARINC was started in 1929 by numerous airlines to provide communications and information processing services for the aviation and travel industries. Its initial focus was on the US but the company now operates numerous networks with international coverage. These networks can be used to pass both inter-company messages between computers in different or the same sectors of the travel industry and can be used by travel firms to transmit their in-company messages between different locations. The networks use both airline-proprietary communication protocols and standard open protocols.

ARINC's most important service for the travel industry is its ARINC Data Network Services (ADNS) which allows travel industry participants to communicate directly with more than 700 other corporate organizational users in the travel industry. The exchange of critical travel information such as passenger name records, seat availability status, hotel and car availability, airway bills, aircraft movement and material management transactions are examples of the kind of data that travel the ADNS network. It is used by the Federal Aviation Administration (FAA) to file flight plans, by airline service companies, by freight forwarders, port brokers and by the airlines settlement bank. In addition, hotels, car rental companies, and other travel suppliers and vendors use the networks, predominantly to handle their reservations processing. General information systems such as the National Weather Service, UK Meteorological Office, US Customs, and credit card companies are also connected to ADNS as are other national networks such as SENEAM, COCESNA and AEROTEL. The other major travel data network, SITA, is also connected to ADNS. Figure 9.1 shows the interconnectivity provided by the ADNS network.

Users can access the ADNS network in a number of different ways, and from local or regional access points. They can access the network through dedicated lines or through modem connections. There are numerous access points and nodes on the network as shown in Fig. 9.2. The network control system is in Annapolis, Maryland, US, with switching and processing centres in numerous locations as shown on the diagram. While it covers mostly the US it also reaches as far as

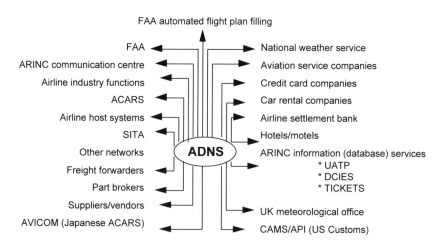

Fig. 9.1. ARINC data network service connections. Source: ARINC literature, 1997.

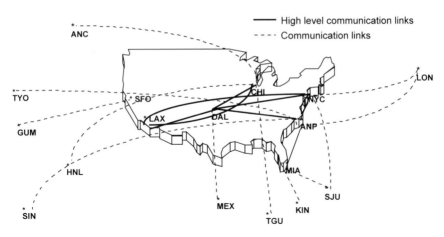

Fig. 9.2. ARINC network. Network control system in ANP, Anapolis. Packet-switch nodes in ANP; CHI, Chicago, USA; DAL, Dallas, USA; LAX, Los Angeles, USA; MIA, Miami, USA; NYC, New York City, USA. Multiplexor access in ANC, Anchorage, USA; GUM, Guam; HNL, Honolulu, USA; KIN, Kingston, Jamaica; MEX, Mexico City, Mexico; SFO, San Francisco, USA; SIN, Singapore; SJU, San Juan, Puerto Rico; TGU, Tegucigalpa, Honduras; TYO, Tokyo, Japan. Message Processor in LAX, DAL, CHI, ANP, LON, London; MIA, NYC.

Tokyo and London. The access speed can be high for high volume users or slower for low volume users. As shown in the diagram, the non-US connections do not yet use high speed data lines. Even so, the average ADNS message has a transit time of 400 ms, and users are charged for using the network on a volume basis.

ADNS supports a number of different communication protocols, the two most important ones supported by the Air Transport Association and the International Air Transport Association (IATA). These two protocols are called Airline Line Control (ALC) and Synchronous Link Control (SLC) and are designed mostly for mainframe communications. In addition, ADNS supports the packet-switched protocol called X.25, the communication protocol for most public data networks. ADNS is also connected to two other networks provided by ARINC – one is called the ARINC Packet-Switched Network (APN) and the other is the Systems Networking Architecture (SNA) network. Each will be discussed below.

APN is a packet-switched network based on the industry standard X.25. Packet-switched networks consist of nodes or computers on the network which transmit small packets of information between each other until the data packet reaches its destination. The packet is enclosed in an 'envelope' with a header and a footer which each computer on the network reads to determine its next destination or node.

Each user appears to have a circuit between their computer and the destination computer, but in reality the data may travel many different routes to reach its destination. Security on the network is tight and users require proper identification codes and passwords before access to APN is granted. This network can be accessed by almost all data communications equipment including PCs, servers, minicomputers, mainframes and LANs. Packet-switched networks are well known for their error-free transmission which is due to a special error detection method called a cyclic redundancy check. Packet-switched networks are also capable of addressing data to multiple destinations simultaneously. Data transmission speeds on the APN network are up to 56 kbps.

A third data network provided by ARINC conforms to the IBM systems networking architecture (SNA) standards using the communication protocol synchronous data link control (SDLC). It also converts messages to the X.25 protocol if necessary. This network is designed more for communications between mainframe computers, minicomputers and front end communication controllers and performs polling of the network terminals when necessary. Polling of network terminals is necessary to control message traffic on many travel computer reservation systems. This network is used to connect together the mainframes that run the airline computer reservation systems, and hotel, car and cruise reservation systems amongst others.

In addition to its main networks, ARINC also provides value-added services on its networks. One of these services is the TICKETS database which is a centralized, real-time database for worldwide identification of lost or stolen airline revenue documents; it is used by 130 airlines around the world. Another is the service called the Universal Air Travel Plan (UATP) which is a database of valid and invalid credit cards. The Dishonoured Cheque Information Exchange Service (DCIES) is yet another database accessible through the ARINC network. ARINC also provides extensive voice and data air-to-ground radio communications and air traffic control communications for more than 4250 aircraft across North America with a service called the Aircraft Communication and Reporting System (ACARS). In addition, ARINC provides telecommunication services for travel firms wishing to create their own LANs and WANs , and is involved with the establishment of technical standards for the global air transport industry.

SITA

The second travel industry network to be created was the SITA network. SITA is the largest global data and voice communication network covering the travel industry in 225 countries. It was started in 1949 by ten airlines belonging to the International Air Transport

Association (IATA) with the purpose of providing communications services to its members. Today the company has a membership of close to 1000 firms in 220 countries worldwide, and provides numerous data communication services to firms in the travel industry. Its networks handle over 42.8 billion messages a year.

SITA supports a number of different networks as does ARINC. Their collection of networks is called Managed Data Network Services (MDNS) and offers a variety of services to large and small travel firms. Communication protocols supported are the packet-switched X.25 and X.28 protocols for those wishing to connect LANs or PCs to the network, and SNA, SDLC and ALC protocols for mainframe and GDS connectivity. Since both airline communication protocols and open protocols are supported, airlines have the option of migrating to the open standards environment if they use SITA. The SITA global network which connects mainframes together (mostly IBM) is shown in Fig. 9.3. This network can be connected via numerous different protocols and from numerous different hardware platforms, even token ring LANs.

SITA operates another network called AeroNet designed to serve the aerospace industry. Airlines can use it to access information from airframe and engine manufacturers in real time via TCP/IP connections, reducing the time and expense of paper communications. CAD/CAM graphical files which are very large and often used by manufacturers, can be exchanged on the network. AeroNet also can be connected to Ethernet and Token Ring LANs at speeds of 9.6 kbps to 2 Mbps. It reduces the cost of international leased lines for airlines since a single connection to AeroNet is all that is needed.

Their most advanced network supports high speed Frame Relay

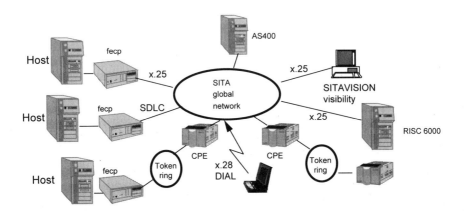

Fig 9.3. SITA MDNS IBM network. Source: SITA literature, October 1996.

communication to connect LANs in different locations and connections with IBM front end communication processors. Their Frame Relay service is available in over 65 countries and is used for client/server communication, terminal to host communication, e-mail, database access and CAD/CAM applications. It is particularly appropriate for firms needing high throughput and low delays in communications between globally dispersed sites. The network transmits data at speeds in excess of 64 kbps.

Users can access SITA's various networks in a number of ways depending on their needs. They can connect via leased lines, public switched telephone networks, public data networks and telex networks. ISDN communications (to be discussed below) are also provided at slower speeds. Once connected, each user is able to monitor the status of their connections to the SITA network using SITAVISION, a graphic display of data communication lines and statistics on the performance of services. SITA has three network control and support centres in Singapore, Paris (France) and Atlanta (US) which oversee the networks.

SITA offers additional value-added services to the airlines which can be accessed via their networks. GABRIEL, a multi-host passenger reservation system can be used by airlines without their own CRS, and currently is being used by over one hundred airlines worldwide. GETS (GABRIEL Extended Travel Systems) is a distribution system which brings travel agents on-line to the GABRIEL CRS. SITA also offers other value-added services to GABRIEL users and others including:

- Automatic Ticketing: a service which provides computer generated passenger tickets and sales reports for management use
- Departure Control: a service which provides improved passenger handling and optimized aircraft payload utilization prior to departure
- TIMATIC: a database of international travel information such as border controls
- SAHARA: a service for hotel reservations
- SITACARS: a service for car rental reservations
- SITAMAIL: a messaging service
- Credit Card Authorization: a service to authorize passenger credit card use

Other systems are available via SITA networks to help airlines with fare quotations, the planning and management of flight schedules, and baggage management. The baggage management service includes the handling of reservations and shipment delivery, in addition to management reporting and revenue accounting. SITA also provides mobile air-to-ground communications for aircraft to communicate with ground personnel, as does ARINC. CUTE (Common Usage Terminal Equipment) terminals in check-in areas of airports to help airlines without their own dedicated terminals to process check-in and departure control information are designed and provided by SITA.

Other firms offer network services to travel industry firms to transmit their messages but ARINC and SITA are the major ones. Still others provide services which perform the necessary translations and emulations so that different computer systems can communicate with each other. The next section of the chapter discusses these services, of which there are many in the travel industry.

9.2.2 Computer Switches

The networks discussed above each require data travelling the network to conform to certain standards and to be understood by the computers which the network connects. If different data formats and standards are in place, computer switches may be required to translate the data before it is received at the other end. There are numerous switches in place which specifically cater to the needs of the travel industry. These switches have been created mostly to allow travel firms to communicate with the GDS in their unique protocols. One example of such a switch is Ultraswitch, another is Wizcom, both of which are discussed below.

The smooth flow of hotel reservations to and from the GDSs has required the implementation of a computer switch called Ultraswitch. This switch allows travel agents to make hotel bookings on-line through their GDS terminals and receive rapid confirmations. As a result of this switch, more travel agents book hotels electronically: in the US more than 50% of hotels are now booked using Ultraswitch. This is predominantly because travel agents are more confident that their electronic bookings are reaching their destination safely since they receive confirmations or cancellation numbers in a few seconds.

In 1989, a consortium of 19 major hotel chains created a company called THISCO (The Hotel Industry Switching Company) to work on this project. THISCO's goal was to provide accurate and rapid information on room availability, rates and confirmation numbers to travel agents through their GDS terminals, and to encourage the electronic booking of hotel rooms worldwide by travel agents. The computer switch they created, called Ultraswitch, performs the necessary translations of messages between all of the GDS and the hotel chain reservation systems involved. Ultraswitch currently claims to be the largest switching company in the world and processes over 40 million messages a month. It runs on a UNIX based computer system, using relational database management software, and supports traditional communication protocols such as SNA, X.25, and SLC. Dedicated data circuits running at speeds of 56–64 kbps link Ultraswitch to each of the four major GDSs and to each of 70 hotel chain CRSs which are part of THISCO.

The Ultraswitch computer allows the GDS and hotel systems to work in their own formats for bookings, room types, property IDs and other information, and contains interfaces for each system connected to it. As Ultraswitch receives transactions from one computer, it translates the message into the format of the receiving system as shown in Fig. 9.4. Ultraswitch accepts messages on bookings, modification and cancellation of guest records, availability data and the ability to display and modify data transactions. It does not connect directly to each hotel property management system but to the inventory in the hotel chain CRS. It is the responsibility of each hotel manager to keep its inventory availability updated in the chain's CRS.

In order to use Ultraswitch, a hotel company must have a computer reservation system which can handle two types of messages. The first type, called Type A or real-time messages allows reservations to be processed and confirmations returned on-line within seven seconds. In this case, product information, inventory status and rate data are maintained within the GDS. The other type, called Type B or teletype messages, allows the travel agent to place a reservation request in

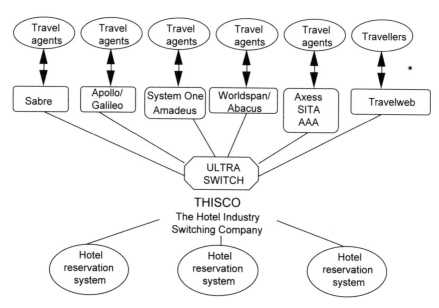

Fig. 9.4. Ultraswitch.

the GDS which is then transmitted to the hotel company's CRS via Ultraswitch. Independent CRSs for non-chain hotels are also connected to Ultraswitch, allowing smaller hotels to benefit from the electronic connectivity provided by the switch. UTELL is the largest of these independent reservation systems. It represents and houses information on thousands of hotels around the world, and is used by travel agents to electronically book hotels which are not part of a large chain. The hotel CRS computer or UTELL must then transmit responses back to the GDS, again via Ultraswitch. Charges to use Ultraswitch are on a transaction basis, requiring all transactions passing through the switch to be logged. Billings of services can then be handled and operating statistics can be maintained.

A recent development to Ultraswitch which further enhances travel agents' electronic booking of hotels is called UltraSelect. This is a database of 19,000 hotel properties which is stored in the Ultraswitch computer. The database contains all the static information (descriptions of hotels, locations, services offered, etc.) on each hotel which agents can search to find the appropriate hotel for a consumer. When a hotel is identified, the agent is then able to connect directly to the hotel chain's own reservation system where it can find status information on rates and availability.

THISCO provides two other technology products for the hotel industry. One is TravelWeb (http//www.travelweb.com), a connection between the Internet and Ultraswitch. By using TravelWeb on the Internet consumers can access information on hotel properties and book them through their PC. More than 8000 hotels are represented worldwide on TravelWeb including 57 different brands. Airlines and car rental bookings are expected to be added to the site soon.

The other product of THISCO is the Hotel Clearing Centre (HCC). This system assists hotels with the collection, processing and reconciliation of commissions due to over 48,000 travel agencies from 38 major hotel organizations. HCC electronically captures check-in information from its participating hotels for all travel agencies. The information is tracked based on the agent's IATA number and stored in the HCC processor. All travel agency commissions are then consolidated and a single commission cheque is sent to the travel agency in the local currency. HCC charges travel agents for this service and many are willing to pay since it ensures that they will receive their commissions on time. THISCO is also an active supporter of the Hotel Electronic Distribution Association (HEDNA) which is an international, not-for-profit organization formed in 1991 by hoteliers to promote and accelerate the use of GDSs and other electronic means for the booking of hotel reservations.

Another company offering interconnect services to the GDS and other travel firms' CRSs is Wizcom, a subsidiary of Avis Rent-a-Car. Wizcom leverages the network that it already supports for its car rental operations worldwide to provide similar services to other travel firms. The switching service provided by Wizcom is called Wizdom and connects each of the GDSs to car and other travel reservation systems not processed through Ultraswitch. Wizcom maintains numerous major international data communication lines to process all of the reservation traffic including two undersea transatlantic fibre optic cables, one transpacific undersea fibre optic cable and one satellite line. This network connects travel firms across the world and handles 1.2 million transactions a day. The Wizcom software allows hotels to update rates and availability in the Wizcom computer which then updates the information in all GDSs, saving each hotel the time of doing it themselves. Fees are charged on a transaction basis. As with ARINC and SITA, Wizcom also offers data communication services such as point-to-point private lines and switched data service for travel companies. They also offer a central reservation system with voice and GDS reservation handling.

9.2.3 Terminal Emulation Systems, Protocol Converters and Gateways

Many travel firms need to communicate data to the GDSs across data lines without computer switches. Examples are hotel chains and car rentals wanting to update their product information on the GDS. They also may use similar lines to connect their own PCs and LANs to their own mainframe CRS hosts. Since the airline systems use the ALC protocol which was developed to connect dumb terminals to their mainframes, when PCs or LANs connect to the GDS, conversion is necessary to transfer the data successfully. In order to do this, terminal emulation software, protocol converters and/or gateways may be needed.

Terminal emulation boards provide the ability for any terminal to be an input and output device for a host system even though the dumb terminal is not designed specifically for that purpose. They ensure that the data shown on the screen is displayed as it would be on a GDS terminal. Terminal emulation systems are used extensively by travel firms wishing to input information into a GDS. They may also be required by companies wishing to connect PCs in various locations to their own mainframe CRS. Terminal emulation systems usually take the form of an expansion board slotted into the PC.

Protocol converters are essential components in networks that link mainframes together. Networks could be between an airline host computer and a hotel, tour operator or car rental host computer, for example.

Protocol converters change the messages from one computer so that they match the protocol of another computer. Since the airlines are most often the ones receiving or sending messages their protocols, ALC, SLC and X.25, dominate. Protocol converters may also serve the functions of character translation, data switching and communications concentration for multiple lines. Protocol converters are usually a separate piece of hardware connected to the PC or LAN. They could also be a card slotted into a PC or are already integrated into a gateway or computer switch.

A gateway is needed whenever networks using different protocols need to be connected. Gateways are required when LANs need to connect to a wide area network, or when two LANs or two WANs need to connect. They provide the necessary translations and conversions to make data traffic flow smoothly. An example of the need for a gateway is when a travel agency LAN needs to connect to an ALC or X.25 protocol network. Apollo is now introducing the TCP/IP protocol into its operations so that users do not need a gateway. To connect two or more like networks together (e.g. two Ethernet networks) a bridge is used. This is a piece of equipment that does not need to perform any translation or conversions.

9.3 IN-COMPANY COMPUTER NETWORKS

Travel firms, like any other firms, have needs to transmit data, messages and files to personnel and departments within the same building or to other branches of the same firm in different locations. Many hotel chains, car rental firms and transportation companies are national or international with many branches and locations. Their data communication needs include local area and wide area data networks. Travel firms also must handle large amounts of voice traffic, and computer–telephone integration systems (CTI) are being applied to this function. This section will discuss all of these options.

9.3.1 Local and Wide Area Networks

Local area networks (LANs) connect computers within a building allowing the exchange of files, e-mail, and other electronic documents, and the sharing of peripherals such as printers and fax machines. LANs from one building can be connected to LANs in other locations via data circuits leased directly from the telecommunication carriers or by using the services of SITA or ARINC as discussed above. A LAN consists of a server and cabling (twisted pair, coaxial cable or fibre optics) to connect the various terminals and components of the network together. Fibre optic cabling, while being the most expensive gives the highest bandwidths and speeds and the highest level of data security.

A LAN may take one of three forms – a star, bus or ring configuration. A star network consists of a central PC which gives employees access to central files and system resources. A bus network allows the sharing of network resources but has no central computer. Ethernet LANs are a common example of this configuration. A ring network connects the individual computers serially to one another, and IBM's Token Ring network is an example of this. Special network operating systems are needed to manage and control the network. Network versions of software such as word processing, spreadsheet software, databases and others provide all users with access to these applications. LANs of all types are found in all travel firms.

Wide area networks (WANs) are necessary for large corporations with multiple branches to allow employees to send voice and data transmissions between locations, and to share peripherals. Travel firms particularly have needs for WANs since their branches and operations are geographically dispersed. Car rental firms and chain hotels are examples of travel firms that exist in many locations who need to connect these locations together electronically. Private WANs require firms to lease communication lines for their data transmission. These are usually 'packet-switched' networks utilizing satellite, fibre optic or microwave transmission which can be leased from ARINC, SITA or other companies who specialize in providing data network services.

The increased need for digital and analogue communications has suggested the creation of a single network to handle all types of data and voice communications locally and internationally. Such a standardized network is in the process of being implemented and is called Integrated Services Digital Network (ISDN). ISDN brings to the user's business or home a communication channel to handle both voice and data communication simultaneously at speeds of at least 64 kbps. One of the most important features of ISDN is that it is evolving from the telephone networks already in place throughout the world. ISDN lines can be connected to any piece of hardware equipment which is able to generate a digital bit stream conforming to ISDN standards. The development of international standards is an important part of implementing ISDN. It is planned that ISDN will use a set of layered protocols that conform to a model for open communications created by the International Standards Organization in Geneva, Switzerland called the Open System Interconnection model. The model which is discussed in detail in many texts (Knight, 1987; Martin, 1988; Stallings; 1989) defines seven different layers of compatibility including compatibility of data presentation, of the transport of data and of the physical compatibility between machines.

ISDN holds great promise for the travel industry as an international standard allowing digital transfers between computers in different countries and different firms. In particular, it will bring multimedia travel information into the home and office of the consumer and travel intermediary, thereby making the travel decision process easier. A multinational pilot project in Europe called Eurotop (discussed in Chapter 3) used ISDN to transmit tour operator brochures from the tour operator's database in numerous countries to the travel agents' PC in other countries.

As ISDN continues to develop incrementally on the telephone systems in more and more countries, the travel industry will benefit in many ways. Travel firms will be able to connect with customers, suppliers, intermediaries, and other locations in their own operations to send data and voice communications more easily and inexpensively. But it may be a considerable time before the majority of countries are connected to ISDN standard networks.

9.3.2 Computer–Telephone Integration

In addition to handling data traffic, travel firms must deal with large volumes of voice communications. Most firms have digital PBXs which are the basis for other voice communication automation. Call centre management systems help to automate voice communications by removing the need for a telephone operator to answer most calls. Call centre management systems announce to the caller a list of departments or functional options they can choose from with their telephone keypad. For example, when a customer calls the tollfree number for an airline, they may hear a listing of options such as 'domestic reservations', 'international reservations', 'flight arrivals and departures'. After they choose an option from their telephone pad, they are connected to a person to answer their questions.

Staffing incoming phone calls from consumers and travel intermediaries can be very expensive, particularly when the agent has to search through a computer database for the answers. Computer systems which provide the consumer with information without human intervention are called computer–telephone integration (CTI) systems, and can make this process more efficient. CTI systems bypass the need for personnel to answer or reply to calls. The consumer's questions are answered directly by the computer.

CTI systems are being employed by many travel companies with the intent of giving consumers faster access to information and reducing labour costs. They operate by having the caller respond to options either with a digital keypad on the phone or by answering questions verbally. The latter require voice recognition systems. In either case the computer takes the response, and uses it to access information in the computer database. Airlines use CTI systems to inform customers of arrival and departure times of flights. The customer enters information on the flight such as origin city, destination city, or flight number and the data is retrieved from the database directly and read to the consumer in pre-recorded or digitized voice. Another application of CTI by the airlines is a service which allows frequent fliers to check the status of their accounts on-line. These systems may involve the caller wending through a maze of options and digitized voice messages, but eventually the required information is usually received. It is expected that CTI will be used more in the future to give customers easy access to product information. Consumer acceptance needs to be studied carefully before travel firms employ this option. Despite the cost savings, negative consumer response could cause firms to lose business as a result of CTI.

9.4 ELECTRONIC DOCUMENT INTERCHANGE (EDI)

As network protocols and computer systems in the travel industry become more standardized, the electronic exchange of more travel documents is likely. Electronic Document Interchange (EDI) is a term used to describe this and is defined as 'the electronic transmission of structured business documents in a predefined, machine-readable format between trading partners' internal computer systems' (Ritz, 1995). EDI is being adopted by selected industries and is facilitating the handling of documents, both within a firm and between firms in a given industry. It has many benefits to do with efficiency and also reduces paper and mailing costs. The tourism industry is using it in selected areas for selected documents but as yet has not embraced it fully. Airline tickets are one form of document that has become standardized and can be stored, displayed and transmitted electronically between two or more different computer systems.

The travel industry generates many other types of documents, and produces volumes of paper in the form of:

- tickets
- coupons
- guest folios
- manifest lists
- confirmations

- itineraries
- schedules
- tariffs

Additional documents found in all types of firms including travel firms include:

- contracts and agreements
- reports
- manuals and handbooks
- business forms
- correspondence and memos
- drawings, blueprints, photographs
- scripts from presentations
- computer printouts
- video clips
- transcripts from meetings

All of these documents contain information that can be used more effectively if they are in electronic format (Sprague, 1995). EDI requires all handling of the documents in an industry to be electronic. It includes the capture and creation of these documents in electronic form, and the transmission of the documents electronically. It also includes the organization, retrieval, synthesis, and of course the printing and display of all these documents. These processes must be done both within a firm and between all firms in an industry for EDI to succeed.

Standards and common protocols are necessary at all of these levels for successful EDI. Since trading partners often operate incompatible internal hardware and software systems using different formats, numerous agreements must be made so that electronic documents can be transferred successfully. In addition to the technical compatibility, however, there are other more challenging obstacles that must be overcome before EDI can become successful in an industry. According to Kubicek and Seeger (1992) there need to be at least four levels of compatibility.

First, there needs to be technical compatibility so that the terminals and computers can actually be connected, requiring standardization of terminals and switching equipment on the communication network. Second, communication protocols must be agreed upon. Third, document formats must be standardized either bilaterally or across the entire travel industry worldwide. This involves the standardization of type, length and sequence of data segments. Given the large number of documents and data types in the travel industry this is a particular challenge, although this has already been accomplished for air tickets.

Fourth, data keys need to be agreed upon that specify the semantics or meaning of characters in data segments.

Some efforts are already being made to create EDI as a successful venture in the travel industry. A symposium was recently hosted by ARINC and United Airlines on the topic of EDI, with the intent of pushing the idea of travel document standardization further. This conference discussed in particular the digitization of technical manuals. Another attempt is by the United Nations which has developed a standard for intra-European trade called EDIFACT which stands for Electronic Data Interchange for Administration, Commerce and Transport. This standard has subsequently been adopted for transborder EDI in international trade and transport. The first EDIFACT document was standardized in 1987 and subsequently over one hundred other documents have been or are in the process of being approved. EDIFACT is the closest thing the travel industry has to an international standard.

SITA has also played an important role in providing EDI capabilities for the air transport and related industries. For example, SITA offers a special PC-based EDI application called SkyForm for airlines and their suppliers. It supports the widely used Cargo-IMP and Air-IMP standards as well as the EDIFACT standard. They are able to provide automatic conversion and exchange between various types of EDI syntax. The air cargo industry also has some successful EDI networks (Ritz, 1995). Cargo Community Systems Switzerland is an EDI network providing connectivity among air cargo forwarders and airlines in the Swiss market. Traxon Europe, set up by Air France and Lufthansa, has created a message switch for freight forwarders, airlines and shippers. The third one is Aviation Exchange which provides services to freight forwarders in US, Canada and Mexico.

For EDI to exist fully in the travel industry much work must be done. It will not happen spontaneously and instigation must come from either government intervention, firms in the industry, trade associations or third party service providers. In tourism there are many possible locations from which the initiative could come, and steps are already being made as mentioned above. Additional support could come from the inter-governmental level in tourism, from agencies such as the World Tourism and Travel Council, the World Tourism Organization and Pacific Asia Travel Association. Each of these agencies is involved in the development of the industry and each has a keen focus on information technology. Most GTOs, however, do not seem to focus in this area, and so they are unlikely to be major players. There are many travel trade associations which could contribute to a move toward EDI by encouraging their members to become involved. HEDNA (a part of THISCO) is committed to increasing electronic connectivity for hotels and so is a natural potential contributor. The Travel Industry Association, the Air Transport Association, travel intermediary associations such as American Society of Travel Agents and their counterparts around the world and the US Tour Operators Association are other associations that could contribute significantly to EDI development and implementation. As independent firms in the industry, the airlines and the GDS firms must become involved since they would be major beneficiaries of EDI in the processing of travel documents. It is also important that contribution and involvement come from different countries around the world. There are many technical, economic and political issues that must be settled by these groups before EDI can become successfully operative in the travel industry.

9.5 SUMMARY

This chapter has presented the various data networks that keep the travel industry connected. The services provided by ARINC and SITA are particularly important to the industry's connectivity, and to leading the way with future telecommunications developments. The technology, standards and protocols used in all networks are rapidly changing. In the travel industry they are becoming more open, making connectivity less burdensome and less expensive. In the past the GDSs have dominated the networks, requiring other firms to match their standards and protocols. This is rapidly changing as the Internet takes over as the predominant network, and open protocols (TCP/IP) and standards are becoming the norm. Travel industry networks, as they grow in coverage, must incorporate more countries of the world, and more smaller suppliers who are not yet connected to them. This will ensure truly worldwide connectivity in the travel industry. These topics will be addressed in the next chapter.

Emerging Trends in 10
Tourism Information
Systems

10.1 INTRODUCTION

Underlying the many systems and applications discussed in this book are certain emerging trends. These trends are changing and guiding the tourism industry as it enters the new millennium, for tourism and information technology are inextricably linked. This chapter examines some of the most important technological trends currently moulding the industry and the touristic experience. There are many more trends and new ones that will emerge in the future. Some will be directly due to new technologies entering the industry, others will be responses to technology already in place. The first three trends discussed in this chapter are occurring as a result of newly implemented technologies. The other two have arisen out of the industry's response to the technologies in place.

The first trend is the increased level of intelligence being incorporated into tourism computer systems now and in the future. As artificial intelligence and robotic technologies are implemented into tourism, fundamental changes in the nature of tourism employment will occur. The second trend is the increased availability of multimedia technology in tourism extending to the use of virtual reality technologies. These are technologies impacting upon tourist choices and touristic experiences directly. The third trend is the increase in connectivity between travel industry computer systems in general, but in particular those of small and medium sized firms and those in different parts of the world. This trend is bringing about more comprehensive tourism networks. The last two trends relate less to the technology and more to the way that the technology is impacting upon the industry. Some tourists now have very high levels of expectation for technological amenities and services offered by travel firms, bringing about a need to segment the travel market based on technical preferences of travellers. Lastly, many significant changes are evident in the structure of the travel industry as IT is incorporated more deeply and broadly.

Each of these trends will be discussed separately below. Even though they are discussed in the context of tourism, these trends could be indicative for other service industries exploring the interplay of information technology and the production of services. Since the tourism industry is one of the largest service industries in the world, the lessons learned and the directions taken with IT may be important lessons for other service industries.

10.2 INCREASED SYSTEM INTELLIGENCE

Recent IT applications are incorporating levels of sophistication and intelligence previously unknown. They are being applied in many diverse situations requiring higher level functioning such as operational analysis and decision support. This emerging trend has spawned an array of software tools referred to as artificial intelligence (AI) and represents the cutting edge of information technology today. AI includes many different branches of computer technology designed to emulate the human thinking, reasoning and decision-making processes. The three branches discussed in this chapter are expert systems, neural networks and robotics. As the tourism industry matures in its use of IT, it is beginning to incorporate AI into its operational and management computer systems.

10.2.1 Expert Systems and Neural Networks

Expert systems contain the knowledge base and decision-making powers of a particular human expert. They can help managers explore new solutions to problems and consider factors that may have been overlooked in the past. Statisticians, doctors and accountants are examples of human experts that can to some degree be replaced by computer expert systems. Expert systems are well established in the airline industry and are now entering the hospitality and travel intermediary sectors also. They consist of a knowledge base, which is a repository of facts and relations about the particular problem or domain, and a set of rules, often called 'heuristics', which constitute the inference engine. The inference engine puts together logical statements to create sets of rules. The knowledge base and the inference engine together suggest decisions and solutions to problems in the field of the expert.

The creation of an expert system requires the purchase of an expert system shell as a building block. The knowledge base and the inference engine are then programmed into the expert system shell. Perhaps the most critical part of designing an expert system is the extraction of the knowledge base and heuristics from the human domain experts themselves. This is usually done with the help of a knowledge engineer – someone skilled in logic and the human reasoning process. The knowledge engineer interviews and observes the expert to understand how decisions are made. Sometimes multiple experts may be interviewed, and the developmental process is iterative, requiring many prototypes before the final version. A user interface then must be created so that the user can interact easily with the expert system. Expert systems are most often used by less skilled staff in the same profession to provide information to the decision-making process of the consumer rather than the consumers using the system themselves.

Expert systems can tolerate uncertainty in ways that regular computer systems cannot. This is an important characteristic for the travel industry which is faced with many uncertain situations such as weather, change of tastes and environments. They do this by incorporating probabilities into their logic often referred to as 'fuzzy logic'. For example, an expert concierge system in a hotel using fuzzy logic is able to respond to requests from a guest requiring information for a restaurant that is 'not too far away' or 'not too expensive' (Cho *et al.*, 1996). It can also attach probabilities to its recommendations. Fuzzy logic is able to deal with vague concepts such as most, few, warm, etc. instead of the precise binary logic of most computer systems.

The transportation sector has two successful examples of fuzzy logic expert systems applications. In 1987, Hitachi installed a fuzzy logic-based automatic control system for the subway system in Sendai, Japan. As a result of this design, the precision of the train system improved dramatically. Each train stopped to within 7 cm of the right stop on the platform, and trains travelled more smoothly and used 10% less energy than their human-controlled counterparts (Price Waterhouse World Technology Centre, 1995). Another example of fuzzy logic in tourism is Nissan, who incorporated fuzzy logic into the intelligent controls of their cars, a development which has subsequently been followed by other car manufacturers. This trend to make vehicles more intelligent is an important development for intelligent transportation systems and is expected to improve the quality of land transportation.

Two other models that incorporate artificial intelligence into computers are case-based reasoning, and natural language processing. Case-based reasoning uses logic gained from previous cases dealing with the same problem area. It has proved to be very useful in automating problem-solving encountered by customer/help desk centres. Since there are many customer help desks in service industries such as tourism this is a valuable feature deserving of more attention by travel firms (Price Waterhouse World Technology Centre, 1995).

Natural language processing brings intelligence into the input–output systems, so that human (or natural) languages can be understood by computers. The travel industry deals in such a multilingual context making translation from one language to another an ongoing and costly challenge, that natural language processing offers significant benefits. It is relatively simple for computer systems to use natural language processing to translate standard technical documents such as tickets and coupons from one language to another, but it is much more difficult to translate free form text. It is here that natural language processing will be particularly helpful. Another important application of natural language processing technology is the ability to create front-end computers allowing customers to query databases verbally and receive responses directly from the computer.

Neural networks take the concept of expert systems one step further, and embed in them intelligence to make the system learn as it operates. They contain dynamic intelligence and incorporate experience into their knowledge base in the same way that humans do. Neural networks are particularly useful in solving pattern recognition problems such as handwriting recognition, and latent patterns in databases. They are also used in natural language recognition and speech recognition. All of these are important components of building more intelligent information systems for the tourism industry.

AI and expert systems are already being used in the travel industry in numerous ways. Not surprisingly the airline industry is exemplary in this regard. Some of its applications already in use are as follows:

- to design and control airline telecommunications networks
- to diagnose maintenance for airframes and engines
- to schedule flight crews
- to calculate complex international fare quotations
- for decision-making support for flight operations personnel
- to reschedule aircraft in bad weather conditions
- for gate management and control

Many more applications are being worked on (McMullen, 1987, Cheong, 1995), but since they represent the cutting edge of technological developments in the airlines, information on the systems is often closely guarded.

In the hospitality industry, the applications of expert systems are fewer, but more are expected to be developed in the future. Three applications are already being implemented. First, expert systems to run hotel yield management systems and to perform room assignment tasks are in regular usage (Gamble and Smith, 1986). One particular system called Eloquent is designed specifically to assist hotel managers with their decision-making tasks such as room assignment, market analysis and reporting (Nissan, 1987). Second, an expert system to replace a hotel concierge is described in Cho *et al.*, (1996). Third, an expert wine steward called the Wine Advisor, designed at Cornell University, advises customers on the type of wine to drink with their meal (Garber *et al.*, 1987). Another food service application to use expert systems for kitchen scheduling is suggested by Palmer *et al.* (1993). Potential applications in hospitality are fewer, since the industry is not as complex as the airlines and guest contact is the major concern.

In the area of travel counselling, a few systems have been designed which assist the traveller in their choice of vacation, their choice of route and their choice of tour package. Crouch (1991) describes how an expert system could help a tourist determine the best type of vacation to suit their needs, and a knowledge based system for travel agent counselling can be found in Dologite and Mockler (1993). An expert system designed to help NTO's with their promotional budget allocations to different international markets has also been worked on (Rita and Moutinho, 1994). Most of these expert systems are in the prototype stage, and have yet to have wide commercial distribution. One fully implemented expert system was used in 1994 to schedule the security forces for the Winter Olympics in Norway (Price Waterhouse World Technology Centre, 1995).

Expert systems pose numerous benefits for travel firms deciding to use them. First, they are able to institutionalize the human expert's knowledge base and keep it within the company for perpetuity. When a human expert leaves the company, an incredible resource of knowledge leaves too. Expert systems prevent this waste and build the level of professionalism within the company. Also, expert systems do not get sick, and can operate approximately 24 hours a day. Second, the costs of creating such a system can be offset in the long run by the salary savings, since less qualified personnel will be needed to provide the same level of service and knowledge to consumers. Without expert systems, the firm requires the time of expert, highly-paid personnel with skills gleaned over a lifetime of experience and learning.

10.2.2 Robotics

Robotic technology is another branch of artificial intelligence which includes the ability to move and manipulate devices. Robotic applications have been popular in the manufacturing sector since the 1950s, but the tourism industry, being a service-based industry, is only just beginning to consider their applications. A certain amount of soul searching by tourism organizations is likely as they consider whether such a service-based industry should use robots. While most observers of the industry would agree that the use of robots for front-line, guest contact functions is unrealistic, there have been examples of robots acting as waiters in restaurants in California, US (Van Warner, 1987). Many back office functions in almost all sectors of the industry lend themselves to the possible application of robotic technology.

Robots are different from automatons in that they are reprogrammable and can perform a variety of tasks. They consist of a number of different components as follows.

- The *control system* is the brain of the robot and contains all instructions for its actions.
- The *manipulation system* is the ability to pick up objects and move them to where they need to go with grippers, tongs and other devices.
- The *motion system* allows the robot to move around with either legs, wheels or tread to accomplish its tasks.
- The *sensory system* allows the robot to sense its environment through vision, infrared, ultraviolet or sonar scanning.
- The *actuation system* powers the robot either electrically, hydraulically (for very light objects) or pneumatically (for heavy objects).

Each of these subsystems must be carefully designed to match the application, and there are some relevant applications in the tourism industry. Robotics in the kitchens of restaurants to perform food preparation and cleaning tasks are possible. Even some cooking can be accomplished with robotic apparatus to ensure the correct temperatures, cooking times and actions. Applications in the laundry and housekeeping departments of a hotel are equally realistic. Robotic devices to change bed sheets and to clean hotel rooms are possible. Robots are particularly well-suited to perform heavy lifting tasks as well as delicate, precise actions. Robotic arms to select the correct data storage devices in an airline reservation system are already in place, and luggage handling systems in airports are also benefiting from robotic technology. Since robots can withstand unpleasant or dangerous environments, such as very hot or cold places, or very polluted places, their application should be investigated so that humans do not have to work in these unpleasant or unsafe environments.

10.3.3 Employment Impacts

Expert systems and robotic applications will undoubtedly impact upon future employment in the travel industry and many questions and issues must be addressed in this area. On one end of the continuum, expert systems have the potential to replace highly skilled employees, whereas on the other end, robots have the potential to replace low skilled, manual labour. This raises concern for employees and future potential employees in both of these positions.

Experts that are 'replaced' by expert systems can use their time to develop the field of their expertise further through research and creative endeavours, and to monitor less qualified personnel in their field. They will also be freer to deal with challenging situations beyond the scope of the expert computer system. The implementation of expert systems in a field may also allow new employees to progress more rapidly up the career ladder, since they have more opportunity to learn by interfacing with the expert system. Not all experts will be replaced, but the application of an expert system could help the experts themselves do their job better. As a result travel firms could benefit by integrating expert systems into decision-making in their fields.

On the other hand, tasks that robots are likely to replace are monotonous and mechanical in nature. They are also ones that humans do not receive much satisfaction from and may even be endangered by. A cause for concern if robotic applications become prevalent, however, is that jobs which now provide employment to non-skilled workers would be less available. The continued application of robotic technology will in the long run require a redefinition of tourism employment to focus on the natural human talents of flexibility, the ability to change and learn, and human interaction skills. It will enhance guest contact positions and permit staff to offer higher levels of service than before, as they are relieved from the tedious, mechanical tasks.

Implementation of both expert systems and robotics can assist in increasing the level of productivity in tourism enterprises. Expert systems can also be useful when adequately trained or skilled personnel are hard to find, and robots are beneficial when people are no longer attracted to menial jobs. Educational institutions must consider the implications of these technologies on tourism employment and educate and train their students to fit the modified job descriptions. Retraining for mature workers will also be important as jobs become redefined. The job descriptions and nature of tourism employment will undoubtedly change over the years as the implementation of technology becomes deeper and broader. Employment is likely as a consequence to become more challenging, and bring more job satisfaction to employees performing tasks more suited to people rather than machines.

10.3 MORE MULTIMEDIA SYSTEMS

Another emerging trend affecting tourism is the increasing availability and transmission possibilities of multimedia information. Information on travel products and the touristic experience itself both lend themselves well to multimedia technologies. In the past, however, their electronic storage, transmission and display have been hampered by the limited hardware of the user and the lack of high bandwidth transmission media. Personal computers with the inclusion of CD-ROM drives and MMX chips are making multimedia information more available to larger parts of the population. Faster transmission speeds at the same time are making it less tedious to use. Transmission technologies are becoming more available and less costly as data compression technology, ISDNs, satellite communications, cable and other network developments are occurring.

The benefits of these developments for tourism marketing are evident since vibrant images and sounds of tourism products and experiences give more realistic impressions to visitors. This assists visitors with tourism destination and product choice processes, leading to higher levels of tourist satisfaction. And when tourist expectations are matched by reality, repeat visitation is more likely. The WWW is already providing many virtual experiences of destinations through multimedia images, thereby helping tourists in their choice of destinations and products. As more home PCs have CD-ROM drives and Internet access, tourist choices and decisions can be expected to be made with more clarity.

Developments in multimedia applications are also affecting the availability of videoconferencing, making it an even more attractive substitute for business and even some family travel. Data compression techniques and high bandwidth lines bring videoconferencing directly to desk top computers as well as hotel ballrooms, airport lounges and corporate offices. The merging of telephone and computers into a single device will make videoconferencing more accessible to the general public with less need for expensive, specialized equipment. As technology improves and costs decline it will become an increasingly popular choice for consumers wishing to forego the rigours of travel. Some business travel situations will, however, never be replaced by videoconferencing, due to the need for face-to-face interaction and the sheer enjoyment of travelling, but many will.

Another area of the travel industry likely to benefit from improved multimedia systems are users of CAD/CAM systems. CAD/CAM systems are important in the design efforts behind many tourism projects, whether it be the designing of a resort hotel, a golf course, ski slope or marina. The transmission of CAD/CAM files between firms is becoming easier with improvements in network technologies also. As new multimedia developments are incorporated into CAD/CAM systems, more sustainable, aesthetic and workable structures should be built.

'Virtual reality' (VR), the ultimate in multimedia, presents definite possibilities to enhance touristic experiences (Cheong, 1995). It has the potential to give travellers a truer 'taste' of a tourism experience before experiencing it in reality, by surrounding them in multiple sensory inputs of a different reality. It could be considered as the ultimate travel brochure. Travel retailers willing to invest in the technology for their clients to use will certainly find potential travellers interested. The possibility of 'trying on' an experience of white-water rafting, walking through the colourful markets of Indonesia or other rich virtual worlds is enticing. It also makes sense for visitors to experience this taste before purchasing an expensive vacation which they may not enjoy.

In a more futuristic sense, VR is often discussed as a substitute for travel. While it removes the need for long air flights, the inconvenience of currency exchange and foreign languages, and exposure to strange and potentially dangerous environments, the realism of someone replacing a vacation with a simulated experience is hard to imagine. VR can probably never come close to simulating the experience that many tourists desire, such as visiting natural environments or cultural and people-related events. Its use in theme parks for short-lived entertainment experiences is more feasible. But a small selection of trips may lend themselves to substitution in the future. Trips with a single purpose, for example to visit a particular museum or to see a particular monument could be replaced by VR. The consumer would have a similar experience of viewing the items in the museum or monument at less cost and inconvenience than an actual trip. The substitutability of VR for tourism in general, however, remains only a distant possibility. Virtual reality is just one of the technologies affecting the touristic experience of the future.

10.4 GROWING GLOBAL CONNECTIVITY

Another trend in full force and currently gaining momentum is the connectivity between information systems across the entire travel industry. Three thrusts are giving this connectivity trend its momentum. First, the developments in data communications technologies and the move towards standardization of protocols (most notably the Internet protocol TCP/IP) are making data communication technologies more accessible. This was discussed in the previous chapter. The second thrust is the increasing connectivity of small and medium sized firms which have previously been isolated from the electronic marketplace and are now becoming part of the networks. A third thrust is the incorporation of more countries in the world than ever before into the travel networks. The last two thrusts are discussed below.

10.4.1 Within and Between Small and Medium Enterprises

Large, multinational firms have been responsible for the development of many travel data networks and have subsequently been the major beneficiaries of them. Some small and medium enterprises have been excluded from these networks due to the cost associated with hardware purchases, but also in some cases due to lack of computer expertise. For example, some small attractions operators or small guest houses have not benefited from electronic connectivity because of the lack of knowledge of its benefits and operation. As the costs of computer technology and data communications continue to decline, smaller firms will be more able to afford the hardware to connect to the networks. Technologies such as ISDN (which brings data communications to their door via phone lines) and Internet connections will allow them more easily to receive and transmit data. Over time, the resistance to technology experienced by some small firms due to lack of expertise is also likely to dissipate. The availability of training sessions on IT applications by educational institutions, GTOs and private firms and increasingly user-friendly software applications will both provide small and medium enterprises with the skills to participate in electronic connectivity.

Once small tourism operators have access to electronic markets their competitive position is likely to improve. They will be accessible to world markets in ways they never were before. This could be through the Internet or through the TCP/IP networks which ARINC and SITA are putting in place. As a consequence, tourists will have a richer travel experience as they discover small and more unique tourism facilities which may previously have escaped them. These types of tourist facilities can often lead to more satisfaction for certain types of guests, which in turn will generate more repeat visits to a destination.

10.4.2 Within and Between More Countries

First world countries have dominated the electronic travel market in
the past because they have had the developed technological infrastructure upon which to build the networks. Some parts of the world
including Africa, Russia, some parts of Asia and Eastern Europe have
had inadequate telecommunication infrastructures to handle high
speed data communication links necessary to be competitive in the
international tourism market. Some have had inadequate satellite connections and no fibre optic cabling, making high speed data communication links impossible. Even local phone lines in some countries are
weak and sporadic, and as most data messages need to begin their
journey on phone lines, connectivity to the rest of the world has been
limited. The issues of cost and familiarity with software are also drawbacks in these parts of the world.

Telecommunication companies are investing heavily in new
equipment in these countries, making voice and data communication
services more accessible and more affordable. This will again mean
more equality for all players in the electronic marketplace, and destination accessibility will be improved. Travel agents and consumer markets in first world countries will be able to research these products and
services electronically for the first time, thereby impacting upon
tourism flows around the world. Destinations may move more rapidly
through the destination life cycle from inception to growth to maturity
if the whole electronic marketplace knows about it. For some destinations and host populations this may be undesirable, and issues of carrying capacity and rapid growth will become major concerns.
Therefore, along with the increase in electronic connectivity for countries previously 'off-line' must come an increase in judicious planning
and control of the destination's development.

10.5 MARKET SEGMENTATION BASED ON TECHNOLOGY

The unrelenting growth in IT applications in tourism carries with it
different consumer and institutional responses. For some travellers,
there is an expectation of higher levels of automation by the travel
firms they deal with. They relish the increased efficiency that IT brings
to their travel experiences. Others see their vacations as escapes from
the modern technological world in which they live and work, and are
seeking experiences that are softer and more human. Travel firms
would be well advised to investigate this technological market seg-
mentation more thoroughly.

Computer literate travellers, especially business travellers, expect the convenience and efficiency provided by many computer operated devices and services discussed in this book. They may not tolerate, for example, hotels that do not have electronic locking systems or teleconferencing facilities, or airlines that do not have Internet terminals in the plane seat backs, or travel intermediaries that are not using the Internet as a search device. Some travellers may expect the use of smart cards to easily access certain facilities while travelling. They may also expect support for the intelligent devices they carry with them. This market segment will also seek out entertainment and attractions that use technology in the creation of the experience. Travel industry firms pursuing this market segment must research not only the latest technologies, but also the needs and expectations of consumers so that they can provide the necessary technological infrastructure and environment. They must also hire employees well versed in these technologies. This may include incorporating rigorous training programmes to ensure staff competency, in addition to hiring staff with experience and certifications in computer skills.

Other firms choosing to focus on the other 'high touch' market segment will not require such high levels of investment or training in technology. This market segment values things done the old, traditional way and shy away from anything technological. They may even view technology as being destructive to the tourism experience. It would, however, behove firms serving them not to ignore technology completely. Technology in these establishments will undoubtedly be kept in the background rather than being visible to the consumers. But there are few operations in tourism today that can ignore IT completely and remain successful. All types of firms and organizations in the travel industry must examine carefully the expectations of their target markets. Differentiation of their products to best match these expectations will be necessary.

10.6 CHANGES IN TRAVEL INDUSTRY STRUCTURE

Information technology is creating fundamental, structural changes in the tourism industry. It is changing the size of firms, the ownership of firms, and the internal structures of firms and organizations. IT is supporting many mergers and acquisitions which are giving rise to large, international conglomerates. Electronic linkages between firms for data communication purposes are often followed or pre-empted by organizational linkages. Technology makes it easier to do business globally and so the economies of scale and the cost structures experienced are creating larger firms. Mergers are occurring both within and between industry sectors. Many of the airline mergers in the 1980s were in part due to airlines wanting to acquire the computer technology of the other. Vertical integration is also occurring as travel agents are acquiring airlines, and airlines are acquiring hotels, for example. This vertical integration may be prompted by information technology in the sense that firms may want to leverage their investments in computer reservation technology across numerous and diverse operations.

Technology also brings with it equalization and democratization which supports the existence of smaller firms. Access to information brings power and as parts of the industry previously without information technology gain access to it, they become more equal with large, multinational firms in the marketplace. Smaller firms can become more competitive by using IT to create competitive advantages. They can also use it to create brand loyalty thereby locking in customers. IT to create product differentiation has been demonstrated in numerous cases in this book. The two trends are having the effect of creating a bipolar industry; one sector is made up of large international firms and the other of small local firms.

IT is also serving to stabilize the industry by creating barriers to entry and exit. It is difficult for firms today to set up in business without significant investments in technology. In earlier times, they could be competitive in some sectors of tourism with little investment at all and certainly without technology. As an example, the tour operator sector in the past has experienced many instances of firms rapidly entering and exiting the industry due to low barriers to entry. Now, since significant levels of automation are required to be competitive, firms are less likely to enter so rapidly due to required costs and will be less likely to exit due to their investments. This stabilization serves tourists well by giving more confidence in the longevity of the firms they are doing business with.

10.7 SUMMARY

This chapter has identified some trends due to technology – the book has identified many applications and impacts of technology. There are more of both. The marriage between information technology and tourism is woven tightly together and is likely to remain strong as the synergy between the partners grows into the next millennium. The relationship between the two partners may change over time but the direction of the change will depend on the aggregate visions of decision makers and policy makers in the industry. As long as technology remains secondary to the process of providing tourists with satisfying experiences in a sustainable manner the relationship will remain strong. If future decisions on technology are based solely on cost and convenience, more technology than is appropriate may be implemented, leaving the industry less effective in the long run. Some sectors can absorb more technology than others. The airlines, for example, seem to be insatiable in their capacity to use technology to their advantage, whereas the hospitality sector is more hesitant, and rightly so. All sectors of tourism must carefully examine their operations, strategic direction and customer needs when deciding to implement new technologies.

References

Abara, J. (1989) Applying integer linear programming to the fleet assignment problem. *Interfaces* 19/4, 20–28.

Alstrup, J., Anderson, S., Boas, S., Madsen, O. and Vidal, R. (1989) Booking control increases profit at Scandinavian Airlines, *Interfaces*, 19 July/August, 10–19.

Alvarez, R., Dunn, J. and Ferguson D. H. (1983) How *not* to automate your front office. *Cornell Hotel and Restaurant Administration Quarterly* , November, 56–62.

Amadeus International (1994) *Information on Amadeus.* 27pp.

Anonymous (1992) Highlights of ticket delivery machines. *Travel Weekly.*

Anonymous (1996), Vehicle Information and Communication System. *New Breeze* 18,

Archdale, G. (1993) Computer reservation systems and public tourism offices. *Tourism Management,* February, 3–14.

Avis, Inc. (1996) Avis leads car rental industry in introducing fighter-pilot 'Head-Up Display' safety technology program to boost consumer awareness. *Avis News Release*, 1–3.

Bartlett, D. (1996) A practical guide to GPS. *Info-Tech.Travel Electronic Bulletin Board.* 25pp.

Bennett, M. (1988) Information technology and the travel agency. *Geographical Papers* 105, University of Reading 42pp.

Bennett, M. (1993) Information technology and travel agency. *Tourism Management*, August, 259–278.

Bieber, T. P. (1989) Guest-history systems: maximizing the benefits. *Cornell Hotel and Restaurant Administration Quarterly,* November, 20–22.

Boberg, K. and Collison, F. (1985) Computer reservation systems and airline competition. *Tourism Management*, 174–183.

Bond, S. C., Brothers, G. L. and Casey, J. F. (1996) Application of the Internet as a tool for enhancing resident involvement for sustainable rural tourism development. In: *Proceedings of Travel and Tourism Research Association 27th Annual Conference*, Travel and Tourism Research Association, Kentucky, US, pp. 120–126.

Borovits, I. and Neumann, S. (1988) Airline management information system at Arkia Israeli Airlines. *MIS Quarterly*, March, 127–137.

Brymer, M. A., Forrest, E. J., Murphy, J. and Wotring, C. E. (1996) Hotel management and marketing on the Internet: an analysis of sites and features. *Cornell Hotel and Restaurant Administration Quarterly*, June, 70–82.

Buhalis, D. (1995) The impact of information telecommunications technologies on tourism distribution channels: implications for the small and medium sized tourism enterprises' strategic management and marketing. Doctorate Thesis, The University of Surrey. 786pp.

Buhalis, D. (1996) Information technology as a strategic tool for tourism. *Revue de Tourisme* 2, 34–36.

Burke, J. F. (1986) Computerized management of tourism marketing information. *Tourism Management*, December, 279–289.

Cash, J.I., McFarlan, F.W., McKenney, J.L. and Applegate, L.M. (1992) *Corporate Information Systems Management: Text and Cases.* Irwin, Boston, Massachusetts, 702pp.

Cheong, R. (1995) The virtual threat to travel and tourism. *Tourism Management* 16/6, 417–422.

Chervenak, L. (1993) Hotel technology at the start of the new millennium. *Hospitality Research Journal* 17, 115–120.

Cho, W., Sumichrast, R. T., and Olsen, M. D. (1996) Expert-system technology for hotels: concierge application. *Cornell Hotel and Restaurant Administration Quarterly*, February, 54–62.

CKC (1993) PMS interfaces: a status report. *CKC Report*, September, 3–7.

Clemons, E. K. and Row, M. (1991) Ahead of the pack through vision and hustle: a case study of information technology at Rosenbluth Travel. In: *Proceedings of the 24th International Conference on Systems Sciences,* January, pp. 287–296.

Clemons, E. K., Row, M. and Miller, D. (1992) Rosenbluth international alliance: information technology and the global virtual corporation. In: *Proceedings of Hawaii International Conference on System Sciences,* pp. 678–686.

Cleveland, H. (1985) *The Knowledge Executive: Leadership in an Information society,* 1st edn. Truman Talley Books, New York, 263pp.

Coddington, P. (1993) The impact of videoconferencing on airline business traffic. *Journal of Travel Research*, Autumn, 64–66.

Collins, G. (1990) Automating properties: understanding the human element. *Cornell Hotel and Restaurant Administration Quarterly*, August, 65–71.

Collins, G. (1991) Selecting point-of sale systems for table service restaurants. *Florida International University Review*, Autumn, 36–46.

Coopers and Lybrand (1995) Videoconferencing: positioning the hotel industry for the next century, *Hospitality Review*, 36–46.

Copeland, D. and McKenney, J. L. (1988) Airline reservation systems: lessons from history. *MIS Quarterly*, September, 353–370.

Crouch, G.I. (1991) Expert computer systems in tourism: emerging possibilities. *Journal of Travel Research*, Winter, 3–10.

Denver International Airport. (1996) Various Fact Sheets, January 1996.

de Pommes, C., Geller, S. and Meyer, J. F. (1995) Voyage into cyberspace. *Airline Business*, October, 56–61.

Desmond, P. (1988) ICA study shows airlines, banks tops in net outlays. *Network World* 5/31, 2.

Dologite, D.G. and Mockler, R.J. (1993) Travel agent business planning consultant: a knowledge-based system prototype, *Proceedings of Hawaii International Conference on Systems Sciences*, 3, 719–727.

Dreistadt, E. and Gardens, B. (1996) A roadside attraction on the info highway. In: *Proceedings of Travel and Tourism Research Association 27th Annual Conference*. Travel and Tourism Research Association, Kentucky, US, pp. 134–141.

Drucker, P. (1990) *Managing the Non-Profit Organization*, 1st. edn. Harper Collins, New York, 235 pp.

Eastman, R. (1996) Hidden drivers in travel distribution. *Aviation Informatics*, April.

Ebner, A. (1994). TIS Tourism Information System for the Tyrol. In: Schertler, W., Schmid, B., Tjoa, A.M., and Werthner, H. (eds) *Proceedings of ENTER Conference: Information and Communication Technologies in Tourism*, Springer-Verlag, Vienna, New York, pp. 201–208.

Engel, D.S. and Ives, T.P. (1982) The call accounting decision: how to select a system. *Cornell Hotel and Restaurant Quarterly*, May, 57–69.

Farris, M.T., Teye, V.B. and Truitt, L.J. (1991) The role of computer reservations systems: international implications for the travel industry. *Tourism Management*, March, 21–35.

Feldman, J. (1994) Airline distribution under siege ... at last. *Air Transport World*, August, 35–43.

Flint, P. (1995) The electronic skyway: after years of promise, ticketless travel is here, offering savings to airlines and convenience to passengers. *Air Transport World*, January, 38–43.

Ford, L., Ford, R.C. and LeBruto, S.M. (1995) Is your hotel MISsing technology? *EIU Hospitality Review*, Autumn, 53–65.

Forrest, D., Murphy, J. and Wotring C.E. (1996) Restaurant marketing on the Worldwide Web. *Cornell Hotel and Restaurant Administration Quarterly*, February, 61–71.

Gamble, P. and Smith, G. (1986) Expert front office management by computer. *International Journal of Hospitality Management*, 3, 109–114.

Garber, S., Nissan, E., and Shur, A. (1987) The 'Wining and Dining' project – 1. 'The Wine Adviser', a deductive database. *International Journal of Hospitality Management*, 4, 203–205.

Gee, C.Y., Makens, J.C. and Choy, D.J.L. (1994) *The Travel Industry*, 2nd edn. Van Nostrand Reinhold, New York, 445pp.

Geller, A.N. (1985) The current state of hotel information systems. *Cornell Hotel and Restaurant Administration Quarterly*, May, 14–17.

Gershkoff, I. (1989) Optimizing flight crew schedules. *Interfaces* 19/4, July-August, 29–43.

Godwin, N. (1987) *Complete Guide to Travel Agency Automation*, 2nd edn., Delmar Publishing Inc., New York, 201pp.

Gray, D. (1993) Consulting concepts come to life for author while working on American Airlines maintenance project. *OR/MS Today*, December, 22–28.

Gray, D. and Kabbani, N. (1994) Right tool, place, time. *OR/MS Today*, April, 34–41.

Greenfield, D. (1996) OR overhaul. *Operations Research Management Science*, April, 12–14.

Guyomard, G. (1994) Information technology and telematics in tourism: a change in systems or policy? *Espaces* 125, 8–12.

Haines, P. (1991) Qualities needed by destination management systems. In: *Proceedings of Information Technology in Public Tourism Offices Conference*. Assisi, Italy, November.

Haines, P. (1994) Destination Marketing Systems. In: Information and communications technologies in tourism, *Proceedings of ENTER – International Conference on Information and Communication Technologies in Tourism*, Springer-Verlag, Vienna, New York, pp. 50–55

Hardman, L. (1989) Evaluating the usability of the Glasgow OnLine Hypertext. *Hypermedia* 1/1 Spring, 34–63.

Harris, L. (1994) US Travel Agency Survey. *Travel Weekly*. 65, 123–149.

Harris, L. (1996) US Travel Agency Automation Survey. *Travel Weekly* 65, 118–134.

Haywood, K.M. (1990) A strategic approach to managing technology. *Cornell Hotel and Restaurant Administration Quarterly*, May 39–45.

Henderson, D. (1991a) Mainframe afterburners. *Air Transport World*, August, 84.

Henderson, D. (1991b) Recipes by videospecs. *Air Transport World*, August, 78.

Henderson, D. (1991c) Software manages flight crews, aircraft. *Air Transport World*, August, 83.

Henderson, D. K. (1995) Airlines in cyberspace: the Internet and the World Wide Web provide new, broad electronic channels for carriers to sell tickets and reduce distribution costs. *Air Transport World*, November, 26–32.

Hickey, J. (1988) Hotel reservation system and sources of business. *Travel and Tourism Analyst*, 23–36.

Hogenauer, A. (1996) Systematic travel information with Global Positioning: changing the face of worldwide travel. In: *Proceedings of Travel and Tourism Research Association 27th Annual Conference*. Travel and Tourism Research Association, Kentucky, US, pp. 127–133.

Intelligent Transportation Society of America (1995) International ITS Information Clearinghouse Fact Sheets, March, 6pp.

ITS (1996) ITS in Australia, *ITS Web Site*, reproduced from *GIS User Magazine* 1, 1–6.

Jones, C.B. (1993) Applications of database marketing in the tourism industry. *Pacific Asia Travel Association Occasional Paper Series*. San Francisco, USA.

Jones, K. (1996) Using hand-held computers to collect intercept data. In: *Proceedings of Travel and Tourism Research Association 27th Annual Conference*, Kentucky, US. pp. 97–103.

Jones, R. (1989) Development of an automated airlines crew bid generation system. *Interfaces* 19/4 July-August, 44–51.

Kasavana, M.L. (1987) *Computer Systems for Foodservice Operations*, Van Nostrand Reinhold Company Inc., New York, 259pp.

Kasavana, M.L. (1996) Slot machines: methodologies and myths. *FIU Hospitality Review*, Autumn, 37–44.

Kasavana, M.L. and Cahill, J.J. (1992) *Managing Computers in the Hospitality Industry*, 2nd edn. Educational Institute of the American Hotel and Motel Association, Michigan, 331pp.

Kay, S. (1989) ACP/TPF spreads its wings. *Computerworld*, April 24, 97.

Knight, F. (1987) CCITT's Director on the evolution of ISDN. *Business Communications Review*, Jan–Feb, 27–32.

Kubicek, H. and Seeger, P. (1992) The negotiation of data standards: a comparative analysis of EAN-and EFT/POS-systems. In: Dierkes, M. and Hoffman, U. (eds) *New Technology at the Outset. Social Forces in the Shaping of Technological Innovations*, Frankfurt/M, New York, pp. 351–374.

Laetz, S. (1994) Application of information technology to meeting and convention planning. Honours Thesis, University of Hawaii, Honolulu, Hawaii, 82pp.

Leshin, C.B. (1997) *Internet Investigations in Hospitality, Travel And Tourism*. Prentice Hall, New Jersey, 180pp.

Loane, T. (1996) Alamo Rent-a-Car. Electronic mail communications, May.

Malone, T.W., Yates, J. and Benjamin, R.I. (1987) Electronic markets and electronic hierarchies. *Communications of the ACM* 30/6, 484–497.

Martin, J. (1988) *Principles of Data Communications*. Prentice Hall, New York, 346pp.

McMullen, M. (1987) Artificial intelligence in the airline industry. *IATA Review*, April–June, 16–18.

Millera, T.E. (1996) Segmenting the Internet. *American Demography* July, 1–3.

Moore, R.G. and Wilkinson, S. (1993) Communications technology. *Hospitality Research Journal* 17, 133–144.

Musselwhite, J. (1996a) Robotic data storage is ready for takeoff. *Aviation Informatics*, February, 10–11.

Musselwhite, J. (1996b) Will airports display the multi-media way. *Aviation Informatics*, February, 4–6.

Nelms, D.W. (1992) Delta's automated cargo. *Air Transport World*, August 57–58.

Nissan, E. (1987) Knowledge-based computer systems for tasks in hospitality management or related areas: accommodation (lodging, alimentation) and leisure. *International Journal of Hospitality Mangement*, 4, 199–202.

Palmer, J., Kasavana, M.L., and McPherson, R. (1993) Creating a technological circle of service. *Cornell Hotel and Restaurant Administration Quarterly*, February, 81–87.

Parker, A.J. (1984) Hotel executive microcomputer use in the United States. *International Journal of Hospitality Management* 3, 147–151.

Peacock, M. (1995) *Information Technology in the Hospitality Industry: Managing People, Change and Computers*. Cassell, London, 121pp.

Pearce, D. (1992) *Tourist Organizations.* John Wiley & Sons, Inc., New York, 219pp.

Peroni, G. (1991) Problems and prospects for the renewal of public tourism marketing in the computer network era. In: *Proceedings of Information Technology in Public Tourism Offices Conference.* Assisi, Italy.

Poling, B. (1992) Transportation department revises CRS rules. *Travel Weekly,* September, 1, 4.

Poon, A. (1993) *Tourism, Technology and Competitive Strategies.* CAB International, Wallingford, UK, 370pp.

Price Waterhouse World Technology Centre (1995) *Technological Forecast 1996.* Price Waterhouse, Menlo Park, California, 718pp.

Reamy, L.M. (1995) The Airborne Arcade. *Institutional Investor* 29/10, 305–310.

Ribbers, P.M. (1994) Strategy and information technology in the tourist industry. In: Schertler, W., Schmid, B., Tjoa, A.M. and Werthner, H. (eds) *Proceedings of ENTER – International Conference on Information and Communication Technologies in Tourism.* Springer-Verlag, Vienna, New York, pp. 9–14.

Rita, P. and Moutinho, L. (1994) An expert system for National Tourism Offices. *Annals of Tourism Research* 1, 143–145.

Ritz, D. (1995) The Start-Up of an EDI Network: A Comparative Case Study in the Air Cargo Industry. PhD Dissertation, University of St. Gallen, Switzerland, 319pp.

Rowe, M. (1990) Technology teamwork. *Lodging Hospitality,* March, 77–79.

Saunders, M. (1994) SITA – harnessing technology to facilitate airport operations. *Airport Technology International,* 109–113.

Sayles, C.I. (1963), New York Hilton's data-processing system. *Cornell Hotel and Restaurant Administration Quarterly,* August, 41.

Schaeffer, B. (1994) Using technology to reach the travel trade. *Pacific Asia Travel Association Conference,* Vancouver, Canada.

Schertler, W. (1994) Tourism 2000 – an information business. In: Schertler, W., Schmid, B., Tjoa, A.M. and Werthner, H. (eds) *Proceedings of ENTER – International Conference on Information and Communications Technologies in Tourism.* Springer-Verlag, Vienna, New York, pp. 20–26.

Schonland, A. (1996) The 1996 Web Traveller Report Executive Summary. In: *Proceedings of Travel and Tourism Research Association 27th Annual Conference.* Travel and Tourism Research Association, Kentucky, US, pp. 142–160.

Sheldon, P.J. (1987) Computers – tourism applications, *Tourism Management,* 8, 258–262.

Sheldon, P.J. (1993) Destination information systems, *Annals of Tourism Research* 4, 633–649.

Sheldon, P.J. (1995) Can travel agents survive the information superhighway? In: Schertler, W., Schmid, B., Tjoa, A.M. and Werthner, H. (eds) *Proceedings of ENTER – International Conference on Information and Communications Technologies in Tourism.* Springer-Verlag, Vienna, New York.

Sloane, J. (1990) Latest developments in aviation CRSs. *EIU Travel & Tourism Analyst* 4, 5–15.

Sprague, R.H. Jr. (1995) Electronic document management: challenges and opportunities for information systems managers. *MIS Quarterly* March, 29–49.

Stallings, W. (1989) *ISDN – An Introduction*. Macmillan, New York, 418pp.

Stipanuk, D.M. (1993) Tourism and technology: interactions and implications. *Tourism Management*, August, 267–278.

Truitt, L., Teye, V. and Farris, M. (1991) The role of Computer Reservation Systems. *Tourism Management*, 21–36.

Tuenissen, W. J. M. (1995) ISDN in the travel industry: a catalyst for change. In: Schertler, W., Schmid, B., Tjoa, A.M. and Werthner, H. (eds) *Proceedings of ENTER – International Conference on Information and Communications Technologies in Tourism*. Springer-Verlag, Vienna, New York.

Tunstall, T. (1996) Emergence of the CRS: industry overview and analysis. Unpublished paper, University of Texas, Dallas, May, 20pp.

US Travel Data Centre, (1995) *1995 Outlook for Travel and Tourism*, Alexandria, Virginia, December 198pp.

Van Hoof, H.B., Collins, G.R., Combrink, T.E., Verbeeten, M.J. (1995) Technology needs and receptions. *Cornell Hotel and Restaurant Administration Quarterly*, October, 64–69.

Van Hoof, H.B., Verbeeten, M.J., and Combrink, T.E. (1996) Information technology revisted – international lodging-industry technology needs and perceptions: a comparative study. *Cornell Hotel and Restaurant Administration Quarterly*, December, 86–91.

Van Warner, R. (1987) Robots: a possible answer to industry's manpower crisis. *Nation's Restaurant News*. April 20, 15.

Vlitos-Rowe, I. (1992) Destination databases and management systems. *EIU Travel & Tourism Analyst* 5, 84–94.

Wagner, G. (1991) Technology meets tomorrow. *Lodging Hospitality*, December, 103–110.

Walle, A.H. (1996) Tourism and the Internet: opportunities for direct marketing. *Journal of Travel Research*, Summer, 72–77.

Waters, S. (1995) *Travel Industry World Yearbook*, 120pp.

Wayne, N. (1991) Hi-Line: A case study of a working computerized central reservation office in the public sector tourism. In: *Proceedings of Information Technology in Public Tourism Offices Conference*. Assisi, Italy.

Weber, M. (1995) Changes in the leisure travel market result in new requirements for tour operator systems. In: Schertler, W., Schmid, B., Tjoa, A.M. and Werthner, H. (eds) *Proceedings of ENTER – International Conference on Information and Communication Technologies in Tourism*. Springer-Verlag, Vienna, New York.

Williams, P.W., Bascombe, P., Brenner, N., and Green D. (1996) Using the Internet for tourism research: 'Information Highway' or 'Dirt Road'. *Journal of Travel Research*, 4, 63–70.

Wober, K. (1994) Strategic planning tools inside the marketing information system in use by the Austrian Tourist Office. In: Schertler, W., Schmid, B., Tjoa, A.M., and Werthner, H. (eds) *Proceedings of ENTER Conference: Information and Communication Technologies in Tourism*, Springer-Verlag, Vienna, New York, pp. 201–208.

World Travel and Tourism Council, (1995) *Travel and Tourism: A New Economic Perspective*. Pergamon, Oxford, UK. 228pp.

Zunkel, D. (1996) Biometrics and border control. *Security Technology and Design*, May

Index